The Smoke-Eaters

A HISTORY OF FIREFIGHTING
IN NOVA SCOTIA

c.1750-1950

MIKE PARKER

NIMBUS
PUBLISHING

Nimbus Publishing Limited
PO Box 9166
Halifax, NS   B3K 5M8
(902) 455-4286

Printed and bound in Canada
Design: Joan Sinclair

National Library of Canada Cataloguing in Publication

Parker, Mike, 1952-
The smoke-eaters : a history of fire-fighting in Nova Scotia, c1750-1950 / Mike Parker.

(Images of our past)
ISBN 1-55109-417-7

1. Fire extinction—Nova Scotia—History. 2. Fire fighters—Nova Scotia–History. 3. Nova Scotia—History. I. Title. II. Series.

TH9506.N6P37 2002   363.37'8'09716   C2002-903974-6

Canadä   The Canada Council | Le Conseil des Arts
for the Arts | du Canada

We acknowledge the financial support of the Government of Canada through the Book Publishing Industry Development Program (BPIDP) and the Canada Council for our publishing activities.

Table of Contents

Acknowledgements:

My thanks to Helen, Matt, and Emily; Nimbus Publishing; Clare Goulet; Joan Sinclair; Garry Shutlak and all the staff at the Public Archives of Nova Scotia; Halifax Regional Fire & Emergency Service; fire departments in Bridgewater, Windsor, Kentville, River John, Amherst, Truro, Upper Hammonds Plains, Glace Bay; Dartmouth Heritage Museum; Cumberland County Museum & Archives; North Cumberland Historical Society; North Shore Archives; Colchester Historical Society Museum; Annapolis Valley MacDonald Museum; Beaton Institute at University College of Cape Breton; Historic Restoration Society of Annapolis County; Maritime Command Museum; Shearwater Aviation Museum; West Hants Historical Society Museum; Antigonish Heritage Museum; Firefighters' Museum of Nova Scotia; Ron Trowsdale, Richard Smith, Reid Whynot, Howard MacKinnon, Vivian Godfree, Kate Currie, Jocelyn Gillis, Lilla Siderius, Joe O'Byrne, Peter Turnbull, Norman Wright, Bill Mont, Fred Fiske, Karla and Larry Kelly, Donal Baird, Steve Nearing, Bill Nelson, Wendell David, Elroy Hill, Dr. Henry Bishop, Graham McBride, Gary Castle, Faith Wallace, Barb Thompson, and Nan Harvey. A special debt of gratitude goes to Don Snider and Ray Beck, who never tired of my seemingly endless requests for favours, information, or contacts, and whose passion for firefighting history and years of research contributed greatly to the book.

A MAP OF NOVA SCOTIA

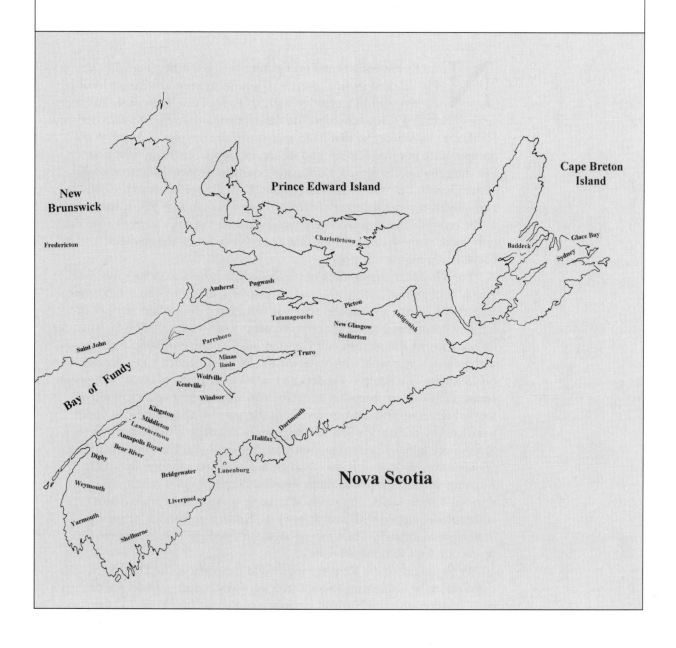

New
Brunswick

Fredericton

Prince Edward Island

Charlottetown

Cape Breton
Island

Baddeck

Glace Bay

Sydney

Amherst   Pugwash

Pictou

Saint John

Tatamagouche

New Glasgow

Antigonish

Parrsboro

Stellarton

Truro

Minas
Basin

Bay of Fundy

Wolfville

Kentville

Windsor

Kingston

Middleton

Lawrencetown

Annapolis Royal

Bear River

Dartmouth

Digby

Halifax

Weymouth

Bridgewater   Lunenburg

Nova Scotia

Liverpool

Yarmouth

Shelburne

Introduction

"Prompt to Rescue"

Halifax Union Engine Company motto

Nova Scotia has a proud firefighting heritage dating back 250 years. The story of its smoke-eaters is significant not just from a local perspective, but in a broader context. Halifax can boast of several milestones, including Canada's oldest fire department and fire insurance company. Halifax is also where the first hand-and-steam fire engines and motorized pumper were put into service, and where, in December 1917, nine firemen lost their lives in the largest man-made explosion before the advent of the atomic bomb. The towns of Windsor and Pictou were home to the country's two longest-serving volunteer firemen; Upper Hammonds Plains lays claim to the only all-Black incorporated fire department in the nation. These are only some of the facts and firsts that make Nova Scotia the cradle of Canadian firefighting history.

For a better understanding of this history, it is helpful to look to the origins of firefighting, and for this one must turn to ancient Greece and Rome. A leather bag with an attached nozzle is considered the earliest piece of firefighting apparatus. Significant improvements were made in 300 B.C. when the Greek scientist and philosopher Ctesibus built a double-cylinder force pump with jointed water pipe, which was capable of being moved both vertically and horizontally. The pump's cylinders and valves were made of brass, with pistons encased in unshorn sheepskin to make them watertight; two men alternately worked levers up and down to force out the water. Pumps similar in design were used by the world's first fire brigades in the days of the Roman Empire. Slaves were initially pressed into duty as firemen, but these members of the *familia publica* proved to be less than enthusiastic and efficient. In 6 A.D., Emperor Augustus replaced them with his Corp of Vigiles comprised of selected Roman males who received training, then were organized into companies equipped with pumps, buckets, ladders, and hooks for pulling down burning thatch. The Corp of Vigiles formed the basis of Roman fire protection for five hundred years.

With the fall of the Roman Empire and the onset of the Dark Ages, organized efforts at firefighting disappeared for many centuries. A revival of sorts came in 1066 with the Norman Conquest of Britain and the introduction of a curfew; open fires were forbidden after sunset at the ringing of the curfew bell. An effective preventive measure against fire, the original intent was to discourage clandestine meetings among Saxons who might conspire to rebel against Norman rule. Interestingly, curfew is a derivative of the French word couvre feu, a metal cover used to extinguish hearth fires. The Portuguese resurrected fire apparatus in the sixteenth century with the introduction of "squirts."

These metre-long syringes were equipped with side handles, which were held by two men while a third man depressed a piston rod to shoot out a thin stream of water. A squirt worked on the same principle as a hypodermic needle: the nozzle was immersed in water, then the piston retracted to fill the cylinder. The first squirts had only a one-gallon capacity, but later German models were considerably larger and mounted on wheels.

In 1666, the Great Fire of London destroyed more than thirteen thousand buildings and homes. This was the turning point in the evolution of fire prevention measures and equipment. From these ruins came new building codes and the division of London into districts, each assigned firefighting tools. The most important development was the establishment of Britain's first fire insurance company. In 1667, the Fire Office organized its own fire brigade to protect properties upon which the company had "accepted risks." This precedent-setting initiative would be adopted by many British insurance companies over the next hundred years. Lead plaques or firemarks bearing the underwriter's emblem were affixed to policy holders' buildings and only that company's brigade would provide assistance in the event of fire. Should another brigade be first on the scene, they simply left the structure to burn. This less-than-civic-minded approach was eventually changed to one where competing brigades raced to fires in hopes of collecting a monetary bonus awarded to the first arrival by the insuring underwriter. (Firemarks were later used in the United States but in Canada, they did not figure prominently, if at all.) Insurance-sponsored brigades were England's only means of fire protection until the early 1800s. Several of these companies—including Hand-In-Hand Fire Office (est. 1696), Sun Fire Office (1710), Union Fire Office (1714), and Phoenix Assurance Company (1782)— would establish fire insurance businesses in Nova Scotia during the nineteenth century.

While Britain and France waged intermittent warfare for control of Acadie during the seventeenth and eighteenth centuries, firefighting made significant headway in colonial America. Boston instituted the first fire-prevention ordinances in 1631, outlawing wooden chimneys and thatched roofs. In 1648 at New Amsterdam (New York), four fire wardens were appointed to inspect chimneys and levy fines against violators for cleaning and maintenance infractions. In what is "generally recognized as the first step in organized firefighting in North America," eight dependable citizens were chosen for the Rattle Watch. Known also as Prowlers, these men (who later numbered fifty) patrolled streets at night, sounding the fire alarm by spinning large wooden rattles that were eventually replaced with handbells. Settlers were compelled by law to keep three full buckets of water outside their door at dark for use by the fire patrols. An additional ten buckets were filled at sunset from the town pump and left in racks for emergencies. Boston purchased the colonies' first fire engine in 1654, followed by Philadelphia in 1719, and New York in 1731. In 1678, Boston organized America's first paid fire department (thirteen men) and, in 1711, established the first mutual benefit fire societies, or salvage companies, for saving removable property from burning buildings. Benjamin Franklin, who was originally from Boston, organized America's first volunteer fire department in 1736 at Philadelphia; this Union Fire Company had thirty members. Franklin was also instrumental in having mutual benefit fire societies established, including the Hand-in-Hand and Heart-in-Hand; these are said to have differed from Boston fire clubs in that Franklin wanted Philadelphia's teams to battle all fires—regardless of affiliation with a particular club or society. In 1740, Franklin also established the first successful fire insurance company in America, the Philadelphia Contributorship.

Edward Cornwallis founded Halifax along the shores of Chebucto Bay in 1749 as a deterrent to the French fortress of Louisbourg on Cape Breton Island. From Halifax, British forces eventually launched sieges that conquered the Isle Royale bastion and Quebec, thereby vanquishing France once and for all in the fight for North American supremacy. In 1880, a series of articles appeared in the *Evening Mail* chronicling the history of firefighting in Halifax up to that time. The Union Engine Company, established on August 8, 1768, was then thought to be the settlement's "Original Fire Company." Such was not the case, however, as "a rediscovered record of a fire department" in the late 1890s turned up in the walls of a Halifax building during demolition. The antiquated document, today preserved at the Nova Scotia Museum, shows that the Union Fire Club—the first volunteer fire company in Canada—originated much earlier, in 1754.

Donal Baird has spent many years researching the history of firefighting organizations and apparatus in Canada. According to Baird, "the French regime in Canada was not such as to inspire local initiatives like community fire protection...it was to come largely from the self-reliant New England colonies." In his book *The Story of Firefighting in Canada*, Baird describes how under British rule in the 1760s "honours for the first firefighting company with a fire engine in Canada would have to go to either Montreal or Quebec, probably the former, the date being 1765." This must be considered an ambiguous "honour," as even he admits "there is a lack of specific detail that would confirm this with any precision." While Baird credits Montreal with organizing a *club de feu* as early as 1763, he does cite conflicting sources which do not place a fire company there until many years later, and he acknowledges the possibility that British garrisons elsewhere may have formed fire clubs or companies and had fire engines earlier than either Montreal or Quebec.

In fact, historian Thomas Raddall in *Halifax: Warden of the North* reports that "The Chebucto expedition [of 1749] was marvelously well organized in view of the inefficiency and corruption of that age. The ships were loaded with everything from fire engines to fishing gear..." While Raddall makes no more than passing mention of fire equipment, Dr. T.B. Akins, commissioner of public records for Nova Scotia, confirms fire engines at the time of Halifax's founding. His book, *History of Halifax City*, published in 1895 for the Nova Scotia Historical Society, lists two fire engines in the settlement's 1749 expenditure accounts submitted to Parliament by the Lords Commissioners. This document places fire engines in Halifax sixteen years before either Montreal or Quebec.

Finally, regarding the first fire company or fire club, there is indisputable evidence that Halifax predates Montreal by nine years. The earliest fire com-

Halifax Fire Insurance Association, 1909

The Halifax Fire Insurance Association published a special annual report in 1909 marking its hundredth anniversary. An accompanying "historical sketch" included this photo of its Board of Directors. According to Secretary-Treasurer Thomas Goudge: "The Halifax Fire Insurance Company has the honor of being the pioneer of Canadian fire insurance companies; many have come and gone in the past 100 years, but the "Old Halifax" is still to the fore and today is in a more healthy, vigorous and sound financial condition than at any previous date in its existence." The first board of directors, all prominent Halifax businessmen, were Andrew Belcher, Charles Hill, Lawrence Hartshorne, Foster Hutchinson, James Fraser, George Grassie, and H.H. Cogswell. For many years, the office was in the home of secretary J.H. Fliegar on Hollis Street. By

1866, the company received thirty-six percent of its premiums from country agencies throughout the province. The first and oldest Canadian fire insurance company is still going strong today, 193 years after its founding.

The beginnings of fire insurance in Nova Scotia date to 1784, when the Phoenix Fire Insurance Company of London "accepted a risk" at Halifax. The Phoenix was followed by several British companies, including the Friendly Society, Hand in Hand, Alma, Union Fire Office, Sun Fire Office, Alliance, and Guardian, as well as American companies, such as Aetna from Hartford, Connecticut. It was in the best interests of these risk-takers to promote fire protection in the communities they insured, and donations of money and fire engines were commonly given as an incentive to establish or strengthen a fire brigade. The Halifax Fire Insurance Association provided a fire engine to Halifax in 1827 and two hundred pounds toward building a water reservoir. In 1834, Aetna donated an engine "built under their directives at New York expressly for this place." In recognition of such generosity, the names of insurance benefactors were often adopted by fire brigades or bestowed upon the apparatus they received.

panies employed buckets and hooks for firefighting purposes but were generally more inclined toward salvage and protection of removable property. In D.C. Harvey's *Notes On Fire-fighting in Nova Scotia*, the provincial archivist states: "As early as 1754, the Union Fire Club had been formed among its citizens to provide equipment for fighting fires and rules of conduct in an emergency." When reading the re-discovered "Rules and Orders" of the Union Fire Club, one finds that provisions were also included to address issues of fire prevention. Members were authorized to inspect their neighbourhoods for faulty chimneys, and to take the necessary measures to ensure that repairs were made. Based upon the aforementioned facts, there can be no question that Halifax had an established fire service and fire engines earlier than any currently on record in Canada.

The Union Fire Club was organized at Halifax on January 14, 1754. Few details about the club exist, though we know it was comprised of approximately thirty-four volunteers and that its original by-laws were revised on January 14, 1759 (See Appendix 1). The formation of the Union Engine Company in 1768 may have been a re-structuring of the Union Fire Club or something entirely new. No one may ever know because "the early minutes of the meetings of the company, if regular meetings were held, have not been handed down." It is noteworthy that both the Union Fire Club and the Union Engine Company incorporated "union" into their name, as did later fire brigades in Shelburne and Dartmouth. The same monicker was used by the Union Fire Office—an insurance company organized in London on February 16, 1714—and by Ben Franklin's 1736 Union Fire Company. This common title comes from British firefighting and insurance practices, which would have first influenced colonial America (Philadelphia's founder, William Penn, experienced the Great Fire in London first hand), then progressed to Halifax before spreading with settlement throughout Nova Scotia.

An inventory of firefighting equipment at Halifax in 1749 would have included three-gallon buckets for carrying water, axes, and hooks for entering and tearing down burning buildings; bags and baskets for salvage of personal belongings; bed keys for disassembling wooden frame beds (which in many cases were a householder's most valued possession); two fire engines; and a few short lengths of leather discharge fire hose. In the beginning "there were very few buildings [in Halifax] above a storey and a pitch and the bucket brigade, with the assistance of a hand engine, were able to cope with a fire at its early stages. If a fire had gained headway, the only remedy was, with the assistance of the military, to blow up one or two buildings in the line of a conflagration and leave a gap which the fire could not bridge."

The most important piece of equipment or apparatus was the hand fire engine. Before 1700, the Dutch were innovators in the development of fire engines and fire hose. By the early eighteenth century, England had become the world leader in fire engine design, the most notable builder being Richard Newsham of London, England. Newsham engines came in six sizes, one model having the capacity to throw 160 gallons of water per minute to a height of 165 feet. The first fire engine built in the New World is said to have been copied from a Newsham, and was manufactured in 1743 by New York cooper and boat builder Thomas Lote, who named his creation Old Brass Back. British-made fire engines were used predominately in North America until about 1840, when American builders took over the market. A number of American engines found their way to Nova Scotia because of close trading ties with the New England states.

Early hand-pumped fire engines were fed water by bucket brigades and had a goose-neck nozzle or short length of hose to spray a stream of water. This placed firemen in constant peril because fires had to be fought at close quarter for any hopes of success and many engines burned up. Later design improvements in leather discharge hose—coupled with the development of hard suction hose for drawing water directly to the engine—were boons to firemen, who could then take an offensive stance against fires rather than always fighting what seemed like a losing, rear-guard battle: one hundred feet of fire hose was the equivalent of sixty men with buckets.

Bucket brigades didn't completely disappear from the firefighting scene until the early twentieth century, although their role had diminished considerably by then. Amherst had a long-established, well-equipped fire department in the mid-1900s, yet fire buckets are claimed to have still been prevalent throughout the town. Interestingly, these buckets were round-bottomed, so residents couldn't use them for everyday storage purposes.

At Kingston, a conflagration in 1925 swept away much of the village centre. Without an organized fire department, ninety percent of the water used in fighting the fire was bailed from a ditch running along Main Street. Early settlers were often required to have two or three buckets made of leather or wood always at the ready. When an alarm sounded, people hastened to form two lines—one carrying water to the fire, the other returning empty buckets for refill. When the fire was finally extinguished, in most cases after having burned the building to the ground, buckets were thrown into a communal pile through which people scoured to find their own. The recovery of buckets was made considerably easier as each bucket had the owner's name or initials painted on it; in the case of firemen this also included the respective company's name or insignia. An account regarding lost fire buckets following a Halifax conflagration in 1833 appeared in the *Acadian Recorder* of April 12, 1913:

> After a diligent search for several days, he [fireman] gave up hopes of finding it and reported the same to the [fire] company according to rule. The orders for a new bucket were deferred about two months, expecting the old one might be found, but ultimately a new one had to be made. The same individual, having occasion to go into the Police Office, shortly after, found his bucket in use for a coal scuttle, with his name in full on one side and the company's badge over it. He asked the reason of its being there and was told that it had not been claimed, and that buckets unclaimed had been kept there. In looking about farther, other buckets were found, one of which proved to be his father's— filled with ashes—which he had lost at a fire in Albemarie Street, and one with the name of Wilkie on it, and some without name legible, being worn out. Each of these buckets cost in making, painting and lettering from 4 to 5

dollars. If the authorities did these things with impunity, there need be no surprise that the vicious element in the community had full swing and that the Phoenix's fire buckets became 'small by degrees and beautifully less.'

Although organized in 1768, the Union Engine Company did not adopt its first by-laws and constitution until January 15, 1793. Quite possibly the members were governed by the amended 1759 Union Fire Club charter until then. Whatever the case, the 1793 rules remained in effect until a new set was instituted in November 1826. Revisions followed in 1835 and 1845, but "no very material alterations were then made, the object being to consolidate the rules and resolutions that had been made from time to time, and to strike out any that had become obsolete, or were inconsistent with others passed subsequent to their adoption." The revised rules and regulations were submitted and accepted on September 16, 1845 (see Appendix 2).

The first records for the Union Engine Company date to 1789:

> On the 12th of May an engine was inspected and found in good order, but the hose was defective and was ordered to be repaired. In November the same year an address was presented on behalf of the Company to the King's Court of Quarter Sessions stating that "an engine lately imported from London for the use of the Company was weak in several points, and not to be depended on in case of an occasion arising for its use" and asking that Court to appoint fit and proper persons to examine it with a view to having its defects remedied....It would appear that a new engine was procured early in May 1790 for a minute of the 11th of that month says "The Company met this evening and worked the new engine and drew it up to the engine house in good order and brought down the old one to Mr. Wisdom's store. On June 1st, 1790, at the request of the Governor, the Company met and worked both of the engines and found them in good order." (*Evening Mail*, August 1880)

Benjamin Bridge was captain of the Union Engine Company in 1789. (Although Bridge had long been retired at the time of his death in 1831, firemen demonstrated their benevolent nature "when application was made to the Company for relief for his daughter who was in distressed circumstances and a collection was made for her benefit.") Only fifteen firemen were listed in 1790 on the Union Engine Company roll. Halifax had one engine house at that time, which was presumably located on or near the Grand Parade in the centre of the settlement. The Duke of Kent is said to have borrowed a naval dockyard fire engine in 1799 for use at the Prince's Lodge. It apparently slipped his mind that the engine was on loan, and the naval storekeeper Alexander Anderson was compelled to write the duke requesting his prompt attention to the matter of its return. By 1812, the company numbers had nearly doubled to twenty-eight volunteers in three divisions of fourteen, six, and eight men respectively. In 1826, the company owned four operational hand engines and had increased its strength to sixty members divided into four engine divisions, with each in the charge of a lieutenant. Firemen then paid an initiation fee of eight dollars each to belong. One of the four fire engines was posted in 1834 to the vicinity of St. George's Church, which was the first attempt "to have a portion of the force placed near the extreme ends of the city so as to be more readily available in the event of fires at a distance from the centre." On April 2, 1835, a fifth division was established to take charge of an engine that had arrived in 1834. Firemen named the engine *Nova Scotian*. In June of 1848, "a new engine was procured and a division bearing the same number [No. 6] was drafted to assume charge and care of it." By 1852, Halifax's six fire engines were posted to four engine houses— three were at the Grand Parade, with one each at Maitland Street, Government House Lane, and City Bridewell.

Fire wrought havoc throughout North America in the mid-1800s. In 1835, New York lost 650 buildings from its business district; in 1845, one thousand were razed in Pittsburgh. Two fires in 1845 consumed three thousand structures at Quebec City, while St. John's, Newfoundland, was nearly annihilated in 1846 with the loss of two thousand businesses and homes. B.E.S. Rudachyk describes the Halifax experience in his paper *"At The Mercy Of The Devouring Element"*:

> Halifax, in comparison with her North American counterparts, was not ravaged by the tyrant flame. From 1830 to 1850, although Halifax firefighters contended with 281 fires, only eleven of these destroyed five or more houses per incident-and only one more than thirty....This represents one of the finest firefighting records, for contemporary cities of comparable size, anywhere in North America. It is a remarkable record considering that during the nineteenth-century any uncontrolled fire—however trifling its initial appearance—could, and regularly did, destroy from 5 to 20 buildings.

Halifax's enviable fire record had nothing to do with its predominantly wood construction and condensed layout of narrow blocks and streets. It was "like all nineteenth-century cities....a fire trap." Rudachyk credits Halifax's good fortune in part to "an all-wise Providence" but more importantly to "the effective organization and zealous co-operation of the fire establishment's personnel. By 1830, Halifax's firefighting forces could draw on over sixty years of unbroken tradition. During this time, each element had come to know and to respect each other's place, rights, and duties. Halifax firemen were organized hierarchically in a system that successfully blended the numerous firefighting tasks with the social conventions of the time. This structure displayed remarkable continuity, remaining largely unaltered from the 1760s until 1861." It was composed of seven separate entities: Board of Fire Wardens, volunteer salvage companies, Union Engine Company, Axe Fire Company, fire constables, engine workers, and military personnel.

Nova Scotia's first piece of fire legislation in 1752 created a Board of Fire Wardens comprised of "prudent persons of known fidelity" who were empowered to take charge "at the times of the breaking forth of fire and during continuance thereof." By 1812, Halifax was divided into twenty small fire districts, each under the jurisdiction of a court-appointed fire warden (also called a fire ward), whose varied duties in his designated district included inspecting chimneys and hearths and ordering necessary repairs; administering laws pertaining to the firing of squibs, rockets, serpents, and other fireworks; maintaining pumps and wells; supervising the formation of bucket brigades; co-ordinating the removal

....

of personal belongings and goods from burning buildings; and ordering the demolition of structures to create fire breaks. These "gentlemen of property and standing" were also experienced firemen who could be easily identified at fires carrying their mark of office—a six-foot-long red staff topped with a six-inch brass spear tip.

Donal Baird believes the five protection and salvage companies that operated in Halifax to have been an inordinately large number for one city. These included the Hand-in-Hand (est. 1789), Sun Fire Company (1801), Heart and Hand (1810), Phoenix (?), and Star(?). Three of the five companies (Hand-in-Hand, Sun Fire, and Phoenix) bore the same names as London-based fire insurance companies and American mutual benefit fire clubs, illustrating once again the close ties that influenced early firefighting development in Nova Scotia. Local fire lore has attributed several hundred men to each Halifax salvage company. Rudachyk's findings, however, show a much smaller and more plausible number of approximately forty select members. The Hand-in-Hand and Sun Fire were considered the most exclusive, with membership drawn from bankers, police magistrates, and "the most prominent merchant families." The Phoenix was described as "very efficient being composed chiefly of young tradesmen of the town." All five companies were volunteer, fell under the jurisdiction of the fire wardens, and followed basically the same philosophy, meticulous rules, and operational procedures as those of the Heart and Hand Fire Company, a portion of which are included here:

> We the subscribers, being fully convinced that it is the duty of every member of society to contribute, as far as in him lies, towards the preservation of the property of his fellow townsmen; and having considered the great advantages that have resulted to this community from well-regulated fire companies; and being willing to assist, as far as lies in our power, so laudable an undertaking, have agreed to form ourselves into a society, to be known and distinguished by the name of The Heart and Hand Fire Company—hereby engaging in the event of fire taking place, to give our ready and cheerful assistance for the preservation of the property of our fellow townsmen in general, but more particularly of the members of whom our society is at present, or may hereafter be composed.
>
> Each person on becoming a member of this Society, shall pay into the hands of the Secretary, by the member proposing him, the sum of five shillings; he shall provide himself, before the next quarterly meeting, under a penalty of ten shillings, with two bags, to be made of raven's duck, one and a half yard long, with proper fittings for tying or closing them; the owner's name to be in black letters on one side, and Heart and Hand Fire Company, in black letters, on the other side lengthwise; also with two buckets and a cap, the buckets to contain three gallons each, to be painted black, with owner's name in white letters on the side near the bottom, with a figure of a heart and hand directly over it: the heart to be painted red, the hand flesh color, and reclining on the heart; the cap to be made of leather, with a helmet top seven inches high, the brim three inches in front and a circular flap behind, to fall six inches below the cape of the coat, with the cape of the coat to be painted black with the figure of a heart and hand in front. There shall be furnished, at the expense of

this Company, six lanthorns [sic] and six bed keys; the rims of the lanthorns to be painted red, with the words "Heart and Hand Fire Company" and numbered; the bed keys to be marked Heart and Hand, and also numbered. They shall be delivered to the members appointed by the President to take charge of them. All the foregoing articles shall be kept hanging in the most convenient part of the house in which the member resides, and never be used or removed except on an alarm of fire, under a penalty of ten shillings. The holders of lanthorns shall keep two candles constantly in them, under a fine of five shillings, and they shall bring them, together with the bed keys, at the annual meeting in February, under a penalty of two shillings and six pence. And any member refusing to take charge of any of those articles shall pay a fine of two shillings and six pence for every refusal. Should any of the buckets, bags, caps, lanthorns or bed keys be lost or damaged at a fire, the owner or holder shall give notice to the Secretary within fourteen days after such loss or damage, under a penalty of ten shillings, and when such notice is received by the Secretary, he shall give orders to have the same replaced or repaired at the expense of the Company, within one month after such loss or damage.

Upon every alarm of fire, each member, not sick or absent from town, shall instantly repair with his bags, buckets, etc. to the house of such person as shall appear most endangered; and shall exert his utmost endeavors to preserve his buildings, and rescue his moveable property, by conveying it to any place of safety the owner may direct, No member shall appear at any fire that may happen after sunset, without his cap, under a penalty of two shillings.

A third key factor in the Halifax fire establishment was the Union Engine Company, charged with the responsibility of operating and maintaining the city fire engines. Firefighting history is replete with tales of fisticuffs among rival companies, one incident at New York in 1843 even involved gun play. Brawling and wild west antics, while common to the United States and some parts of Canada, were not manifested in Halifax, nor in other parts of Nova Scotia. Rudachyk attributes this to the Union Engine Company being a multi-division company:

Most contemporary North American engine companies consisted of one engine, one captain, one or two lieutenants and approximately fifty men. The Union Engine Company, on the other hand, by 1848 had six divisions under one captain, twelve lieutenants (six first and six second) and a membership of only eighty men....What the company lacked in manpower, it compensated for with unity of purpose and fellowship. The direction of one company of six engines and sixty to eighty well-trained property owners under one popularly elected captain, eliminated the rivalries, jealousies, and rioting among the companies so common throughout North America. This unity of purpose was translated into early arrival at the scene of alarm and the swift deployment of the various engines, which in turn, did much to prevent small fires from spreading.

Entry to the Union Engine Company was select, as it was in many later fire brigades, with admittance granted by a majority vote of existing members.

....

Coloured beads, beans, or paper were cast in a secret ballot—"white for, black against"—giving rise to the nomenclature of "blackballing." Although a volunteer position, there were enticing job perks for firemen, including ample socializing opportunities and exemptions from jury, constable, and militia duty and the paying of road taxes. Some men joined solely to escape certain of the aforementioned unpleasantries, but their lack of dedication to the business at hand soon became evident, and they were usually dismissed forthwith. In 1846, a man's name was stricken from the books "as he had not met the Company after being two months balloted in. It was supposed that he had his name put on for the purpose of not paying his road tax the present year."

Another important component was the Axe Fire Company, organized at Halifax on July 12, 1813 and credited by Donal Baird with being the first axe-and-ladder company of its kind in Canada; comprised of tradesmen, there were twenty or thirty firemen under one captain and one lieutenant. According to Rudachyk, this select group was "skilled in the use of the axe and saw, knew where to cut to best expose the flames; and, when necessary, where to place the fire hooks to the greatest advantage in order to pull down those houses contiguous to a fire to create a firebreak. This was by far the most dangerous branch of the service as chimneys, roofs, floors, walls, and beams could collapse and fall without warning." The Axe Fire Company also came under the jurisdiction of the fire wardens, receiving the same benefits and travelling in the same social circles as their engine-company counterparts.

Two special categories of the Halifax fire establishment were engine-workers and fire constables. Fires tended to draw crowds of idle onlookers who were often forced into working the hand engines to spell off exhausted firemen. A more popular custom used in England than this press-gang approach was the provision of unlimited beer, which enticed men into working "with a rhythmic chant of 'Beer-Oh! Beer-Oh!' pumping and drinking until they were too duddled to do either." It was common to read in the London morning tabloids of arrests and charges for "drunk and disorderly conduct" on the heels of the previous night's fire. Although men such as noted brewmaster Alexander Keith held fire warden posts, Haligonians appear to have been more temperate in this respect, although, on one occasion at a brewery fire, the press noted that all furnishings and stock were lost, with the exception of "ten casks of spirits which were got out." Halifax fire wardens complained so vigorously in the 1830s of the "most listless and uninterested manner" exhibited by crowds attending fires and their "outright refusal" to obey direct orders to man engines that in 1835 the House of Assembly created a special group of three hundred "engine-workers" whose sole duty was working the pumps. Special constables were appointed at the same time to relieve beleaguered fire wardens of some of the "more disagreeable aspects of policing a fire," such as mustering civilians for bucket-brigade duty.

The last element of the Halifax fire establishment was the military. Many fires were first detected by sentries posted about town, who then blew trumpets to sound the alarm. Large numbers of able-bodied men could be drawn from the garrison, dockyard, ordnance, and naval vessels in the harbour. Thanks to the military, Halifax had more fire engines at its disposal than any Canadian city in the early nineteenth century. At a waterfront fire circa 1840, it has been said that twelve fire engines were operational within ten minutes of the alarm. Toronto, by comparison, had approximately the same population as Halifax at that time (15,000) but could muster only four engines. The reason for such a high number in Halifax was that several of the engines belonged to the British military garrison and naval dockyard.

Military sentry stands guard at Windsor following fire of 1897

Halifax firemen, however, spoke disparagingly of these as being small and "inefficient" when put against their apparatus. The *Acadian Recorder* gave this account of military fire procedure (circa 1817):

It was in General Orders that on an alarm of fire the several Guards and Picquets were to be immediately under arms and to wait the orders of the senior officer in the garrison or the field of the day. All officers and men were required to repair as expeditiously as possible, without arms, to the regimental parade and each corps to remain in Barracks until it received orders to be marched toward the fire. It was then the duty of the commanding officers of corps to detach such men as might be required, with officers, and non-commissioned officers in proportion to form Ranks and assist in passing water or otherwise as the Firewards might desire. Any soldier found out of the Ranks or absent from the post assigned him, was liable to be punished by a Court Martial. The field officer and captain of the day (in concert with the Firewards and Magistrates) directed the employment of the Picquets in

Looting was a universal problem at fires, so much so at Halifax that "scarcely a pile of furniture or goods could be observed without a sentry over it with fixed bayonet pacing up and down." Authorities in Halifax held such a dim view of looting that severe measures were adopted to rectify the situation. On October 9, 1816, a conflagration destroyed a number of businesses and dwellings along Bedford Row and Hollis Street. Shortly thereafter, the administrator of the government issued a proclamation stating "it had been represented that many evil-minded persons took advantage of the dreadful calamity of Wednesday evening last, and did rob, plunder, embezzle and convey away, or conceal the goods, merchandise and effects of the distressed inhabitants. All persons who shall be convicted of having, or detaining in their possession of the goods before mentioned for the space of Two Days after making the Proclamation, such person or persons are liable by Law to be declared Felons and to suffer Death."

the most advantageous manner for the security and protection of property. The Military Fire Engines were required to be moved without delay towards the fire and the commanding officers of corps who furnished men for the engine stationed in the North and South Barracks were required to detach a subaltern officer to take charge of their men with the Engines who was directed to report to the Firewards and then take care to cause their direction to be strictly adhered to. Any non-commissioned officer or soldier who was found employed otherwise than his special duty demanded, or who was detected in taking away goods or furniture, without orders from the magistrates or Firewards, was immediately taken up and confined. The Town Major patrolled the streets contiguous to the fire and took up all straggling soldiers who were found out of the stations allotted to them. Commanding officers of corps were required to be near the station where their men were employed and it was their duty to see that the orders were punctually obeyed, keeping always a proportion of officers with the men so employed. One hundred buckets were placed near the Guard Rooms in the North and South Barracks. The officers in charge of the Guards were responsible that these buckets were never taken from their places, except when to be made use of in the event of a fire or when the engines were ordered out.

It is interesting to note that the military fell under directives of the civilian fire wardens when attending to fire duties. This caused more than its share of problems at times, but city officials were quick to publish an appreciative post-fire acknowledgment in the newspapers:

> The Mayor, on behalf of the citizens, returns his thanks to Major-General Doyle for his promptness and willingness in affording the assistance of the Military when requested. To the officers and men of the Naval and Military Fire Companies and the officers and men of the Dartmouth Fire Department, for their praiseworthy exertions in assisting to arrest the progress of the disastrous Fire which occurred on Tuesday morning last.

Another contentious issue between the Union Engine Company and the military was the matter of "engine bounties." While the British practice of issuing firemarks to specific insurer's properties never materialized in Nova Scotia, insurance companies in Halifax did offer money or engine bounties to the first engine division, civilian or military, arriving at a fire. This may have prompted speed of response but it generated feelings of ill will. The Union Engine Company felt that the military had an unfair advantage as sentries routinely sounded alarms, giving their engines a head start. Following vigorously written complaints that "this Company are fully aware that the compensation now received by them is not adequate to the labor performed," the insurance underwriters agreed to give a "bonus" to the first civilian and military engine arriving upon the scene. This resolved that particular issue, but inter-division quarrelling continued and the Halifax Fire Insurance Company finally eliminated engine bounties in January 1849, giving an eighty-dollar honorarium to the Union Engine Company, a practice thereafter followed by other insurance companies. The Axe Fire Company also benefited from similar donations in recognition of their specialized work.

It was common during the hand-engine era for firemen to stage "public trials" demonstrating the pumping prowess of their machines. Shooting a stream of water over the tallest church spire was one of the more popular exhibitions, drawing large crowds of townsfolk. The following account from an 1880 issue of the *Evening Mail* described the Halifax Union Engine Company's first "trial," held on November 10, 1858 :

The Fire wardens, Fire Constables, Union Engine and Axe Fire Companies with their apparatus mustered on the Grand Parade at the hour appointed and at one p.m. moved off in the order agreed upon. The pageant was headed by the fine band of the flagship and the procession was marshalled by Thomas Hume, the Marshal of the Union Engine Company. The whole passed through Barrington, Argyle, Jacob, Brunswick, Gerrish and Upper Water Streets to Her Majesty's Dockyard, the band playing the old popular airs. The umpires headed the procession. The trials were witnessed by their Excellencies the Lieut. Governor and the Vice Admiral, the Major General commanding the troops in Garrison and a host of leading gentlemen in Halifax.

Arrived at the Dockyard the engines took up positions at the jetty and the trials began with No. 6 ("Alma") through 18 feet suction and 120 feet leading hose. The several engines followed as quickly as possible in the order decided upon by the committee. It is proper to remark that, although the Naval and Military engines did not join in the procession to the Dockyard, yet they were up to time and all ready to participate in turn at the trials. The Royal Artillery sent 40 men with their engine; the 62nd. and 63rd. 30 men each; and the Dockyard and Ordinance tubs were fully manned-the former had her brakes full of Jolly Tars and the latter by good men and true from the Garrison. The several military and naval engines were all small machines, and with the exception of the Sailors', the "Red Lion Saucy", were not named.

The following are the figures reached by each machine. No. 1 engine *Rapid* threw 102 feet; No 2 engine *Alliance*, 94 feet; No. 3 engine *Halifax*, 188 feet; No. 4 engine *Resolute*, 126 feet; No. 5 engine *Aetna*, 121 feet, No. 6 *Alma* engine, 116 feet; Dockyard engine *Red Lion Saucy*, 92 feet; Ordnance engine, 66 feet; Artillery engine, 58 feet; 62nd. Regiment, 67 feet; 63rd. Regiment, 58 feet. All things considered No. 5 *Aetna* played the best horizontal stream of any tub on the ground. She is the senior engine in the city, having been added to the Department as far back as the summer of 1834. No. 3 the "Cock of the Walk" on the present occasion was built by Old Tilley, of London, and was imported by the city in 1844.

The order was then given for Captain Roome's very efficient Axe and Ladder Company to show what they could perform. In considerably less than fifteen minutes, the whole roof of the issuing store in H.M. Dockyard was covered with ladders, etc. The next trial was alongside the steamer Styx, Commander Vesey, at the Dockyard wharf. The engines taking part in this display drew a supply of water through 18 feet of suction hose, and threw it over the fore-royal mast truck-a distance of 135 feet. This was very handsome practice and all that tried succeeded except No 2 whose water only reached the top-gallant yard and cross trees.

After the trial was over, the Mayor addressed the men complimenting them highly on their efficiency. In the evening the firemen and their friends were entertained to a sumptuous supper at Mason Hall by the several Fire Insurance Associations and Agencies in the city.

The importance of the hand fire engine lessened in the mid-1800s with the arrival of the steam engine. George Braithwaite and John Ericsson of London, England are credited with building the world's first steam fire engine circa 1828—a ten horse-power engine that could pump 150 gallons of water per minute to a height of ninety feet within twenty minutes of firing the boiler. The engine's worth was proven at a fire "in the depths of winter" when the steamer worked non-stop for five hours while hand engines around it froze up. Most people, however, were hesitant to endorse "such a controversial device." A humorous anecdote involving the engine designers' early frustrations involved a London brewery. Following a fire on the brewery premises, at which the steamer was used, the proprietors asked for the lend of the engine on a one-month trial basis. Braithwaite, seeing a possible sale, was only too happy to accommodate their request. The steamer was subsequently used day and night for the entire month to pump not water, but beer, and then returned to Braithwaite without an offer to purchase. Eventually, of course, the steam engine came to be accepted in British firefighting circles. The technology spread to the United States, and by the mid-1800s Seneca Falls, New York, was touted as the "fire engine capital of the world." Philadelphia was also noted for its steam-engine manufacturers, and in 1859 hosted a "great trial of steam fire engines" considered to have been "the first real public demonstration of the state of the art of building and operating steam fire appliances." A similar international exhibition was staged at London, England in 1862.

At least twenty-seven steam fire engines were used in Nova Scotia between 1861 and 1907. Seven manufacturers produced them, including Shand-Mason (a British firm); Amoskeag, Silsby and Cole Bros.(American); and Ronald, Waterous, and Burrell-Johnson (Canadian). Waterous began in Brantford, Ontario, but later moved to St. Paul, Minnesota. Burrell-Johnson Iron Company was a Yarmouth, Nova Scotia, foundry that built only two steam fire engines— one stayed in Yarmouth, the other was sold to Digby. As mentioned regarding hand engines, one hundred feet of fire hose could do the work of sixty men with water buckets. In the evolutionary process of fire apparatus, a single steam engine operated by only three men was claimed to produce the same results as one hundred men on hand engines. This revelation led to considerable unrest in the old garrison town.

Things went smoothly for Halifax firemen until 1861 when members of the Union Engine and Axe fire companies resigned. The reason for such audacious behaviour was in large measure due to the arrival of Canada's first steam fire engines in Halifax. Firemen saw the steamer as not only a new-fangled contraption but a threat to their very existence. Because of the nature of their work and the influential composition of their membership, fire companies in cities across North America had become a force to be reckoned with in the political arena. Halifax City Council viewed the steam engine as a means to lessen the political clout that firemen had come to wield.

After a firefighting candidate for the Union Engine or Axe Fire companies was successfully voted in, his name was forwarded through the Board of Fire Wardens to the Court of General Sessions—later city council—for final approval. The same procedure was followed for officer nominations. Except on rare occasions, this was a mere formality. Refusal to rubber stamp a captain's appointment in 1835 had led to a major rift in the company with the majority of firemen resigning. In 1861, a similar occurrence tore the fabric of the Halifax fire establishment asunder. On May 6, 1861, Alderman James Duggan moved the following resolution at a meeting of council:

> That in future no person be acknowledged a member of the Fire Company of the city, or entitled to receive the privileges allowed by law to firemen, unless they shall be elected by the Council in accordance with the law, and that the Captain of Union Engine Company shall report to this Council through his worship the Mayor, any vacancies that may from time to time occur in ranks of the Engine Company, in order that the same may be filled by the Council.

Infuriated firemen gave council forty-eight hours to change their minds. When the time elapsed without conciliation, the two fire companies, along with four fire wardens, tendered their resignations. There was no dearth of volunteers to fill the void; in fact, more applied than required. Less than two weeks later, on May 21, 1861, 150 firemen in six divisions assumed their duties as the newly appointed Volunteer Engine Company (this name change didn't catch on and firemen retained the traditional Union Engine Company). As for the disgruntled ex-members, they re-organized themselves into a salvage group to be known as the Union Life and Fire Protection Company ("Life and Fire" was later dropped) and worked independently under separate charter until they disbanded circa 1919. Despite the fact the newly formed Union Engine and Union Protection companies "were for several years bitter rivals," both performed their fire duties side by side for the common good of the community. Over time, "the feeling of antagonism happily died out" and they became amiable partners in the working and social life of Halifax. As for the ancient salvage clubs, their role and existence seems to have faded away with the dawn of a new firefighting era. The military, while not as prominent in later years regarding city firefighting, still provided mutual aid when required until Imperial forces were called home from Canada in 1905-06.

So far, our discussion has focussed on Halifax, and for good reason: it was there that Nova Scotia's fire roots took hold. Widespread settlement in the province didn't begin until the late 1700s with the Acadian repatriation and the influx of thousands of Scots, Planters, and Loyalists. The province's second-oldest fire company was established at Shelburne in 1784, one year after the town's founding. The Friendly Fire Club—a mutual benefit protection and salvage group—had a membership restricted to forty men "dedicated to assist each other in time of fire." Each fireman was responsible for providing two three-bushel bags, two leather buckets, and a round hat with black brim and white crown inscribed with the letters "F.F.C." When the alarm sounded, generally a church

Union Engine Company 1860 banner

On June 8, 1860, the Union Engine Company marched in a procession as part of festivities celebrating Halifax Natal Day. "On that day the City Corporation presented the Company with a banner." Minutes of a June 19 firemen's meeting indicate the passing of a motion ordering "a suitable box be procured to contain the splendid new banner...also suitable belts for carrying the banner [and] two suitable wreaths for the banner be procured." Both the Union Engine and Axe Fire companies possessed banners that were boldly displayed at every opportunity, whether it be marching in one of their numerous parades or sleighing through city streets en route to one of many favourite "watering holes." As the Prince of Wales was due to visit Halifax in the summer of 1860, the new banner was no doubt intended as a replacement for an older one that had reportedly been undergoing much-needed repairs. April 1860 was also the first mention of a fireman's uniform, which indicates that the Halifax smoke-eaters were preparing a grand show for His Royal Highness.

Union Engine Company coat of arms on reverse of 1860 banner

The Union Engine Company's original banner had been donated by William Caldwell many years prior to 1860. Caldwell joined the Union Engine Company in 1821, serving as its captain from April 1839 until his retirement in August 1846. On August 31 of that year, Caldwell was given a testimonial dinner, where he was presented with a gold-inlaid walking cane and bestowed the special rank of honourary assistant captain. In regards to retirement, it was noted in May 1843 that "all members desiring to retire after 16 years service must signify such intention in writing three months before leaving or forfeit their certificate of past membership." Further to this, Halifax City Council donated a generous sum of money to the company on February 17, 1857, "to procure an engraving for the purpose of furnishing members with a certificate of the period of their service." For their part, the Union Engine Company ordered a copy of the fireman's retiring certificate be framed and presented to city council. A resolution had been unanimously passed on June 18, 1839, "that a member after serving sixteen years and having arrived at the age of 45 shall be exempt from all fines unless he is an officer of the Company or holds a commission as such." Sixteen years must have been the standard for firemen, as similar retirement provisions were adopted by several fire departments.

bell, men raced to members' homes most threatened, where entry was gained only by using a password. Fines were levied for not having equipment at the ready or failing to give the secret code. The Friendly Fire Club was still operational in 1795, with sixteen members.

Organized efforts at early fire protection were few and far between in Nova Scotia. When looking through local histories, one invariably finds exhaustive records relating to commerce, religion, and education but—with few exceptions—little or no mention of fire departments. There could be several reasons for this. Fire brigades came and went, depending upon the enthusiasm of those involved. River John, for example, had a Hook & Ladder Company in 1869 but it died out; efforts were then made in the 1930s to re-organize, but these, too, petered out until a third and successful attempt circa 1950. Volumes could be written on Nova Scotia's firefighting past, but all too often, the consuming flame swept through unsuspecting towns, reducing valuable municipal records to ash. In many cases, organized fire protection simply didn't exist. Dartmouth was settled in 1750, but its Union Engine Company was not established until 1822; Germans and Swiss immigrated to Lunenburg in 1753, but it was 1820 before the first fire brigade was organized. Loyalists founded Digby in 1783, but it would be one hundred and three years before that town had its first fire department. Sydney, too, was settled by Loyalists, in 1785, but not until 1852 did a fire brigade materialize. These are but a few examples of a province-wide trend that saw decades, sometimes a century or more, pass from the time of settlement to a concerted effort at establishing fire protection. Even then, it was often the larger towns which took the initiative; for the fishing village or farming hamlet it would be the mid-1900s or later before a volunteer fire department became reality. Of the 314 fire departments in Nova Scotia today, the majority were not started until after World War Two.

Fire can be a comforting friend or formidable foe. Settlers certainly knew its danger, speaking derisively in terms of "fiendish monster," "tyrant flame," "fiery serpent," and "devouring element." When hacking out an existence in a new land, however, mere survival took precedence over preventive and protective fire measures. Land had to be cleared; streets laid out; homes, outbuildings, stores, and churches erected; fields tilled and crops planted; vessels built; trade and fishing pursued. Wood was king, open fires the norm—a perfect recipe for trouble. It often took little time for the "devouring element" to pay a visit. The following account of a fire at Truro illustrates the typical resourcefulness and resiliency necessary for those early times:

> On May 8th, 1796, being Sabbath, Mr. Cock was preaching….The people being nearly all at Church, his house took fire on the roof by a spark from the chimney, and before assistance could be had the house was in flames. George Wright ran to the Church for assistance, a distance of about two miles. He went to the door and cried out fire! fire! and returned with haste. Few persons heard him, and those who did hear began to go out, which created quite a confusion in the house. It was some time before the cause of the stir was

Introduction

generally known. At length his youngest daughter went up to the Pulpit and told her father that his house was burning. He closed the Bible and stepped down from the Pulpit, quite composed, and recommended the people to try and save the Village. It being a very dry time, and the wind blowing very strong from the southeast, the fire soon caught on Major John Archibald's three barns. The burning shingles were flying, and the smoke so thick it was with difficulty that the people got up through the Village. John Logan's barns next took fire, and then William Logan's barns. The fire continued to sweep the buildings of the Village to the lower end of it. The number of buildings destroyed that day was eighteen. The dwelling houses were saved, with the exception of Mr. Cock's and William Flemming's. Thomas Dickey's house was in great danger, the chips catching fire at the door; and, as there were neither men nor water at hand to save the house, Mrs. Dickey took her churn full of cream and applied it to quench the fire, and by doing so made out to save her house. (Thomas Miller. *Historical & Genealogical Record of First Settlers of Colchester County*)

Accounts of fires and their aftermath generally relate a very matter-of-fact, get-on-with-life attitude. Following a 1892 blaze at Stewiacke that destroyed the Presbyterian manse, "with characteristic promptness and energy the people at once undertook the work of rebuilding." A year later the church caught fire. "The immense crowd of people who gathered could do nothing but stand and see the old church burn to ashes. At once, measures were adopted which resulted in the erection of the present church in the course of the summer of that year." Following the Great Middleton Fire of January 27, 1911, which "wiped out" the town's business district, an upbeat article appeared one week later in the *Outlook*:

> The most encouraging feature of all is the manly way in which our business-men have faced the situation. To see the results of years of labor swept away in an hour and to be obliged to begin again where one started 10 or 20 years ago is discouraging. Yet we hear no suggestion of giving up in despair, nor see any sign of lack of faith in the future of our town.

Middleton had at least taken initial steps toward organized fire protection before its catastrophe. Fire department budget for 1911 amounted to $285, of which $216 was spent on apparatus and $48 dollars on firemen. Generally, however, when communities suffered fire losses there was invariably talk of better fire protection but little transpired and, human nature being what it is, complacency set in until the next fire. This is not to imply that people did nothing, but action would appear to have been more spontaneous than organized—ringing the church bell or banging on doors to raise the alarm, running with buckets, shovels, water-soaked blankets or whatever could be hastily found to stay the fire's progress, salvaging as many personal effects as possible, and then rebuilding when the ruins cooled. At some point, patience wore thin and a fire brigade or protection and salvage company materialized, as did fire wardens and fire constables. Merchants and businessmen were the catalyst in most cases, as they stood to lose the most in the event of fire. Rudachyk's ideas on why men joined the Halifax Union Engine Company could be applied to fire brigades in general:

> Quite apart from motives of public spiritedness, the thrill and excitement of firefighting, the camaraderie occasioned at the companies' numerous social events, the special privileges enjoyed by members of the companies or even the inside track on departmental supply and repair contracts, these men fought fires out of sheer self-interest. Every alarm of fire meant the potential loss of the fruits of a lifetime of toil.

With Halifax having the oldest fire service in the province, the organizational structure of its Union Engine Company often served as a blueprint for other towns. When Truro established a volunteer fire brigade in 1868, James Publicover (an ex-fireman from Dartmouth then living in Truro) "provided a printed constitution and by-laws of the Halifax Engine Company as a guide." Dartmouth assuredly copied its cross-harbour neighbour when setting up its own Union Engine Company in 1822. The structure and composition of most early fire brigades differed only from Halifax in that they were on a smaller scale. New Glasgow was a good example. In his book *More About New Glasgow*, James Cameron writes that the town had a hand engine and firemen prior to incorporation in 1875 but existing records are "unusually sparse." In 1876, six fire wardens and an equal number of fire constables were appointed. New Glasgow purchased its first steam fire engine and one thousand feet of hose in 1877 for six thousand dollars. A year later, three men were hired to operate the engine—one at fifty dollars and two at twenty-five dollars, per annum. Whenever the engine raised steam, the men received a two dollar bonus.* In 1879, New Glasgow's fifty-man fire brigade was divided into three companies: a steam engine company comprised of twenty-two men, a hook-and-ladder company of ten men, and an eighteen-man hand engine company. By 1883, brigade strength had been increased to five companies (possibly a hose company and a salvage company), and in 1885 a second steam engine was purchased. A piped water system and forty hydrants were installed circa 1888, with each hydrant costing thirty-five dollars.

It was all well and good to have a measure of fire protection within town limits, but Nova Scotia was very much a rural province where people often lived far from any hope of assistance. In those cases of fire, people were left to fend for themselves. No one was immune from threat, not even Nova Scotia's most notable seasonal resident. On January 11, 1892, Alexander Graham Bell wrote to his wife Mabel Bell in the United States from Beinn Bhreagh, their estate retreat at Baddeck on Cape Breton Island.

---

* In some cases, a town council had the money to hire a select number of firemen on a permanent or call basis for key positions within the department. Halifax firemen were still volunteers in 1890 with the exception of twenty-six in the Union Engine Company who were paid on a permanent or call basis. Full-time included one caretaker, electrician, storekeeper and chemical engineer, and seventeen drivers who "literally sleep alongside the apparatus, ready for instant service by day or night, never leaving the engine house." Five steam engineers were remunerated as call men to operate the fire engines when needed.

Laboratory is now closed for the season. Mr. Ellis will spend tomorrow in putting tools and etc. away. Just as we had concluded experiment of boiling water we were all startled by the appearance of Mrs. Martin who rushed almost breathless into the laboratory and subsided on a stool with a gasp of "Fire." Instantly laboratory was vacated—Mr. Martin, Mr. McInnis and John McKillop ran a race to the Lodge. I followed more leisurely.

Stove pipe red hot-showers of sparks from chimney—that was all—no cause for extreme alarm displayed. Everyone seemed in a panic—Mr. Martin had the fire-hose out—squirting water all over himself in so doing. [few had the resources of Mr. Bell to have what appears to have been a privately owned fire pump]. Johnny seemed to be everywhere at once—I caught Mr. McInnis rushing wildly to the stove in the hall with a large tin of water. I stopped him just as he was about to throw it on the fire. A nice mess he would have made of your parlor had I been a moment later.

I didn't think the stove much mattered when the trouble was in the stove pipe higher up. Real danger in the attic where nobody was. Went up there with Mr. McInnis and Johnny. Found some brown paper on floor on fire— smouldering. Put it out. Stationed Johnny there to watch it-with water from cistern. Then sent Mr. McInnis up ladder to roof outside with fire-hose to deluge roof as the quantity of burning stuff out of chimney decidely alarming.

Found fire-hose worked admirably—wet the whole roof on both sides—let chimney blaze away. Fire soon burned itself out."
(Alexander Graham Bell Papers; Library of Congress)

The late 1800s was the era of town incorporation. With a change in civic status came an increased responsibility for better fire protection. At the behest of underwriters, and driven by upward-spiralling fire insurance rates, several communities organized their first fire departments—Windsor (1881), Amherst (1883), North Sydney (1885), Kentville (1888), Parrsboro (1889), Wolfville (1890), Middleton (1890), Stellarton (1893), and Lawrencetown (1898). Back in Halifax, it wasn't organization but disintegration that had the venerable Union Engine Company worried.

By 1893, the city's fire establishment had four components: the Board of Firewards; the Union Engine Company (126 active members in five engine and three hose divisions, plus fifty-nine honorary members); the Union Axe Company (forty firemen in two divisions, North and South); and the Union Protection Company (forty-five active and forty-one honourary members). The *Daily Echo* of October 30, 1894, reported that "for some time matters have been tending in the direction of a radical change in the fire department." Like the old days of 1861, the Union Engine Company and city council drew battle lines. It was reported that only forty firemen were available for fire duty on a regular basis. This would have been the entire force for most towns, but in the provincial capital it meant only a twenty-five percent turnout. The *Daily Echo* kept Haligonians apprised of developments, even going so far as to survey firemen to determine the reasons for their absenteeism. They were as varied as the men who comprised the company: steamship engineer— "at sea"; lineman—"out of of town much of the time"; merchant— "awkward to leave business"; dry dock worker— "cannot attend in day time"; policeman—"cannot leave his beat"; roofer—"liable to be in any part of the city"; hackman—"1 mile from apparatus." Published results concluded:

> The fault does not lie with the firemen, most of whom are always willing to give their time and services when time is their own....In day time the city is worst off. Most of the men are not employed in the evenings or at night and are always ready to turn out to answer an alarm. But in daytime they find it impossible to respond or if not impossible not judicious as but few of them would care to jeopardise their position.

Valid reasons to be sure, but too many firemen were far from their apparatus. An extreme example was William Hughes, who would have had great difficulty hearing the alarm considering he lived in Windsor, forty-five miles from his assigned engine house!

In 1894, Halifax had a substantial investment in its fire establishment— $43,850 in real estate and personal property, $22,490 in five steam engines, $8,700 in fire hose, $4,200 for hose and ladder tenders, and $3,450 for twenty-three horses. City Hall believed the volunteer system was no longer viable. Bickering went on for nearly a year in council chambers and the press. On October 17, 1894, the following resolution to dissolve the Union Engine Company was tabled and passed by a vote of nine to seven.

> Whereas it is in the opinion of this council essential to the good government of the city that the city council should have absolute control over the fire apparatus and appliances belonging to the city and also control over all persons in charge of such property; therefore resolved that the services of the U.E. Co. be forthwith dispensed with, and that the city clerk be instructed to notify the said company accordingly.

The *Daily Echo* of November 2, 1894, announced the formation of a newly structured and renamed Halifax Fire Department based on a part-paid, part-call format. The days of the Union Engine Company were over, and it wasn't a smooth transition.

> There is likely to be some little trouble between some members of the Union Engine company and the new department. It seems that late last night or early this morning all articles of furniture, pictures, etc. belonging to the different divisions were taken from the rooms in most of the engine houses. In one house two men are known to have removed a bookcase and a number of other articles and it is probable a warrant will be issued at the instance of other members of the division who have an interest in the furnishings. The flag on the engine house on Spring Garden Road was put at half-mast.

The first half of the twentieth century brought a whirlwind of change. Halifax organized a fully paid, permanent fire department in 1918. Hay burners gradually gave way to gas guzzlers as horse-drawn steam engines were replaced by triple combination motorized fire engines, each capable of doing the work of three separate pieces of earlier fire apparatus. At the close of

World War Two, Federal War Assets provided cheap, surplus equipment that for many communities was an affordable means to finally organize a fire department of their own. Just as important was a shift in philosophy from one of fighting fires to that of identifying causes and preventing fires. This was unfortunately a concept that took many years to develop .

One of the first fire-prevention measures at Halifax addressed the number of bush fires that were becoming "a menace to the buildings and fences about the town," measures that included this 1753 proclamation:

> All persons are hereby forbid to burn any bush on their lot or otherwise but at such times and in such manner that the fire will not spread. And notice is hereby given that all persons who shall light fires are liable by law to any damage that shall accrue therefrom. And owners of lots who intend to clear and fence the same are hereby advised that a law is ordered to be prepared for the better securing them from accidents by fires carelessly lighted.

It was previously noted that one of the duties of Halifax fire wardens in 1752 was the inspection of chimneys to ensure proper cleaning and maintenance. Similar steps were taken at Shelburne in 1784, when fire wardens were assigned to the five town divisions and two directors of chimney sweeps appointed. Edward Elliot, the licensed chimney sweep in charge, inspected all flues in new buildings to ensure there was sufficient width to accommodate his sweeps, who were generally small boys capable of squeezing into tight spaces. The sheriff and town constables were empowered to tear down such chimneys and flues found defective or not meeting Elliot's code.

Another fire-prevention measure came after a forest fire-ravaged Shelburne in June 1792, destroying fifty farm houses, barns, and out-buildings, as well as a mill and several bridges along the Jordan River. The result of this was a Court of Sessions order similar to one in Halifax banning all burning of brush, meadows, and marshes between May 15 and October 15.

Arson was a plague which had no respect for preventive ordinances and by-laws. In 1802, it was recorded at Halifax that "several fires occurred in June which were supposed to be the work of incendiaries. It had been proved beyond all doubt that buildings in several parts of the town had been set on fire. A patrol of militia under Colonel Pyke was ordered to patrol the streets from sunset to sunrise and all suspected persons who could not give a good account of themselves at night were ordered to be arrested. A reward of 100 pounds was offered for discovery, and several arrests were made. A boy who confessed to having attempted to set fire to the Dockyard was sent out of the province." Little could be done to keep arsonists in check, but increased pressure was applied by fire wardens for residents to assume more responsibility for their chimneys, as these were the number one cause of fires. Notice was given that anyone's chimney catching fire "unless such chimney had been swept by a licensed sweeper within one month of the date of the fire" would be prosecuted "with the utmost vigor." The cost of chimney sweeping, to be borne by the home owner, amounted to one shilling for a two-storey dwelling, ninepence for a one storey. Further measures in 1830 banned smoking on wooden planked sidewalks.

A noteworthy feature of this fireman's portrait is the Maltese cross on William Settle's tunic breast pocket. Known also as the cross Pattee-Nowy or the Calvary cross, it has long been the universal fire service insignia. The origin of the cross dates to the eleventh and twelfth centuries, when it was adopted by the Knights of St. John of Jerusalem (Knights Hospitallers), a charitable order serving the sick and poor, as well as providing military assistance to the Knights of the Crusades on the island of Malta—thus the name. Adopted as the symbol of the Crusaders, the Maltese cross served a practical purpose as well, distinguishing friend from foe in battles that featured similarly clad combatants. Its association with fire-fighting resulted from the heroic deeds of knights rescuing comrades who were targeted by enemy incendiary bombs and fire ships containing naptha. In recognition of these gallant acts, the Crusaders' crosses were adorned with decorative inscriptions. Through the ages, the eight points of the Maltese cross have come to represent the principles of gallantry, sympathy, tact, observation, explicitness, dexterity, loyalty, and perseverance.

Many of the firemen's badges adopted the Maltese cross in some form. Dartmouth's first firemen's badge was a roughly cut Maltese cross with "1822" inscribed upon it. When Halifax reorganized its volunteer firemen into a part paid, part call force in 1894, one hundred and fifty new badges were purchased that were no doubt the same or similar to the one worn in this photo. An earlier badge resembled a western sheriff's star. Truro firemen ordered new silver badges in 1895 at a cost of seventy-five cents each, which "remained the property of the Company and in the event of a member leaving the Company, his badge is to be returned;" a year earlier, the fire brigade had presented Captain A.E. McKay with a gold badge in recognition of services rendered. New Glasgow spent three dollars in 1882 for badges to be worn by its six fire wardens; warden and fire constable badges were more inclined towards a shield design.

Thomas Raddall believed that destructive fires did have their positive side. "In truth fire was a benefactor in the old crowded wooden city, whatever the momentary suffering….A great fire [1816] swept away the sprawling rookery of old wooden shops and warehouses between Sackville Street, Hollis Street and Bedford Row, and these were replaced very rapidly with new and better structures, often in brick or stone." Raddall points out that, thanks to fire, Halifax had thirty-seven brick buildings and seventy-three built of stone by 1827. Fire, especially in its conflagration state, also caught the attention of towns outside of the provincial capital. Unfortunately, it often took more than one visit to warrant changes. At North Sydney on May 5, 1913, forty-one businesses were reduced to ashes. This in itself was disastrous, but the same area had been burned over in 1881. Finally, in May 1916, the Nova Scotia Legislature acted upon a resolution submitted by North Sydney officials that "all buildings, hereafter to be erected on either side of Commercial Street within the town of North Sydney, extending westerly from the ICR crossing to Peppett Street shall be constructed of brick, concrete or stone." New Glasgow took similar steps in 1910, when all wooden construction was forbidden within an area designated the "brick district." The February 3, 1911, issue of the *Middleton Outlook* reported, in regards to the town's "great fire," that brick would be used to rebuild the business district as "to do otherwise appears to be inviting another disaster and indicates a failure to learn from sad experience."

Building with stone was a positive first step, but it gave a false sense of security. The 1944 annual report of the Department of Labour, Fire Marshal Branch, emphasized that "contrary to general belief, the interior of brick and wooden buildings may burn as rapidly as buildings of entire frame type." Statistics released by the Fire Marshal's office for 1943 showed 1,328 fires in the province that year accounted for $1,627,644 property damage, with thirty-three people losing their lives and sixty-six injured.

> In nearly every case the cause of death and injury has been faulty building construction which has permitted rapid spread of fire and trapping of occupants....The Fire Marshal's conclusions are none of these fires would have happened had standard precautions in construction of chimneys, correct installation of heating equipment and smoke pipes, standard electric wiring and control of the smoking of tobacco in all forms been practised.

Sprinklers were in their infancy then, but the consensus was that "this is a protective device that should receive the earnest consideration of all Board of Commissioners." Fire-prevention education was just becoming "recognized as a most important section of work done by the Fire Marshal service."

Nearly sixty years have passed since the first concerted efforts at fire prevention in Nova Scotia were undertaken. The most recent report available from the Fire Marshal's Office (for the fiscal year ending March 31, 1999) shows that great strides have been made in some areas while at the same time giving one a sense of déjà vu. The leading causes of fire are still traceable to heating, cooking, and electrical sources. The number one cause of fire deaths is cigarette smoking related. For the ten-year period between 1989-90 and 1998-99, there were 184 fatalities and 592 injuries in Nova Scotia attributable to fire. While a single loss of life is one too many, there has, at least, been a steady decline in numbers, from thirty-five in 1989-90 to ten for 1998-99. There are a number of reasons for this, including improvements in fire-retardant construction materials, stricter building codes, and early warning systems, such as properly installed and maintained smoke detectors. Public fire safety awareness has been heightened through various educational media, including the "Learn Not To Burn" program introduced to schools and a "Retire Your Fryer" campaign to rid households of that outmoded, dangerous cooking appliance. Home and business fire-hazard inspections are readily available, as are continually improving fire-related training programs for civilian and fire service personnel. Most recently, the Fire Prevention Act has undergone a full review, its first in twenty years. One of several recommendations made by an all-party committee to the legislature is for the Nova Scotia Government to adopt the Canadian National Fire Code as a provincial standard. Thanks to ever-improving technology, firefighters have never been better prepared, equipped, or protected than they are today. A Nova Scotia Firefighters School has been operational for more than thirty years. Special HazMat teams address the increasing challenges of hazardous materials, and many firefighters are trained now as medical first responders. Despite safety advances, the dangers of the profession are manifested in the fact that fourteen Nova Scotia firefighters were listed among the injured in the 1998-99 Fire Marshal's report, and a firefighter was killed in the line of duty as recently as 1997.

Nova Scotia currently has nine thousand firefighters serving in 314 fire departments, of which approximately 8,500 (or ninety-four percent) are volunteers. A press release dated September 19, 1999 proclaimed that "history was made in Halifax on August 15th, 1999 [when] more than 65 representatives from volunteer fire departments from British Columbia, Saskatchewan, Ontario, Quebec, Nova Scotia, New Brunswick, Prince Edward Island, Newfoundland, and Nunavut were represented for the first meeting of the newly created Canadian Volunteer Fire Services Association." Future plans included appointing representatives from Manitoba, Alberta, and the Yukon. As of the 1999 report, there were "more than 120,000 volunteer firefighters in Canada, a number which makes up more than eighty percent of the firefighters across the country." Donal Baird writes that in all of Canada "possibly the most notable hotbed of volunteer firemen is Nova Scotia."

The era of the bucket brigade and men working hand engines to exhaustion passed long ago into the pages of time. Gone are the days when the tolerance to "eat smoke" was as much an accepted part of the job as it was a badge of courage. There are few left who can recount seeing fire horses race madly through streets with steam engines in tow. The purpose of this book is twofold. As a historical essay dependent upon photographs and anecdotal facts, it tells the story of the first two hundred years of firefighting in Nova Scotia, circa 1750 to 1950—the equipment and apparatus, engine houses, the men, their work and leisure, and some of the great fires and disasters they faced. As a tribute, it honours society's vanguard in times of need: smoke-eaters of the past, firefighters of the present and future.

....

Introduction

Engine house mascots

A book on firefighting would be incomplete without mention of mascots. Jack Russell terriers Nix (black eye patch) and Girlie were mascots of the Halifax Fire Department in 1910; they appear in many photos with Chief Patrick Broderick. The Dalmatian has long been cast in fire lore as the typical engine-house mascot. Blessed with stamina and the innate ability to run among horses' hoofs without being trampled, these "carriage dogs" were used to protect stage coach travellers from highwaymen. In the days of horse-drawn fire apparatus, they guided teams and firemen through busy streets. Dalmatians are also said to have formed strong bonds with fire horses and served as a calming influence during times of crisis and chaos. Some even claim they prevented rats from chewing up leather fire hose. Despite the Dalmatian's numerous merits, it cannot be said that the breed figured in the Nova Scotia firefighting story. The only mention was a short-lived venture in the 1950s, when the Oland family of local brewing and political fame donated a Dalmatian to each Halifax fire station. The dogs apparently developed sore feet and cracked pads, from the concrete floors, and had to be given away. The occasional cat found its way into the hearts of firemen—West Street had Madame Queen, Morris Street was home to Rusty, Bedford Row was patrolled by Jean, while many others went nameless. A much-heralded canine mascot belonged to fireman Patrick Connors, who joined the Union Engine Company in 1861; an undated newspaper account reported the following:

A splendid animal, a cross between a Newfoundland and a Retriever, for many years accompanied her owner to all the gatherings of No. 6 Division and was always the first in case of an alarm to seize the end of the rope and help to haul the engine to the fire. She was an active and valued attache of the Division until her death, resulting, as was supposed, from injuries received at a fire at which she assisted…Mr. Connors' dog Darky was known by every fireman. Although a most intelligent and sagacious animal it had some bad traits. After nearly every fire, Darky would return to his home intoxicated. Ale was his favourite beverage and he imbited freely.

Chapter 1

Apparatus & Equipment

c.1785–1907

Halifax Fire Chief Patrick J. Broderick and driver, c.1910

Halifax provided its fire chief with a horse-and-rubber-tire patrol buggy to assist with his daily duties of overseeing eight engine houses and for quick response to emergency calls. A gong, as featured on the front of this buggy, was standard with all early fire apparatus and served to warn pedestrians and traffic to clear the street for oncoming firemen. The only piece of equipment carried on the chief's wagon was a first aid kit "for men and horses." Horses were high maintenance. A Dr. Jakeman provided veterinary care to Halifax "hay burners" for many years. The cost of these services was put out to annual tender. In 1907, Dr. Jakeman was the only veterinarian to submit a bid to the Board of Fire Commissioners, but his fee of six dollars a horse "was thought to be too high, and was on motion filed." An agreement must have eventually been reached, as Dr. Jakeman was still listed on engine-house log books seventeen years later.

This Newsham fire engine was named in honour of King George III, England's reigning monarch from 1760–1820. Preserved today in the Shelburne County Museum, it is one of North America's oldest surviving relics from the eighteenth century firefighting era. Two of these London-built engines were ordered for Shelburne in 1785 through local merchants Benjamin Davis and James Robertson. The following advertisement appeared at the time in the *Port Roseway Gazetteer and General Advertiser*:

c.1785 hand fire engine *King George*, Shelburne

The Chamber will receive proposals in writing from any person or persons willing to contract for the building of two houses, proper for the reception of the fire-engines, making ladders, fire hooks etc. on ground that will be pointed out by applying to the subscriber, with whom a plan of the whole is left for that purpose.
By Order W. Branthwaite, Secty.

One engine was stationed at opposite ends of the town in North and South Divisions and manned by a small contingent of firemen. The standard design used in North America during the late 1700s, these "petty engins" have been described as "nothing more than bathtubs on wheels [with a pump and chain driven pistons] that were filled with buckets of water which was then sprayed onto the fire by means of side or end mounted handles." (Bucket-fed engines were referred to as "tubs," while later models using suction hose were known as "hand engines.") A drawback to engines such as *King George* were fixed wheel axles, which limited their manoeuverability. To compensate for this, the front end of the engine had to be physically lifted when cornering. If going any distance, firemen sometimes found the chore easier than towing the engine with hand ropes to carry it in a wagon or to simply pick it up and run to the fire. Both Shelburne engines were used until circa 1834. Many years after its firefighting days were finished, *King George* was unceremoniously filled with dirt and left as a planter on the front lawn of a Shelburne home until rescued by local firemen. Legend also contends that American millionaire Henry Ford tried unsuccessfully to purchase the venerable artifact for a curio. The other engine is said to have been broken up for firewood.

Industrialist John P. Mott of Dartmouth purchased this Perry fore-and-aft hand fire engine in 1844 to protect his chocolate factory and spice mill from the "devouring element." George Perry & Brothers of Montreal are considered to have been the only builders of hand fire engines "of any significance in Canada." In business from the mid-1800s until circa 1870, their machines won "Great Medals" for design and working efficiency over numerous British and European models at London in 1851 and again at Paris in 1855. The Halifax Union Engine Company received two Perry engines on October 4, 1858, naming them *Rapid* and *Resolute*. On April 25, 1859, the *Halifax Morning Sun* reported "The

Perry fore-and-aft hand fire engine, Dartmouth

Engine Company entertained Mr. Perry, the maker of several of the newly imported Engines now in use in this city at a supper in the large room at the Engine House, on Tuesday evening last." One of these engines replaced a pumper lost while fighting an 1857 conflagration that destroyed St. Matthews Church. Fanny Lenoir wrote of the fire in her memoirs:

The heat was so intense that the hair and whiskers of those working the engine were singed, and in some cases their hands and face blistered. The men kept bravely on, but soon were obliged to abandon their apparatus, which was burned up where it stood on the street. The bell tolled as the steeple of St. Matthews fell and was soon a mass of molten metal.

Fire engines improved significantly by the early 1800s. A movable front wheel axle allowed for better steerage. In 1822, suction hose—which carried water directly from its source to the engine—began replacing bucket brigades of the earlier "tub" era. By 1849, Halifax averaged twenty-seven feet of hard suction hose for each of its six hand engines. Note the copper strainer on the hose to filter out dirt, and the extra length of suction hose carried on the backside of the engine. Wooden poles stabilized the front wheels while firemen worked the end-mounted levers or "brakes" as they were more properly referred to. The custom of manually pulling fire engines continued for many years, a team of twenty firemen or more running with the wagon tongue and tow ropes.

William Hunneman from Roxbury, Massachusetts, and James Smith from New York City are said to have been the principal builders of American hand fire engines used in Nova Scotia. The Hunneman Company produced hundreds of engines and is credited with being the largest of all the hand fire engine manufacturers. On September 2, 1840, two Hunneman fore-and-aft engines were delivered by ship from Boston to the Yarmouth Fire Engine Company. Annapolis Royal owned a Hunneman engine in 1877 that was praised in the *Annapolis Journal* as "one of the best for a long siege." George Perry learned his trade under William Hunneman before striking out on his own, and experts

c.1854 Smith piano hand fire engine, Halifax

claim it is difficult to distinguish between the designs of the two builders. This derelict Smith side brake piano engine, so named because its lines apparently resembled pianos of the era, was restored years ago as a museum piece. The cylindrical cannister (left) served as an air chamber for the pumping mechanism, while the ornate lantern on the front would have lighted the way through darkened streets and provided illumination for the men toiling at the brakes. Two Halifax hand engines, *Aetna* (1834) and *Alma* (1852), were both Smith models. Another builder of note for Halifax engines was W.J. Tilley of London, England. One early engine nicknamed *Temeraire* gave dependable service for many years and was then sold to Dartmouth. The Union Engine Company's No. 3 engine *Halifax*, another Tilley acquired in 1844, was considered "the city's finest" for that time. With a capacity to pump 149 gallons of water per minute, it nearly doubled the output of the company's smallest No. 5 engine. Crewing a hand engine of the size featured here was "back-breaking and exhausting work." Between twenty and forty men worked in two platoons to maintain an average of sixty strokes a minute; on occasion firemen could be asked to double output to 120 strokes a minute; an engine crew in Britain is said to have once reached an incredible 170 strokes. Few men, however, could last more than ten minutes at a sixty-stroke pace.

In 1837, the Yarmouth Fire Engine Company was organized to take charge of an engine purchased in Halifax (possibly second-hand) that was similar in design to Shelburne's Newsham engines. By 1857, Yarmouth owned four hand engines with each assigned to a fire engine company—St. George Co. No. 1, Milton Engine Co. No. 2, Reliance No. 3 and H & L Co. (for Hook and Ladder). With four fire engines, Yarmouth firemen had the capability to pump water great distances through relays, which often resulted in company rivalries. The engine crew closest to a well or reservoir pumped water to the next engine in line, which in turn pumped it to the next or onto the fire. The first engine crew pumped furiously in an attempt to fill the tub of the engine ahead to overflowing while that crew pumped just as strenuously to pass it on. To have a company's engine run over (or "washed") was especially degrading. Conversely, an engine that had never been washed was referred to as an "old maid." Bragging rights also went to the

Early Yarmouth hand fire engine with hose reel on parade

company getting "first water" onto a fire. In 1867, a blaze broke out while Company No. 1 was holding a banquet. Rushing off in hopes of arriving first, a hose water fight ensued with Company No. 3, with one man knocked from a ladder. In the end all was forgiven; Company No. 3 stayed to fight the blaze and Company No. 1 returned to their banquet drenched. Fire engines were continually being replaced or shuffled about. An interesting account involves Yarmouth, Tusket, and Saint John, New Brunswick. Circa 1863, Emerald Co. No. 4 in Saint John became embroiled with City Council over a matter that led the company to dismantle its hand engine, with each fireman taking a piece of it home since he had helped pay for it. News of this somehow reached the village of Tusket, NS, which was in need of a fire engine. A representative was dispatched to Saint John where an agreement of sale was reached, the pieces were returned and re-assembled, and the engine shipped off to Tusket. It was used there for several years but was found to be too large for village needs and was in 1872 traded to Yarmouth for a smaller engine.

Sydney experienced its first major fire on November 28, 1851, when four buildings were destroyed. With no firefighting apparatus available at the time, damage could have been much worse had not the Black Watch Highlanders garrisoned in the town turned out with their military hand engine. In the aftermath of the 1851 fire, "an agitation sprang up for the purchase of a fire engine and the raising of an efficient fire brigade in connection with it." Halifax was then advertising to sell a used engine for sixty pounds, but after acquiring the necessary money from door-to-door canvassing, Sydney officials determined the engine was not suitable for their needs. Unable to afford the expense of a new appara-

1869 Hand fire engine, Central Engine House, Sydney c.1943

tus, the town was again saved by the Black Watch Highlanders, who donated their engine to Sydney in 1852; a fire brigade was organized that same year, with Henry Ingles its first captain. The military engine provided dependable service for many years, being "easily worked and gave a good stream of water." A second engine was purchased sometime later (possibly this one above) but it was such a "man killer" that crews could apparently only work it in five minute shifts. Adapters or connecting boxes were often needed to accommodate hose connections from different makes or different sized engines if using them in relay. Halifax had an elaborate connecting system in 1850 for each of its six hand engines. No. 2 Engine for example had a "double headed box to connect with numbers Three, One and Four [engines]—two single Boxes to join with Six and Five [engines]—and also a connecting Box to join on the Ordinance Hose. The Dockyard Hose will likewise fit on No. 2….It may be proper to bear in mind the following arrangements which may be made according to circumstances: All the Hose may be extended in one line by placing them thus: One, Three and Four on the Fire Plug—then Six and Five—then Two next the Fire." With each engine having its idiosyncrasies laid out in such complex jargon, one is left the impression that a building could burn to the ground before a neophyte figured out what connected to where.

Truro purchased its first hand fire engine in 1868 from Boston. Firemen named their hand engine the *Honeyman Tub* after the builder Honeyman, a subsidiary of a British company bearing the same name. Originally hand-drawn, the 2,750-pound engine arrived unassembled and was put together by James Publicover, who had been a fireman in Dartmouth for five years before moving to Truro. Note the brakes, or pumping levers, which folded up on some larger engine

Honeyman Tub, Truro's first fire engine, 1868

models to make it easier navigating narrow spaces. This type of engine was referred to as a "squirrel-tail" because its suction hose remained connected to the intake pipe when not in use, and was bent over the back of the engine like a tail. Truro kept the *Honeyman Tub* for only six years before selling it to the Dominion Chair Company at Bass River. Ironically, plans were being made to buy back the antiquated pumper for display at a firemen's tournament that Truro was hosting when a fire in 1909 destroyed both the factory and "Tub."

In 1849, the six divisions of the Halifax Union Engine Company (*Rapid, Alliance, Halifax, Resolute, Aetna, Alma*) were each equipped with a hand engine. Dartmouth owned three engines—the first purchased in 1822, another in 1847 for £150, and a third in 1857 for £275. Dartmouth firemen also had the good fortune of borrowing used engines from their cross-harbour Halifax brothers. As mentioned, Yarmouth owned four engines by 1857. Few Nova Scotian towns were fortunate to have one fire engine, some makes and models costing in excess of £400. Small communities often found such a price tag "rather more than could be afforded" and water buckets remained their principal means of fire protection even as late as the 1900s.

Hand engines came in a variety of shapes and sizes. This small pumper served the citizens of Amherst prior to the organization of a town fire department in 1883. Blacksmiths and foundries sometimes tried their hand at building fire engines with mixed results. In January 1834, the Halifax firm of Guthrie & Turner proposed to build an engine for the city at a lower cost than an import from England. Their offer was accepted, and "an engine quite as satisfactory as #2 was ready for use by mid-summer." It cannot be said with any degree of certainty how many hand engines were used in Nova Scotia. Liverpool owned two, circa 1868, named *Rapid* and *Rescue*; the Pictou Hook & Ladder Company, circa 1870, had the *Phoenix* and *Volunteer*. Antigonish operated an 1864 model, while New Glasgow's lone engine of unknown origin predated the town's 1875 incorporation. Evidence suggests that Windsor circa 1881 had a "sidewinder" (side-brake) engine, while the Windsor Fire Department Museum today displays a small wheelbarrow design hand pumper dating to circa 1831, thought to have been built in Connecticut and used on a private estate. North Sydney bought an engine in 1873, which was used until 1885, when it was relegated to an auxiliary role after the town acquired a steam fire engine. The arrival of steam engines provided an affordable opportunity for communities to pick up used hand engines from larger centres like Halifax and Saint John. Bridgetown and Annapolis Royal both benefited from Saint John discards, as did Dartmouth which obtained a hand engine from the Loyalist city in 1872 that required "considerable repair work." In 1892 Dartmouth sold it to Boston interests for display at the Chicago World's Fair. Yarmouth auctioned off its 1857 *Reliance* engine for fifty-three dollars to the nearby village of Hebron circa 1903; Hebron, in turn, sold it three years later to Clark's Harbour for that community's first fire engine. Interestingly, Hebron purchased another hand engine in 1905, which Yarmouth firefighting historian Paul Cleveland believes to have been "the last new one ever to come to Nova Scotia."

Early Amherst fire engine

Halifax has the distinction of being the first in Canada to own a steam fire engine. The impetus to move from hand to steam engines was a series of devastating conflagrations that ravaged the Halifax business core within a span of four years. On January 1, 1857, fire destroyed twenty-two buildings along Hollis and Prince streets, including St. Matthews Church and nine legal offices. Then came the Granville Street Fire of September 9, 1859, which burned four acres, including sixty "of the finest buildings in Halifax." Two years later on January 12, 1861, with the temperature at -13 degrees fahrenheit and water hoses frozen shut, fire

Canada's first steam engine *Victoria* c.1861

swept through George and Prince streets, Bedford Row, and Cheapside, eventually reaching Hollis Street before being checked. When the smoke cleared, forty-four stores and offices, and four houses, had been razed. With the local fourth estate clamouring for a steam fire engine, city council voted $1,500 for a new apparatus and sent the mayor and an alderman to Boston in search of one. This Amoskeag engine was purchased from Manchester Locomotive Works in Manchester, New Hampshire in March 1861 and named *Victoria* in honour of England's long-serving monarch. A second Amoskeag was added within months and christened *Albert* for the queen's husband and prince consort. In 1862, Halifax could boast of having "two first class steam engines," five hand engines, seven hose reels, eight thousand feet of hose and an assortment of equipment "all in prime order and of the best material and style."

Horses came into prominence during the late 1800s as manufacturers turned out increasingly heavier steam engines. An interesting comparison can be made between the photos of *Victoria* and *Albert*. Note the engine rope traces on *Victoria*. Firemen of the Halifax Union Engine Company were leery of change in 1861 as the newfangled steamers arrived. For many years after they continued to manhandle *Victoria* and *Albert*, using tow ropes in the tradition of earlier hand-engine times. This was an amazing feat considering the steepness of Halifax streets and the fact that a steam engine of this design weighed five thousand

Steam fire engine
Albert

pounds. Halifax operated six engine houses in 1861, with all divisions reportedly facing a downhill run to the principal mercantile district of the city. This would have resulted in some harrowing experiences, since restraining ropes attached to the rear of the steamer and manned by gangs of firemen were the only means of slowing down on hilly descents before the advent of rear-wheel hand brakes. There was, of course, the chore of pulling the steamers back to the engine house after the fire. Firemen finally succumbed to the changing times in 1873 when the city purchased a 6,500-pound Cole Bros. steam engine. Then *Victoria* and *Albert* were converted to horse draught (as seen here) and nine horses contracted out for service. This effectively ushered in the era of the Halifax fire horse. By 1884-85, city-owned horses were being used. When Halifax later added a 7,800-pound Amoskeag engine and a 9,900-pound Waterous, its stable grew. The annual civic report for 1911-12 listed the fire department owning thirty-four horses; five had been recently sold for $711.30, with their replacements costing $1,480.

THE
SMOKE-EATERS

Six steam fire engines followed *Victoria* and *Albert* into service with the Halifax Fire Department between the years of 1873 and 1907. Included in these were a Cole Bros. (*Chebucto*, purchased 1873), two Amoskeags (*Halifax, Columbia*, 1888, 1892), two Shand-Masons (*Battenburg, Alexandra*, 1896, 1907) and a Waterous (*King Edward*, 1906). All but one were reciprocating, double-piston pump engines with working capacities of 250-800 gpm. With regular overhauls and boiler replacements, four of the six engines were still serviceable in 1916, the other two being kept as reserves. No. 4 Engine *Alexandra*, a Shand-Mason, is

No. 4
Steam fire engine
Alexandra

thought to have been the last new steamer purchased in Nova Scotia. It was certainly the heaviest ever used, weighing 11,400 pounds. Alexandra was such a brute to move about that only on the rarest of occasions was it taken from the Bedford Row Engine House on a first alarm. (The severity of a fire was determined by the number of times an alarm was repeated. Ringing it once signified a minor blaze that could be handled by the equipment and men assigned to that district; a third alarm brought every piece of available apparatus in the city.) Even when needed, *Alexandra* was usually placed at draft along the nearby waterfront. Steam engine capability far exceeded the old hand-engine days when two pumpers or more were often needed in relay at intervals of three hundred feet if bringing water uphill from the harbour. *Alexandra* had a rated pumping capacity of eight hundred imperial gpm. It was reported in 1940 that in three days the steamer pumped 1,500,000 gallons of saltwater from Halifax harbour into a storage tank owned by Provincial Oils Ltd. to test it for leaks prior to being filled with gasoline. A December 31, 1941, Halifax newspaper account claimed that *Alexandra*, even at that late date, "considerably" outperformed all motorized fire engines then owned by the city's fire department.

Apparatus & Equipment
c.1785-1907

In May 1876, Bridgewater organized its first fire department, the Hook & Ladder Protection Company, comprised of twenty-seven members. A collection of $156 was taken to buy two hose reels and a ladder cart. In 1880, a Ronald steam engine was purchased and named the *J.A. Curill* in honour of the company's first secretary; in 1883, the name was changed to the *Alert*. Of the seven manufacturers that produced the twenty-seven steam fire engines used in Nova Scotia (out of which only four survive today as museum pieces), Canadian-built

Ronald steam fire engine *Alert*, Bridgewater, c.1890

Ronald engines were the most popular. Shelburne, Lockeport, Liverpool, Bridgewater, Lunenburg, Windsor, New Glasgow, and North Sydney all used Ronald models. John D. Ronald first began building fire engines in Brussels, Ontario circa 1870. His design was said to be strikingly similar to that of Cole Bros. from Pawtucket, Rhode Island, which produced sixty steam fire engines between 1867 and 1880. (On this note, firefighting historian Donal Baird believes Halifax to have owned the only Cole Bros. steamer used in Canada.) Ronald engines competed at the 1893 Chicago World's Fair, where they were awarded first place over many American-built designs. Ronald appealed to the "small town market" because their engines were relatively light, designed to be hand or horse drawn, and came in two sizes—a "village" model capable of pumping from 300 to 600 gpm and the "standard" 600- to 1200-gpm engine. The majority of Ronald engines were in the 500-gpm class. They reached working steam in three or four minutes using cold water, and could have water on a fire in five to eight minutes from the time of lighting the fire box. North Sydney incurred its first debt in 1885 (which required ten years to pay off) when the town spent $5,500 on a Ronald engine. New Glasgow purchased a Ronald the same year for $3,600. Bridgewater is claimed to have spent only five hundred dollars for its Ronald, indicating that the engine must have been a second-hand model.

This rare photo depicts Digby's steam fire engine *Victor*, one of only two built in Nova Scotia by the Burrell-Johnson Iron Company of Yarmouth. An increase in fire insurance rates was often the impetus for a town to improve its firefighting capability. In January 1886, an editorial in the *Digby Courier* addressed recent premium hikes and urged officials to consider purchasing a steam fire engine. On November 5, 1886, the town organized its first fire department, comprised of thirty volunteers, and a few days later took delivery of the Burrell-Johnson engine. The *Victor* arrived amid much hoopla, accompanied by a contingent of

Digby's Burrell-Johnson Steamer *Victor*

Yarmouth firemen who were met by Digby's newly formed brigade in full dress uniform. A trial demonstration of the engine's pumping prowess was staged for inquisitive townsfolk, followed by a firemen's banquet at the Royal Hotel. A two-wheeled hose reel and 700 feet of hose accompanied the *Victor*, as did a four-wheeled hose cart "capable of carrying a like amount of hose when required." The November 12, 1886, edition of the *Digby Courier* carried a descriptive account of the *Victor*'s attributes:

The engine...makes a very handsome appearance. The boiler is steel, fitted with copper tubes. The frame is "crane necked" to allow short forward wheels to turn short around, and while light and graceful in appearance, is very strong and stiff. The water tank is mounted over the forward axle forming a seat for the driver, carrying a pair of handsome side lights—one on each side of the seat. The engine, a single one, is placed with the pump vertically, just forward of the boiler. The large burnished copper air chamber stands just in front of the steam cylinders. All the ornamentation is of brass, highly polished. A reel, carrying the drag rope, is fitted to the forward axle and the tongue is arranged for running the machine either by hand or by horse. Two polished brass hose pipes are mounted just in rear of the driver's seat and the suction hose is carried in three lengths on brass brackets.

On February 13, 1899, the town suffered a disastrous fire during "one of the worst northeast gales and blinding snowstorms known in Digby's history." The *Victor* was unable to halt the inferno that razed forty-four buildings along Water Street by daylight (see Chapter 6). By 1918, Digby had a twenty-five-man volunteer fire department, two hose houses, three hose reels, 1,500 feet of hose, grapnel hooks, ladders and ladder cart, a piped water system, and twenty-two fire hydrants.

New Glasgow owned two steam fire engines, this 1877 Amoskeag nicknamed *Lulan* (derived from Mi'kmaq mythology) and a 1885 Ronald engine dubbed *New Glasgow*. The Ronald performed poorly from the outset and efforts were made to sell it three years later; it was still on the market in 1899 for $650, the last known party showing interest being Saint Raymond, Quebec. There was little incentive possibly to sell the engine because both steamers were in much demand from other towns. Pictou rented the Ronald in 1888 for one dollar a day

New Glasgow's *Lulan* in front of town hall/engine house

while its own steamer was being repaired. Antigonish hired *Lulan*'s services in 1889, as did Truro in 1910. Pictou again leased the Ronald in 1893, agreeing to pay transportation costs, twenty dollars if its boiler was fired, and posted a three thousand dollar security for loss or damage. In 1894, Pictou hired out the steamer a third time, paying fifty dollars on this occasion to cover five months use. *Lulan* was sent by rail to Halifax following the 1917 Explosion but never left its rail car. The steamer last pumped water circa 1925. Pictou owned two steamers of its own—the *Empress of India* (Silsby) and the *Dr. Dean* (Amoskeag). The Amoskeag was purchased second-hand from Boston, where it had fought that city's Great Fire of 1872. Pictou retired the old engine in 1931 but returned it to active service in World War Two to provide protection at the town's naval refit wharf. Mothballed again after the war, the engine survives today as a museum piece. A humorous story surrounds Liverpool's Ronald steamer, the *Rapid*. During downtimes at the engine house, firemen indulged in the odd game of poker, along with an "ample supply of demon rum." Ronald's engine stack was said to be a convenient repository for the empty bottles. With more free time than fires, the hidden stash grew. When an alarm came at long last, kindling was lit in the fire box and the engine hurried off, leaving steam to build en route as was customary. To the firemen's chagrin, nary a drop of water could be raised upon arrival at the fire. With rising temperatures, the bottles had apparently been turned to a "molten mass" of glass, rendering the steamer inoperable.

THE
SMOKE-EATERS

A two-horse hitch was the most commonly used on steam engines in Nova Scotia. Liverpool's circa 1892 steamer could be pulled using one horse while Pugwash's engine was "fitted out for horse or human locomotion." Larger engines like Halifax's *Alexandra* and *King Edward* (pictured here), required a three-horse hitch, sometimes a four in winter conditions. Fire horses held a place of high esteem within the engine houses and communities they served, and as such were affectionately looked upon as pets. Some Halifax horses were adept

On parade near Halifax Citadel Hill, early 1900s

at more than pulling fire apparatus. The team of Tubby and Buster developed the unsavoury habit of enjoying a chaw of chewing tobacco. A horse named Colonel did them one better, chewing tobacco and smoking a pipe, skills taught him by ladder-man William Powell at Morris Street Engine House. Fire horse Frank provided comic relief by removing hats from the heads of unsuspecting visitors (and firemen) at Bedford Row Engine House, a penchant that landed him in trouble when he once lifted not only a lady's bonnet but a mouthful of her hair as well. That particular stunt required intervention by the Board of Fire Commissioners to soothe the somewhat injured and very indignant victim. Frank did have his useful side however, holding a broom in his mouth and shaking his head in a sweeping motion as he moved across the engine house floor. On a more serious note, Frank survived the 1917 Halifax Explosion unscathed although the wagon he was pulling while responding to the initial alarm was "blown to bits"; his harness-mate Tony lost an eye and their driver, Johnson, was found hours later unconscious. Twisty owns his place in history as well, having pulled carts of water needed for embalming the bodies of *Titanic* victims in the temporary morgue set up at Mayflower Rink in April 1912. Bedford Row Engine House was home to the 1750-pound Farmer, described as being "gentle as a kitten" when he searched for sugar in the pockets of visitors. Upon his death, Farmer's "handsome tail, well over five feet in length, carefully plaited, was hung amid trophies in the station's recreation room."

Apparatus & Equipment c.1785–1907

**Filling a water cart
from fire hydrant on
Brunswick Street,
Halifax, c.1916**

Halifax fire horses were reported to be "well selected, fairly well trained and in good condition." Most were exercised four times a week, with some used on a daily basis for several hours pulling water carts for truckmen, whose job it was to "lay the dust on busy streets during dry summer months." Filling up from one of Halifax's 435 public hydrants, as depicted in this photo taken at Saint Georges Church, was both convenient and widely practised. It was frowned upon by firemen, however, as precious water resources were drained and hydrants often damaged. An early 1900s civic report claimed Halifax's Low District (comprising the harbour area, older residential and principle mercantile districts) used water at "an enormous rate of consumption," in excess of three times the actual need. With fire horses out and about "sprinkling streets," firemen's response times were dramatically slowed. Thomas Raddall writes in *Halifax, Warden of the North:*

"When the bells rang an alarm the drivers had to lash their steeds in the direction of the stations, with the carts swaying dangerously and spraying furiously regardless of the traffic."

THE
SMOKE-EATERS

Dartmouth purchased its first steam fire engine in 1878 after fifty-six years of using hand engines. The brand-new Silsby from Seneca Falls, New York, served Dartmouthians until 1919 and was christened *Lady Dufferin*, in honour of the wife of the Marquis of Dufferin and Ava.

Fire horses were either owned by a town and stabled at the engine house, or hired out on a contractual basis with local truckmen. North Sydney accepted Bart Musgrave's tender of ten dollars a year in 1891 for the use of his horses. Harry MacKean rented his horse to Stellarton and, when not on fire duty, had it doing road work for the town. At the first blast of the fire whistle, the horse would bolt for the engine house regardless of whether or not its driver was on the cart. In 1905, Amherst's fire chief described how they "purchased a pair of horses and placed them in No. 1 station for the exclusive use of the department as they [firemen] were seriously handicapped before from the fact town horses were used for other purposes." A prompt first response was critical for any hope of containing a fire. The slightest delay, according to one old-time Sydney captain, meant firemen "usually saved the chimney and cellar." A case in point was Dartmouth in the late 1800s. Contracted fire horses were quartered at W.H. Greene's Stables near the ferry terminal. When the alarm sounded, a designated driver ran to the stables, harnessed the horses, then hurried them off to the King Street Engine House to be hitched. The inefficiency of this was proven one winter's night when firemen watched helplessly as a two-storey boat house burned to the ground "almost within shouting distance of the Engine House and within pumping distance of salt water" because their equipment was late arriving. The story goes that the driver first misplaced the keys to unlock the stables. Then, in his haste, the harness became entangled. More delays ensued because icy streets made for treacherous footing. It was not until 1906 that Dartmouth finally purchased horses and quartered them at the rear of the engine house.

Silsby steam fire engine *Lady Dufferin*, **Dartmouth, c. 1900**

Truro Fire Brigade horses

"It was the proud boast of the leading fire brigades that they could have their horses harnessed into the shafts…and ready for action within 10 seconds of receiving the call to duty; one company even claimed that it could be ready for action in just six seconds." While the latter may have been stretching the truth somewhat, such claims were not idle braggadocio. A documented case at Halifax circa 1894 involved a trial inspection by the mayor, fire wardens, and insurance underwriters. They commended the chemical division of the Union Engine Company for taking just seventeen seconds "from the first sound of the gong until everything was ready for a start." Two Halifax divisions, however, were given a failing grade because "the horses are too far from the engine house"; Queen Street clocked in at four minutes, Gerrish Street at six minutes. Gerrish Street times must have gotten progressively worse because in 1895 it was condemned— "the building was almost useless for an engine house…the ladders cannot be stored in it and there is no place to keep horses. The latter are 100 yards away from the building and it takes twelve minutes to get the apparatus out for a fire."

When New Glasgow purchased a chemical engine circa 1910, fire horses were "to be stabled in the central station with a teamster on duty there by day and sleeping in the building at night, ready always to drive the engine in response to an alarm." The team was exercised daily pulling the engine "so horses and driver could become accustomed to handle this work." The fire brigade, however, encountered difficulty procuring a suitable pair from any of the horse traders in New Glasgow, Halifax, Charlottetown, Montreal, Truro, or Saint John. A team was finally purchased locally for $550 from the superintendent of the county asylum; should one of the horses become sick or injured, provisions were made that a replacement be hired for fifty cents a day.

Quick hitch collar, Central Engine House, Truro c.1900

A key factor affecting response times was the type of harness used. Rigging traditional harness was time consuming. An "ingenious contrivance for automatic harnessing" was the "quick hitch collar" or "hanging harness," a prefabricated apparatus suspended from the engine house ceiling. It was developed at St. Joseph, Missouri, in 1871 and arrived in Canada at Montreal circa 1883. Halifax first used the harness in 1893, and made reference to "Montreal Fire Collars" in 1907 when ordering a double set of harness with quick hitch collars for ninety-five dollars. Featured in this circa 1900 photo are the Truro Fire Brigade's ladder truck, chemical engine, and hose wagon, all three waiting at the ready connected to a hanging harness. When the fire gong sounded, horses were trained to leave their stalls and go to a designated spot under the harness which was then dropped over them and snapped securely into place. One Halifax veteran recalls how department horses were groomed for this by continual practice – ringing the alarm, then slapping them on the rump to move into position. After a time, horses would anxiously paw the stall doors to be let out when the gong rang. The procedure was speeded up by having the stall door latches connected to a single cable that, when pulled, freed all the horses at once.

Sutherland & Craig hose reel, 1887

With the development of leather fire hose and the evolution of fire engines from tubs to powerful steamers, a means to convey thousands of feet of hose was needed to effectively fight fires. The answer was the hose reel or hose jumper. Fire hose was heavy. A 50-foot length of one-and-one-half inch or two-inch double-rivetted leather leading hose, with brass couplings and iron hand rings for lugging, could weigh eighty pounds. The typical nineteenth-century two-wheeled, hand-drawn hose reel carried 500 feet of hose, sometimes more, and could weigh 600 pounds fully loaded. Several manufacturers of firefighting apparatus sold hose reels, and new fire engines often came with a reel. The Truro firm of Sutherland & Craig built hose reels in the 1880s. J.L. Sutherland (L) and S. Craig pose beside one of their products, which had been decorated for Truro's Natal Day on September 13, 1887. New Glasgow paid one hundred dollars for a hose reel (excluding freight) in 1904 from an unknown supplier. Firemen sometimes turned to local blacksmiths and wheelwrights to fashion their own. The Lawrencetown Fire Brigade built two-wheeled hose carts in 1917 with boxes added to hold axes and other firefighting equipment. These were initially hand drawn but then became horse drawn and were later towed behind automobiles.

THE
SMOKE-EATERS

Parrsboro Volunteer Fire Brigade

Members of the Parrsboro Volunteer Fire Brigade (est. 1889) muster with three hose reels and a horse-drawn ladder truck.* In 1857, Halifax had nine "effective hose reels." Bridgewater owned three reels in 1882, New Glasgow had five in 1895, Amherst three in 1905, and Wolfville four in 1912. Two or three reels were the average for most fire brigades. The earliest reels were attached to the rear of hand engines, but as the amount of hose wound onto the spindle increased, so too did the weight, and reels were later pulled separately. Firemen took great pride in their ability to muscle reels through all manner of weather, but even they had their limits, and, in 1835, Halifax firemen requested that five "respectable" truckmen and their horses be hired to provide assistance when needed. Passersby would sometimes lend firemen a helping hand or the occasional horse would be commandeered from its buggy. Manning a hose reel could be a "perilous undertaking." Halifax firemen James McGuire and John Spruin learned this the hard way one winter's night when they were the first to reach Central Engine House in response to the alarm. "The red glare from the fire indicated that it was more than an ordinary blaze. The two decided to take the reel alone, down George Street. The streets were covered with ice….They took the tongue between them and started [but] soon found the task was too much for them. They were carried rapidly down the icy incline. On they rushed towards the [Grand] Parade fence. In an instant they were upon it, and reel and men were hurled into the Parade. They crashed through the fence and they and the reel were found in a heap in the centre of the square." Fortunately, both men lived to fight another day.

* In early firefighting terminology, a horse-drawn ladder wagon was referred to as a "truck"; a hand-drawn ladder wagon was a "cart."

Hose cart
Perseverance

Hose was sometimes carried on four-wheeled carts. As was the custom with fire engines, hose reels, and carts were often named, some Halifax favourites being *Perseverance, Salamander, Dreadnought, Vesta,* and *Alert.* In 1879, Halifax had 3,000 feet of rubber hose and 5,500 feet of leather hose, which reports indicate was "proportionally about average for the major cities." Halifax fire wardens were highly complimentary toward the hose purchased from Gutta Percha Rubber Company of New York. "One thousand feet of the Carbolized Rubber Hose has been added during the year to the supply previously on hand which is enough to provide against any contingency that may arise for sometime to come. Too much cannot be said in praise of this quality hose, as it has given the utmost satisfaction in every manner it was possible to test it. The first lot that was purchased some five years ago does not yet show any perceptible sign of wear, not a break of any kind having yet occurred in any portion of it."

Fire hose in general had to be continually repaired and replaced. The Amherst Fire Department in 1905 reportedly had 3,500 feet "of good hose" and 500 feet "of old hose not to be depended on." In 1908, the town allotted nearly one quarter of its $5,400 fire budget to purchase new hose. In March 1895, Halifax fire commissioners reported that 650 feet of hose had burned up, and another 600 feet had burst at a recent fire; this was in addition to 800 feet destroyed earlier. Commissioners also complained about damage sustained on more than one occasion from teamsters driving their wagons over hose, and "in future the police will be requested to report all those who do so." The town of Parrsboro ordered 500 feet of new hose in 1897 for five cents a foot. Rubber hose circa 1905 sold for $1.10 a foot, while cotton hose, with couplings included, cost forty-five cents a foot. New Glasgow spent $650 on hose in 1883, generally placing orders in 500-foot lots from companies such as Gutta Percha and Maltese Cross. In 1888, the town purchased 800 feet of unlined cotton hose in 200-foot lengths and were forced to order 3,000 feet in 1919, after complaints from fire underwriters that eight sections had recently burst.

Hose cart *Alert*

Hose carts were converted on occasion to a temporary hearse for firemen funerals. The March 11, 1898, *Daily Echo* carried this account:

> The funeral of Lieut. William Lewin of the Halifax fire department, who was fatally injured by the falling chimney at the Tower road fire, took place yesterday afternoon from his late residence, Maynard Street, and was very largely attended by civic officers, firemen and citizens generally.
>
> The casket was drawn on the hose reel 'Salamander' which had been very neatly draped and decorated. The whole of the upper part of the reel was covered in black and the casket rested on a stand in the centre. From four supports extending from the corners of the reel and joining above the casket was suspended a crown covered with crape, while hanging below the crown was a small bell which was kept tolling as the funeral procession moved. A miniature fire ladder rested on the front of the carriage and led up to the bell. The ladder and supports were in black and silver, and the design of the arrangement of the carriage was a good one. On top of the casket, and immediately below the bell, rested the white hat and belt of the late lieutenant; at either side of it, as well as on the carriage, were the many floral tributes that had been sent. They included a miniature fire ladder, at the top of which was a dove, from the members of No. 1 steamer and No. 2 hose divisions; a handsome wreath from the mayor; wreaths from the fire commissioners, St. Mary's Young Men's Society and the Union Protection Company; a cross from 'brother firemen,' and an anchor from C.W. Davies and employees. The reel ropes were covered in black and white.

By 1880, low-maintenance rubber hose was quickly replacing the standard copper-rivetted leather variety, which tended to dry out and crack if not kept pliable with regular oiling or popped rivets from the pressure of steam engines. A further improvement in hose design was the later development of unlined and rubber-lined cotton hose, which tended to be lighter, stronger, and easier to store. Hose wagons became widely used in the late 1800s as the new types of hose could be folded, giving wagons double the carrying capacity of reels and carts. Halifax first used horse-drawn apparatus in 1884, which were converted circus wagons purchased at a bankruptcy sale. By the early 1890s, eight hose wagons were in service. Hose wagons carried an array of firefighting equipment, including assorted nozzles, hydrant connectors and pipes, universal couplings, axes, crowbars, rubber gloves, ropes, oil torches, lanterns, wire cutters, shingle lifters, and door openers. In 1905, the Amherst fire department owned three hose wagons and two ladder trucks. Six horses were available to pull the apparatus, but two of the horses were privately owned and two others were shared with the "street department." Town council was asked to purchase an additional pair of fire horses because "the hose wagon and ladder truck are entirely too heavy for one horse. The weight of the hose wagon being 2230 pounds and of the ladder truck 2037, with the additional weight of four or five firemen on these wagons, you will readily see the necessity of having two horses in order to reach the scene of fire quickly." In 1908, the Glace Bay Fire Department received a two-horse hose wagon that carried one thousand feet of hose; it was purchased for $365 from the Truro Carriage Company. The Halifax civic report for 1916 listed the fire department owning 12,600 feet of two-and-a-half inch hose with 2,300 feet in reserve; each engine company averaged 1,800 feet of hose in service. Three-quarters of the hose was double-jacketed cotton rubber lined with the remainder being rubber, and none was more than eleven years old with eighty percent of it being in service for less than five years. One or two thousand feet of new hose was purchased annually through local dealers.

Dartmouth hose wagon

Ladders were indispensable for reaching the upper stories of buildings to fight fires, rescue people, and salvage property. In 1828, Halifax struck a deal for a truckman's wagon and services to carry hooks and ladders to fires in exchange for his exemption from "statutory" road work. By 1849, the city owned two hook-and-ladder carts; each carried hook ladders and wall ladders forty feet long, support poles for large ladders, and two grapnel hooks and chains for pulling down walls and roofs of burning buildings. In 1893, Halifax had seventeen

Halifax ladder truck

ladders and two Bangor extension ladders (fifty and sixty-five feet) valued at $593.90. A 60-foot Seagrave ladder truck was purchased in 1910; a similar American-LaFrance model was added the following year. Both were horse drawn and carried 60-foot ground extension ladders, as well as six or eight assorted ladders, including two roof ladders. By the early 1900s, Halifax owned ladders totalling 769 feet in length with 150 feet in reserve. An array of tools were also carried on ladder trucks, including plaster hooks, pitch forks, pickaxes, wrecking hook, shovels, buckets, saw, wall cutter, sledge hammer, hose hoist, life net, scoops, sponges, maul, and surgical kit.

Wooden ladders were the norm until the mid-1900s, when metal began to be more widely used. Some wood ladders could be quite heavy. The Tatamagouche Hook & Ladder Company found theirs to be so unwieldy that they decided, in 1903, to plane roof and short wall ladders at the mill to lighten the equipment. Some fire brigades purchased ladders—New Glasgow ordered six in 1881 for $42.65—while others built their own. Halifax firemen were still building wooden ladders as late as 1941. A price quote received by the Kentville Fire Department from Bickle-Seagrave Ltd. in 1938 shows aluminum single wall ladders (22'-26') sold for between $88 and $107, while aluminum roof ladders (16'-20') went for between $62 and $77. Wooden wall ladders with solid sides (22'-26') cost as much as $65; an extra $6 was charged for wooden roof ladders to cover the expense of folding hooks.

Apparatus & Equipment c.1785-1907

Ladder sleigh, Grafton Street Hook & Ladder Company, Halifax c.1885

Wagon wheels were often replaced by ski runners for winter travel, or ladders switched to long sleighs and bobsleds, as featured here. It was also customary to convert hose reels, fire engines, and chemical engines to skis for snow conditions. In January 1839, a committee was appointed in Halifax "to devise some means to prevent engines from sliding down the hills in slippery weather in cases of alarm of fires." What recommendations made, if any, are not known. In 1894, the Parrsboro Fire Brigade rented a "fire sled" for ten dollars. Halifax used sleds for hand-engines as early as 1820, and by 1910 owned fifteen hose-and-ladder sleighs. Each Halifax steam engine and ladder truck was outfitted with an "ice wheel" for winter travel. What constituted an "ice wheel" is unclear, but some veterans believe it may have been a standard wagon wheel equipped with iron studs to enhance traction.

THE
SMOKE-EATERS

American Alanson Crane is credited with patenting the first fire extinguisher on February 10, 1863. A year later, the French formulated a fire retardant by mixing sulfuric acid and sodium bicarbonate to produce carbon dioxide. A chemical engine or wagon (like the one featured here) was basically "a large soda-acid extinguisher on wheels." Thousands of two- and four-wheeled models were built and operated in North America during the late 1800s. Of the approximately one hundred chemical units used in Canada, only one is said to survive today, that being the Halifax Fire Department's *Acadia*, which is preserved at the Fire-fighters Museum in Yarmouth, Nova Scotia. Chemical engines were popular

Early chemical engine, Sydney Fire Department

because they did not depend upon a water supply and could be more quickly pressed into service than steam engines, which took time to build up working pressure. When chemical tanks were expended, a special coupling device on some models allowed the engine to be hooked into a hydrant system to pump water. The Truro Fire Brigade was one of the first in the province to own a chemical unit. An American-built Babcock engine, known affectionately as "Baby" to Truro firemen, was purchased and operated privately by the Truro Foundry & Machine Company before being turned over to the town circa 1874. The acquisition of this piece of horse-drawn equipment may have been the impetus for Truro to part with its *Honeyman Tub* hand engine the same year. New Glasgow purchased a "triple combination" chemical, hose, and ladder horse-drawn wagon in August 1910 for $2,100, a price that included thirty electrical warning "tappers" or alarms for firemen's homes. The occasional private citizen had the financial means to own a chemical unit, in all probability to protect a place of business. The Clish & Crowe Foundry in Truro reportedly had a Babcock engine in September 1882. W.F. McKenzie from New Glasgow owned a Babcock (circa 1878) that was seized by town officials in lieu of unpaid taxes.

Halifax operated three chemical engines. The first was *Acadia* (1892), an American Holloway engine weighing 5,300 pounds that was equipped with two 60-gallon chemical tanks, 300 feet of one-inch rubber hose, two 3-gallon fire extinguishers, a 20-foot ladder, and a 12-foot ladder. In April 1893, W.F. Pickering, chairman of the Board of Fire Wardens for Halifax, reported to City Council:

> Too much cannot be said in favor of the chemical engine placed in service during the year. It has proven itself worthy of the consideration of the board, and its usefulness warrants its purchase by the council. This machine answers promptly to every call or alarm from any part of the city, the limits of which are so extensive that renders it almost impossible for her to perform efficient service in every instance. I hope the day is not far distant when the council in its wisdom may see its way clear to purchase another chemical engine and thus give the firewards an opportunity to divide the city into districts whereby efficient service can be assured.

**1892 Holloway
Chemical Engine**
Acadia

A Babcock engine (*Micmac*) was added in 1896. It weighed 4,700 pounds and was outfitted with tanks and hose similar to Acadia but carried only a three-gallon fire extinguisher and a twenty-four-foot ladder. A Canadian-made Seagrave combination chemical engine and ladder truck (*Alert*) was put into service in 1907. The apparatus weighed 3,500 pounds, measured 35 feet in length, and carried two 35-gallon tanks, 150 feet of one-inch chemical hose, two 3-gallon fire extinguishers, and 8 ladders totalling 155 feet in length. The *Acadia* was assigned to Grafton Street Engine House, the *Micmac* to West Street, and the *Alert* to Morris Street. All three chemical engines required a two-horse hitch. By the early 1900s, sixty-five percent of all fires in Halifax were put out using only chemicals. The city of approximately 50,000 residents was divided into three chemical districts, with one engine assigned to each. On still (telephone) alarms, only a chemical unit was sent. Other times, a hydrant line with shut-off nozzle was laid as a back-up for chemicals. Firemen carried alarm box keys, and if additional help was required, a box was pulled or assistance called in from the nearest telephone.

THE
SMOKE-EATERS

Following town incorporation on January 30, 1901, Glace Bay officials debated the merits of fire protection for several months. Their decision was hastened along by a near-disastrous July blaze which would have razed the community had it not been for the heroic work of resident bucket brigades and firemen from the local collieries. Finally, on September 24, 1901, Glace Bay organized its first fire department, with fifty men volunteering to form two hose-reel companies, a hook-and-ladder company, and a salvage company. Less than one month after

Glace Bay Fire Department chemical engine, c.1913

first meeting, the entire force, with two hose reels, rushed off to Sydney by special train in response to an urgent request for assistance in fighting a conflagration ravaging the town (see Chapter 6). On January 15, 1902, this state-of-the-art horse-drawn Holloway chemical engine—which came highly recommended by Halifax firemen—was placed into service. In addition to two chemical tanks and one hundred feet of hose, it was equipped with four hand fire extinguishers, two short ladders, an axe, pike, and two lanterns. In 1904, the town purchased a horse-drawn ladder truck and a $4,700 Waterous steam fire engine. The steamer was last used on December 30, 1917 during a blinding snowstorm. When horses bogged down in heavy drifts, townsfolk latched onto the steam engine, named *John Leaman* for the department's first chief, and pulled it to the fire by hand. Unfortunately, St. Ann's church, convent, and glebe house were totally destroyed, with losses amounting to $125,000. In 1927, Glace Bay suffered its greatest loss to fire when seven buildings, housing twenty businesses, were destroyed, totalling $450,000 in damages.

Apparatus & Equipment c.1785-1907

Despite the advent of chemical retardants, water remained the key to combatting the "tyrant flame." From the earliest days of settlement, every available natural source of fresh and salt water was tapped. Contingency plans were also made early on for artificial safeguards. In 1758, Governor Lawrence had wells dug and pumps installed at Halifax "as reservoirs against fires." Small portable pumps were also used to bring harbour water onto the wharves for filling buckets. In the spring of 1785, Shelburne petitioned the Court of Sessions for the provision of wells and pumps at strategic locations for "the Safety of the Town in case of Fire." Blockmaker David Whipple was paid an annual salary of fifteen shillings a pump to keep them in working order. Monies for this were raised through increased town taxes and a special water tax of fourpence per hogshead of sixty-five gallons levied against any vessel that filled up from town wharves. Circa 1817, Halifax began constructing a series of underground tanks on upper streets to hold salt water expressly for fire emergencies. Several were built between 1830 and 1840, with twelve in operation by 1847. Each tank was about thirty-

Craig Bros. Fire, George & Barrington streets, Halifax, January 12, 1912

one feet long, sixteen feet wide, and twelve feet deep, with a capacity to keep a single hand engine pumping for thirty-nine minutes at an average of 150 gallons of water per minute. In 1825, fire wardens pressed for a restraining order prohibiting ships from filling casks at Halifax wells "lest the water supply should be depleted on the outbreak of fire." Additional measures were proposed in 1828, when Halifax fire wardens recommended a box or trough and two casks be filled with water and mounted on wheels to get the tub engines operational at fires until bucket lines could be formed.

THE
SMOKE-EATERS

West End Supplies Fire, Cunard Street, Halifax, January 4, 1955

Towns throughout Nova Scotia followed Halifax's lead in digging reservoirs and wells. Some also mobilized water tenders. Dartmouth officials purchased livery-stable-keeper George Turnbull's street watering cart for thirty-five dollars and hired a horse from Greene's stable to pull it for three dollars a day when needed. The cart was filled with salt water from Mosley's wharf, or fresh-water from the Starr Manufacturing Company's stream, and kept at the ready in the event of fires. A truckman in New Glasgow presented town council with a bill for fifty cents on February 8, 1881, to cover his expenses for winter hauling of water barrels for fire purposes.

There were few fire hydrants in Nova Scotia until the late 1800s, when many towns began installing waterworks—Dartmouth, 1874; Truro, 1876; Yarmouth, 1881; New Glasgow, 1887; Stellarton, 1892; Lunenburg, 1893; Digby, 1895; and Lawrencetown, 1898. Halifax was the exception, having piped water by 1848 which included twenty-five fire plugs and eighteen hydrants. How hydrant and fire plug became synonymous is noteworthy. The earliest water mains were generally constructed from sections of hollowed-out logs joined with staves and hoops covered with tar. Fire plugs preceded hydrants and as the name implies, were wooden plugs in the water mains that could be accessed at the bottom of a catch pit and removed for fighting fires, then replaced when finished. When a fire plug was not readily accessible, firemen were faced with the "slow and cumbersome" task of having to first dig down through sometimes rock-hard, frozen earth, then bore into the wooden water main using an auger. A long stand pipe would be inserted, or possibly a portable collection dam erected, into which a suction hose from the engine was run. When hydrants eventually replaced fire plugs, the name stuck. Hydrants were supposed to be the last word in fire protection, but many of the early town waterworks and hydrant systems were incapable of producing sufficient pressure to be efficient, so steam engines (and motorized pumpers later) were still required as boosters.

*Apparatus & Equipment
c.1785-1907*

Supply wagons

Steam engines carried a minimal amount of coal to reach working pressure. Supply wagons similar to this hose wagon were then needed to bring additional fuel. When a steamer ran out, the engineer blew its whistle as a signal that more was needed. Halifax owned three supply wagons in the early 1900s, wagons that were also used to exercise horses and to run supplies and tools between engine houses. A wagon generally carried sixteen to twenty bags of coal, with as many as forty bags kept at each engine house. According to a 1911–12 fire department report, it was common for ten thousand feet of hose and eight to ten tons of coal to be used at a three-alarm fire. When the Halifax Board of Fire Commissioners called for coal tenders on October 4, 1898, four companies vied for the contract–Cunard & Co., McKenzie & Co., Halifax Coal Co., and William Roche. The lowest bid for Sydney coal, considered to be "the real thing," was four dollars a ton, submitted by Cunard & Co. Coal expenditures varied greatly; New Glasgow in 1881 spent only two dollars on coal for its steam engines, while the 1908 Amherst Fire Department budget showed an outlay for coal of $165.16. Coal was also a primary heat source. It was reported on August 9, 1946 that, for the winter season just ended, Halifax had used eighty tons of coal to heat its five engine houses.

   The fireman featured in this photo is hoseman John Duggan. He responded to the first alarm on December 6, 1917, with this hose wagon from Isleville Station on Gottingen Street, and was at ground zero on Pier 6 when the munitions ship *Mont Blanc* blew up in Halifax Harbour (see Chapter 6). The dead horse and wrecked wagon were later recovered, but Duggan's body was never found. The horse collar was picked up nearly two miles away.

Awaiting the call   Two Halifax fire horses harnessed to a turret wagon wait patiently under warm blankets for the call to action. The triangular nozzle visible at the rear of the wagon was called a "turret pipe," and became common with larger fire departments (such as Halifax) in the 1890s. A LaFrance firefighting equipment catalogue touted the advantage of turret pipes:

> Used for safely controlling large streams [of water] at dangerous locations since service of firemen is not required to hold it while stream is playing. Nozzle can be swung up and down vertically and requires no locking device....Made in two styles or models, non-revolving and revolving [which] can be turned in complete circle. Furnished either with or without shut-off and with either 2-way or 3-way siamese connection. Quick-action bracket for mounting on fire apparatus furnished.

Similar wagon units could be purchased from local manufacturers. The Truro Carriage Company ran the following advertisement circa 1910 for a variety of apparatus:

> We Make A Speciality of Hose Wagons of Different Capacities for One or Two Horses. We can fit them with Two or Three way Turrets when wanted. Ladder Trucks, Ambulances, Buck Boards, Delivery Wagons and Carriages of Every Description.

This small, hand-drawn salvage cart was used in 1861 by the Union Protection Company of Halifax to carry bags and tarps. In later years, the cart was replaced by a two-horse wagon equipped with four lanterns, two torches, twenty waterproof covers, fifteen canvas bags, a life net, two 3-gallon fire extinguishers, 480 feet of rope, smoke protectors, and an assortment of small tools. In 1916, a salvage corps of forty volunteers (there were more than eighty in 1897) and one paid driver worked from a "commodious" three-storey building on Jacob Street.

Union Protection Company salvage cart

The first floor included sleeping quarters for the driver and two meeting rooms connected by a doorway to the wagon house and stables. The second floor had accommodations for the caretaker and his family, as well as a spacious billiard room and smoking lounge. While in no way connected with the fire department and "the chief exercises no supervision over it," Halifax nevertheless provided the Union Protection Company with a wagon and pair of horses, equipment, and two thousand dollars annually for maintenance.

Similar salvage companies operated throughout Nova Scotia, with some working independently while others operated as a division under the auspices of the fire department. A Yarmouth Salvage Corps was organized in 1891 but remained separate from the main body until after 1900, when its members received the same benefits as firemen (exemption from poll taxes, jury duty, and compulsory road work). Listed here is an inventory of equipment and initial expenses incurred by the Yarmouth Salvage Corps in 1891: wagon, $150 (this was a partial payment with the remaining $75 paid the following year); harness, $13.25; blankets and rubber fire buckets, $159.28; fire extinguisher, $32.50; belts, $8.40; bags, $15.15; axes and hatchets, $8.25; lanterns, $3.30; hooks, $1.75; baskets, $7.00; duty, $10.20; expressage, $5.19; total costs: $414.27.

The age of the steam fire engine began to wane throughout North America circa 1909, with the advent of motorized apparatus. Much like the earlier hand fire engines, a number of Nova Scotia steamers were recycled throughout the Maritimes to fire departments and businesses, including sawmills and coal mines. Canada's first steamers *Victoria* and *Albert* survived fifty years with Halifax until they were sold circa 1911—one to Charles Brister & Son for $150, the other to Thomas Hogan for $175. Sydney Mines purchased Yarmouth's Burrell-Johnson

Amherst steam engines

steamer in 1905; Digby shipped its aging Burrell-Johnson to Lancaster, N.B., where it was burned up in a 1921 engine house fire. Dickie & McGrath lumber company at Tusket procured a second-hand steam engine from Fredericton, N.B. in 1906, while Oxford, N.S. bought Pictou's Silsby engine, then scrapped it and installed the pump on the popular Pierce Arrow chassis. Steam engines were still operational in Halifax as late as the 1930s and served as back-up pumpers during World War Two. In 1940, some of the city engines were sold to the French Islands of St. Pierre-Miquelon and the New Brunswick towns of Sussex and Dalhousie. In March 1945, the Brookfield Construction Company from Mahone Bay paid $350 for the *Alexandra* and the chemical engine *Acadia*. North Sydney's 1885 Ronald engine was finally scrapped, unfortunately, in 1950 "after many years of service and no public interest." Yarmouth historian Paul Cleveland writes in his article "The Steam Fire Engine of Nova Scotia," "When the fires were put out under their boilers, and the horses put out to pasture, the most colourful era of the 'Fire Service' came to an end."

The fire horses' farewell

The Truro Fire Brigade races down Prince Street in the early 1900s. Horses running at full speed hitched to heavy fire apparatus were said to slow down noticeably after only one-half mile. Feasibility studies conducted in the early 1900s showed that a motorized fire department could be maintained for one-third the cost of a comparable horse-drawn department. Halifax Fire Chief Patrick Broderick claimed in 1915 that a savings of $1,695 could be realized if the department sold five of its fire horses in exchange for a motorized fire engine. Most fire departments throughout North America, including Nova Scotia, began the change-over from "hay burners" to "gas guzzlers" by the early 1920s. Chicago stopped using horses on February 5, 1923, while most of San Francisco's 450 were gone by 1925, as described in a municipal report that year: "The motor has driven the horse from the field of activity in man's behalf. A few are still eking out a comfortable old age in some of the City's less strenuous departments." Victoria, British Columbia, was one of the first Canadian cities to go fully mechanized, their last horse being decommissioned in 1919. Toronto followed in 1931, while Montreal took the last of its horses out of service in 1936, a few being kept on the city ledgers for the unpleasant task of pulling garbage wagons. The town of Kentville, N.S. was still advocating the acquisition of horses to haul equipment in 1923, despite the purchase of its first motorized pumper two years earlier. Horse-drawn fire apparatus in Halifax began to disappear in 1926 and were gone by 1929. The following requiem in the Halifax *Chronicle Herald* entitled "The Fire Horses Farewell" marked their passing:

> We played the game and played it square, at every call of the gong.
> We gave our speed, upheld our breed, now our life's not worth a song.
> Our time is past, the die is cast; perhaps it's just as well.
> So to our Halifax friends and the Fire Brigade,
> We neigh our last farewell.

Chapter 2

Apparatus & Equipment

C.1912–1950

Out with the old, in with the new

Members of the Bridgewater Fire Engine Company pose with a 1920 hose truck, 1876 hose reel and 1880 Ronald steam engine. The decision to go motorized was made after the Methodist Church burned to the ground on an "icy night" in March 1919. Bridgewater's first acquisition was this Model-T, purchased in August 1920, after which a town-owned service truck was used as a back-up to pull hose reels. Enclosed custom-built cabs first appeared on fire trucks in 1928, but open cabs remained the norm until the 1950s because they gave better overall visibility. Half-doors were introduced in the late 1930s, although it was felt that this somewhat hindered firemen from "springing into action." Note the right-handed steering wheel. Nova Scotians followed the British custom of driving on the left until the 1920s.

Halifax firemen pose proudly with Canada's first motorized pumper, the *Patricia*, a 1912 American LaFrance Type 12 triple combination pumper, chemical engine, and hose wagon. Named in honour of the governor general's daughter, the state-of-the-art pumper cost $10,800 and came with the latest equipment—a six cylinder, seventy-three horsepower motor, Dayton airless tires with dual on the rear, five hundred gallon-per-minute rotary water pump, thirty-five gallon chemical tank, twenty-two feet of 4 1/2 inch and 2 1/2 inch stiff suction hose with suction siamese and reducers, divided hose body for twelve hundred feet of 2 1/2 inch fire hose, and two hundred feet of chemical hose. An engine test conducted in 1916 showed that the *Patricia* "made a good run," the operator taking one minute to start her motor. Some believed the *Patricia* was "hoodooed" because she arrived in Halifax on March 13, 1913. "Delivered on the 13th day of the month and in 1913? She'll never be a success," they said. In some ways the doomsayers were correct. Four of the men featured in this photo—Condon, Brunt, Killeen, and Hennessy—were among nine firemen killed in the Halifax Explosion of December 6, 1917. The *Patricia* itself was a casualty, suffering $7,500 in damages. She was rebuilt by LaFrance in Elmira, New York, which wrote-off $1,500 of the repair bill. Returned to active duty within a few months, the *Patricia* remained in service until retired in 1942. Three years later she was put on the auction block. A February 26, 1945, *Halifax Herald* article reported that, "The 'Daddy' of Halifax fire pumpers, which led in the fight against most of the city's major fires for more than three decades, has pulled down its battle flag at the end of its days of action-and now nobody wants it…. The scrap pile will likely be the answer."

Canada's first motorized pumper
Patricia

L-R: Chief Edward Condon, Comptroller Hines, Deputy Chief William P. Brunt, Capt. John Brommit, unidentified, unidentified, Hosemen William Connors and Ned Strachan, driver Billy Wells, Claude Wells (Chief Condon's driver), Hosemen Frank Killeen, Art Sheehan, Joseph Ryan, and Walter Hennessy.

THE
SMOKE-EATERS

Halifax purchased this motorized aerial ladder truck in 1919 for $17,900. The *Halifax Mail* of March 1, 1932, claimed it to be "the first 75' aerial ladder truck in the Dominion." Halifax also owned a horse-drawn seventy-five-foot aerial ladder designed locally by William Horton in the 1890s (see Chapter 4, Bedford Row Engine House for photo). Horton's extension and fire ladder was displayed at a Montreal firemen's convention in 1894, where a judging committee "was favorably impressed with it." In March 1895, Halifax aldermen debated the merits of purchasing a Horton for the fire department. Some were against the idea, claiming that the machine was too heavy, while others said that the city didn't have an adequate building to house such a piece of equipment. A Horton representative speaking to council claimed that, at seven thousand pounds, the aerial "was one of the lightest and best ladders manufactured in the world." The decision was finally made to purchase one for $3,500 but by 1916 the apparatus was considered "too unwieldy to use" and was stripped of its ladders and placed in storage. The first aerial ladder was patented in 1868 by American Daniel Hayes. Early models were hand raised by several firemen using a system of gears and pulleys but, circa 1902, a more efficient spring-powered aerial was introduced. Numerous companies in the early 1900s built aerials in varying lengths of fifty-five to eighty-five feet. Air-operated hoists came on the market in the 1920s followed by hydraulic-mechanical systems in 1931, which, for the first time, allowed the ladder to be raised, rotated, and extended by a single fireman. One-hundred-foot aerials arrived in 1935; ladders then were built in two sections of Douglas fir with hickory rungs and steel reinforcing rods. Speaking to a local Rotary Club in 1950, Halifax Fire Chief Fred MacGillivray stated that his department had recently purchased the first hundred-foot "metal" aerial in Canada.

1919 LaFrance aerial ladder truck

R-L: unidentified civilian, driver Charles Thomas, Fire Chief John W. Churchill, Matt Young, Chief Mechanic Con Leahy, Ray Beck Sr., William Howley, John Brooks, Ed Strachan, unidentified.

Apparatus & Equipment c.1912-1950

Motor section of the Halifax Fire Department, 1919

Photo above:
L-R: supply car, pumper Chebucto, *salvage car, pumpers* Cornwallis *and* Patricia, *chief's car, aerial ladder truck.*

This rare photo depicts the motorized pool of the 1919 Halifax Fire Department, including the pumpers *Chebucto, Cornwallis,* and *Patricia*. The Chebucto and Cornwallis, like the *Patricia,* were triple-combination fire engines. The *Cornwallis* was purchased in 1917, while the *Chebucto* was obtained by the Halifax Relief Commission in 1918 as a replacement for the damaged *Patricia.* Both engines pumped 750 gpm (gallons per minute) and remained in service until replaced in 1944 by two 1000-gallon pumpers—an American LaFrance and a Canadian Bickle-Seagraves—each costing $17,000. The *Chebucto* was then sold for $200 to Dartmouth for spare parts. The aerial ladder truck was disposed of in 1945 for $115 and replaced by a new $20,500 eighty-five foot model. Considerable debate ensued as to the fate of the *Patricia,* "the still shiny red old warrior whose roaring motor and clanging bell thrilled children and adults alike when it raced through the streets of Halifax in yesteryears." Some wanted her designated a firemen's memorial, but council frowned upon that proposal. A purchase offer of $125 with the intent of converting Patricia into a wood-hauling truck was also rejected. The decision was made in 1945 to give both the *Patricia* and *Cornwallis* to Chief Mechanic Con Leahy as retirement gifts. Sadly, *Patricia* ended her days stripped of parts and left to rust alongside the highway at Gold River. Some interesting end notes: when Halifax began its permanent force on May 1, 1918, the proposed budget called for a staff of seventy-seven men, with the majority to be paid seventeen dollars a week plus one week's annual vacation. The chief was to receive a salary of $1,800, the assistant chief $1,400, the chief mechanical engineer $1,500, and the carpenter and property overseer $1,000. Comptroller J.J. Hines and Fire Chief J.W. Churchill argued: "This will cost the taxpayers $15,000 more than they are paying today. Can they refuse to pay it? Can you [council] refuse to vote it? Is $17.00 a week too much for a fireman who is on duty and subject to discipline 24 hours a day for seven days of the week?"

Bridgewater fire apparatus c.1927

Bridgewater firemen pose with their 1925 LaFrance motorized pumper, 1927 ladder truck, and 1920 hose wagon in front of a new fire station built in 1922. Standing to the far left is Walter Gow, who served as fire chief from 1914-1945. Bridgewater traded in its Ronald steam engine in 1925 for seven hundred dollars on a fifteen-thousand-dollar LaFrance 625-gpm pumper. Two years later an International truck (centre) was purchased, and ladder racks installed, at a total cost of $2,100.

> The most significant tactical development in apparatus was the combination of the pumping duties of the steamer, the hose laying capacity of the hose wagon and the first aid fighting of the chemical engine into one vehicle. The majority of pumping engines built in the motor age have performed all these functions and thus are called triple combinations. The remainder simply lacked the chemical tank which might be carried on a hose wagon.
> (Donal Baird, *A Canadian History of Fire Engines*)

By 1911, there were two hundred companies specializing in motorized fire apparatus, as well as several automobile manufacturers, including Ford, Chevrolet, and Pierce-Arrow. But it was the American LaFrance Fire Engine Company of Elmira, New York that controlled the lion's share of the Canadian firefighting market. By 1930, ninety percent of the country's fire departments used LaFrance pumpers, hose wagons, and ladder trucks. Between 1910 and 1926, LaFrance built more than four thousand pumpers. Wolfville, Kentville, Windsor, Dartmouth, Sydney, North Sydney, Glace Bay, New Waterford, Truro, Amherst, New Glasgow, Bridgewater, and Yarmouth all had purchased combination pumpers—mostly LaFrance—by the early 1920s. Size and price varied with 350-1000 gpm rotary gear motor designs costing between ten thousand and twenty-two thousand dollars. It seems not everyone welcomed the new machines. New Glasgow's five fire companies were disbanded and merged into one "central" company with the arrival of a LaFrance in January 1919. Shortly thereafter, the pumper suffered mysterious maladies—lost pressure due to being "tampered with" and coal found in the fly wheel "that could only be put there with human hands." As with the earlier hand and steam engines, firemen gradually adapted to the changing times.

The Great Chicago Fire of October 9, 1871, consumed more than two thousand acres in twenty-seven hours. Left in its wake were three hundred dead, one hundred thousand homeless and the smouldering ruins of seventeen thousand buildings. To mark the fortieth anniversary of the conflagration, the Fire Marshals Association of North America (FMANA) observed the inaugural Fire Prevention Day in 1911. Canada's first national Fire Prevention Day was proclaimed by the Governor-General in 1919; four years later, a National Fire

Fire Prevention Week, Halifax c.1925

Prevention Week was established. The United States took similar steps by presidential order in 1920 and 1925 respectively. Nova Scotia's first Fire Prevention Act was introduced in 1919, but there would be few significant improvements until after World War Two. A check of several Halifax engine house logbooks of the 1920s shows the most common entries for fire responses were sparks from chimney, defective flues, faulty wiring, oily waste, lamps catching curtains on fire, fat fires, and overheated stove pipes. In 1925, Dominion Fire Commissioner J. Grove Smith claimed overheated stoves, furnaces, and stove pipes to be the number one cause of fires in Canada. Between 1921 and 1946, there were 33,538 fires in Nova Scotia, with $207 million in losses. Five hundred and fifty people died, including 208 children, 206 men, and 136 women. Fires ran rampant through wartime Halifax. "Scores of deaths" were attributed to a lack of fire escapes because of a shortage of labour and materials. Firemen called Saturday night in downtown Halifax "mattress night" because of the high number of smoking-related fires. These were usually extinguished quickly because "there was always someone walking around at two or three in the morning selling rum and they would pull an alarm box." Building codes were in their infancy, with ancient structures merely a fire waiting to ignite. A classic example was the Morse Tea Fire of 1927, which resulted in $400,000 damage. The cause of the Halifax blaze which started in an 1812 building known as the Jerusalem Warehouse was attributed to a rafter that ran directly through the chimney!

Shortly after Samuel Morse invented the telegraph in 1844 came the idea that this invention could be incorporated into a fire alarm system using a series of signal boxes wired to an engine house. Boston is credited with having the world's first telegraph fire alarm in April 1852. Halifax installed a system circa 1861 at a cost of ten thousand dollars. In 1902, this system was replaced by the popular Gamewell telegraph alarm. In addition to a gong, five Halifax engine houses also had tower bell strikers. Historian Thomas Raddell writes that "the alarm was

Gamewell fire alarm system, Halifax

sounded over the city…ringing the location by a code which every housewife kept posted on her kitchen door." Electrical storms played havoc with early systems, setting bells to ringing and firemen running. In some cases, warning "tappers" were also wired to firemen's homes. At Halifax in 1902, firemen were generally summoned by a beat policeman who was often the one to pull the alarm. This arrangement didn't always work well, as telephone calls first went to off-duty constables who faced fines if they failed to turn out for fires. A new Gamewell system, pictured here, was installed by Northern Electric circa 1945 in a brick building on Summer Street which served the city until the early 1990s. Forty new alarm boxes (to go with the 150 already in service) were installed throughout the city at a cost of $12,000. A coded series of printed-out taps gave signal box location to the alarm headquarters and engine houses simultaneously. Phoned-in alarms first went to headquarters and were then relayed using a transmitter wheel, as shown on the table. If sent from a street box, the location code was repeated four times in engine houses; from headquarters it was given three times. Fire calls in many communities went directly through telephone operators who triggered general alarms or called firemen directly. A memorable case took place at Weymouth in 1929; switchboard operator Mary Hankinson was on duty the night of October 2 when word arrived that the town was ablaze. With flames on the doorstep, she remained at her post to telephone firemen, then narrowly escaped dressed only in her nightgown.

1926 American LaFrance fire engine
Village Queen

Not all fire engines of the motorized age were self-propelled. One example was this hand-drawn American LaFrance pumper with a Model T Ford gasoline engine. Weymouth purchased the *Village Queen* in 1926 for $2,100. Unfortunately, it failed its baptism by fire on the night of October 2, 1929, when a conflagration swept through the town's commercial district. The fire began as many did: from carelessness. It was believed that a lit cigarette butt had been left smoldering in a garbage can at Captain Donald Barkhouse's general store. The close proximity of buildings and strong winds combined to fuel flames which soon engulfed both sides of the main street. Captain Barkhouse, a West Indian trader in lumber and pulpwood—who ironically was also the fire chief—had only limited success in getting the *Village Queen* up and running. With telephone lines down, cars were sent to Digby and Yarmouth for help. Townspeople cut a hole in the wooden sidewalk of the bridge and dropped fire hose to the Sissiboo River below, but the tide was low and efforts to raise water were fruitless. Digby's fire department arrived in quick order, but without hydrants their equipment was useless. Yarmouth sent a chemical engine, which helped somewhat until a heavy rain and the returning tides finally beat the "fiery serpent" into submission. The final tally was devastating: twenty-five buildings razed with losses of $250,000, only $20,000 of which was insured. The village of 1,200 residents rebuilt, but with the throes of a Great Depression ahead, the once-prosperous shipping and lumbering centre never regained its glory years.

The earliest aerial apparatus were confined to large urban centres like Halifax. More common to smaller rural fire departments were motorized trucks carrying eight or ten portable ladders varying in length from ten to sixty feet. These were referred to as "city service ladder trucks" in firemen's vernacular. Hose trucks and pumpers were also outfitted with short wall ladders. Manufacturers such as

Bickle-Seagrave and LaFrance built standard fire apparatus or customized orders to a fire department's needs. This 1935 Yarmouth Bickle-Seagrave ladder truck may have been a specialized unit, as it features not only ladders but also a booster tank, fire hose reel, and what appears to be a deluge nozzle with hydrant connectors. Cash-strapped fire departments often performed their own speciality work. In 1930, Truro converted its horse-drawn ladder truck to a motorized Model A , then to a Model T with an extended chassis of eighteen feet. This do-it-yourself vehicle carried fourteen ladders, including a 55-foot extension ladder, three straight 30-footers, and several short wall and roof ladders. A variety of additional equipment was packed on board—twelve tarpaulins, twelve fire helmets, rubber clothing, first aid kit, rope, lanterns, axes, shovels, picks, forks, and a large safety life net. This proved to be a tremendous amount of weight for a home-made special to convey, and there was a noticeable sag to the mid-section as the truck raced through Truro streets. As was customary with fledgling fire departments, Bible Hill's fire brigade purchased the truck in 1953 when Truro received its first aerial ladder.

Truro purchased a LaFrance 700-gpm pumper in 1919, nicknamed *Nancy*, which firemen were still using in 1960. In 1929, the town's 1874 horse-drawn chemical engine *Baby* was converted to this motorized unit appropriately named *Baby II*. A Model T Ford truck chassis was outfitted with the original two 60-gallon chemical tanks and four hundred feet of chemical hose, an additional eight hundred feet of two-and-a-half inch hydrant hose, two fire extinguishers, nozzles, crow bars, roof ladder, extension ladder, rubber clothing, and first aid kit. Due to the lack of Model T parts ten years later, equipment was transferred to a Model A Ford chassis. *Baby II* served the citizens of Truro until 1953 (eighty years in total), when its tanks were stripped for junk and the chassis sold to a

Truro's chemical engine *Baby II*

resident in Saltsprings, Pictou County, where it was used to haul wood until the 1960s. New Glasgow undertook a similar conversion of its 1910 chemical/horse combination in 1918 when the town purchased a White Company chassis for $2,522.50. This coincided with the acquisition of a $15,000 LaFrance, Type 12, 350-gpm combination pumper. Two drivers were then hired—A.E. MacDougall at ninety-five dollars a month and John "Speedy" MacEachern at eighty dollars a month. Speedy lived up to his name when MacEachern was commended by town council in April 1919 for reaching a fire at Roger's Garage with his chemical unit before the alarm had stopped ringing. Chemical apparatus generally fell out of favour in the early 1930s; they were messy and expensive to operate, and their tanks had a relatively small capacity. Tests had also debunked earlier theories that chemicals were superior to water when fighting fires. Existing chemical tanks were converted by simply filling them with water, or were replaced by larger eighty- or hundred-gallon water units called "boosters." According to the Hon. L.D. Currie, minister of mines and labor, circa 1945, "It is still true that the best extinguishing agent is the one which reduces the temperature most and nothing has been found to equal water in doing this."

Halifax fire boat
Rouille, c.1941

Rouille pumped water for nine hours into the French Ship M.V. Maurienne *at Pier 28, during a fire on February 7, 1942*

A little-known aspect of firefighting was the role played by Halifax fire boats in the protection of harbour shipping and waterfront stores. As early as 1847, it was proposed that a city fire engine be placed on the steam ferry between Halifax and Dartmouth for such a purpose. In 1879, the Board of Fire Wardens reported that "an effort has been made during the past year to ascertain the cost of fitting up some of the tug boats in the harbour with a pump and hose that could be made available in case of a fire breaking out on the water's edge." Steam fire engines were later placed on board harbour vessels. *The Daily Echo* of February 23, 1895, reported that the chairman of fire commissioners had called a meeting "to fix a sum to be charged for the services of the fire engines on the steamer *City of Wakefield.* One steamer worked forty-seven hours and the other twenty-eight hours. The tugs received $10 an hour and after some discussion it was decided to charge $5 an hour for the use of the steamer, hose and labor. The total amount to be charged will be $375." In 1898, Halifax reportedly had fireboats owned by the shipping firm of Lawson Harrington and Company. Two fires along the waterfront within four days of each other in September 1904 caused $500,000 in damage. Coverage in Halifax newspapers reiterated "the need of a properly equipped and thoroughly up-to-date fire boat was evident to everyone who watched the progress of the conflagrations." Cost was a factor, and city council hedged committing the necessary money as it was rumoured that the federal government was planning to build a new boat for the quarantine service. For the interim, Judge's "water boat" the *Water Witch* was tendered for fire service, as was a private tug equipped with pumps from A.C. Whitney. The idea of placing a steam fire engine on a barge in the harbour expressly for firefighting purposes took hold. Aldermen suggested that information from Boston, New York, and Montreal be gathered as to how those cities maintained their harbour fire protection. By 1915-16, seven privately owned tugs, each equipped with 600-gpm pumps, were operating in Halifax Harbour and "would respond on a telephone call if within reach." The press, however, lamented that "the chances of getting them are remote as shown by experience in the past." Harbour protection at Halifax remained a problem for many years.

During both world wars, Halifax was arguably the most important convoy staging point on the North American Atlantic coast. Thousands of damaged Allied vessels limped into the port city, impregnating wharf pilings with leaking Bunker C and carpeting harbour waters with oil. Halifax Harbour was patrolled during World War Two by the fire boats *James Battle* and *Rouille*, both chartered to the National Harbours Board for wartime service.

Apparatus & Equipment c.1912-1950

Halifax Harbour Ferry *Governor Cornwallis* **on fire, December 23, 1944**

Four hundred passengers escaped injury but the $300,000 vessel was a total loss

Although ingredients for a repeat of the 1917 Explosion passed in and out of Halifax Harbour daily for six long years, disaster was somehow averted. What makes this even more amazing is that firemen and their boats contended with more than five hundred fires associated with vessels and the waterfront. The three most famous and potentially hazardous episodes, involving the *Rouille* and *James Battle*, were the scuttling of the burning British munitions ship *Trongate* in Halifax Harbour in April 1942, the fire aboard the American munitions ship *Volunteer* in November 1943, and the Bedford Magazine Explosion in July 1945. At war's end, the *Rouille* was returned to its marine construction and dredging owner J.P. Porter & Company in 1946; eight years later, while returning from contract work related to the building of the St. Lawrence Seaway, it sank off Cape Smokey, Nova Scotia, with a loss of five lives. The *James Battle* remained in service for general towing, firefighting, and salvage purposes at Montreal and on the Great Lakes from 1945 to 1991, after which it was broken up for scrap. The port of Halifax at present depends upon its fire protection primarily from the Canadian Forces auxiliary vessel *Firebird*. Built in 1975 at Vancouver Shipyards, her sister vessel, *Firebrand*, is stationed on the West Coast at Esquimalt Naval Dockyard. The *Firebird*, a part of the Halifax Naval Dockyard Fire Department, is designated as YTR 561 (Yard Tug, Rescue). Her fire pumps have the output capability of 6,000 gpm, with each of the three fire guns rated at 1,250 gpm. Potential fire response duties are varied, and involve regular marine traffic, an oil refinery, autoport, container ports, naval dockyard, and availability to Halifax Regional Fire and Emergency Services.

THE
SMOKE-EATERS

**The saga of
RCN 1000**

"RCN 1000" is a 1942 American LaFrance 1000-gpm pumper that was originally built for the City of New York. The Canadian government obtained the wartime services of "Big Bertha" (a nickname given by firemen) and assigned her to HMC Halifax Dockyard. Known officially thereafter as "RCN 1000," the pumper was quartered under tarp outside a small, sparsely equipped naval fire station in the basement of building D-14. In 1944, naval firemen burned the motor out of "Big Bertha," and it was taken out of service for the duration of the war and stored at the Naval Maintenance Garage. In 1946, the pumper was repaired and returned to active duty until extensively damaged in 1949, while being used to teach firemen safe driving techniques. The story goes that buckets were used to hold pieces of grille, bumper, fender, and radiator picked up from the roadway, then parts and pumper were sent to the Dockyard Transport Section for safe keeping. "RCN 1000" was later given to Crown Assets, which in turn sold it to the Lawrencetown Fire Department in Nova Scotia's Annapolis Valley. Subsequently repaired and renamed, Pumper No. 5 remained in Lawrencetown until circa 1987 when it was sold to an individual living in Paradise, Annapolis County for one thousand dollars. Later, stripped of parts needed to restore a 1942 pumper owned by the Halifax Fire Department, "Big Bertha" sat idle in a farmer's field for two years, along with three other pieces of derelict fire apparatus. In September 1990, an astute passerby spotted the old pumper gathering rust near the highway. When word reached naval authorities in Halifax that "RCN 1000" was still alive, but not well, little time was wasted before sixty Department of National Defense firemen had chipped in the $1,000 needed to buy her back. Returned to the dockyard on a flatbed truck, along with some of her original loose parts, "RCN 1000" was placed in the same bay of D-26 she left forty years before. Today the vintage pumper has been restored to working order and is driven on special occasions.

*Apparatus & Equipment
c.1912–1950*

Naval Dockyard fire hall, Halifax, 1945

Halifax was Britain's key military and naval installation in North America for more than 150 years. From the time of its founding in 1749, ordinance and dockyard fire engines manned by "good men and true from the garrison" and naval "Jolly Tars" provided mutual aid to Halifax smoke-eaters in times of trouble. As late as 1904, British military units were called out to battle a conflagration at Pickford & Black's on the waterfront, where they "gave every assistance, bringing hose with them, and aiding the firemen in every possible way. A detachment of sailors were landed from the *Ariadne* whose help was most valuable in carrying lines of hose and raising ladders." With the recall of Imperial forces in 1905-06, Canada was left to develop its own military fire service. Initial steps were taken during World War One, when the British Royal Flying Corps—from which the Royal Canadian Air Force was born seven years later—was first stationed in 1917 at Camp Borden, Ontario. An on-site fire brigade was essential due to the quantities of flammable fuel stored at the base and the ever-present danger of crashes during pilot training. Canadian army firefighting procedures were based on directives laid out in British army fire manuals, while Royal Canadian Navy shore establishments in Halifax were dependent upon the city's fire department for assistance. What advances were made in Canadian military firefighting during World War One became lost in the years between 1919 and 1937 because of peace time federal military budget cuts. Captain E.J. Evans of Air Command Headquarters, Winnipeg, writes in his brief history of the Canadian military fire service, "The fire services of the three arms of the forces were in a rudimentary state just before the Second World War, lacking adequate equipment and a practical training program." In light of this, it took civilian fire officials to persuade military brass of the devastating losses fire could inflict upon the war effort. At Halifax, it would be 1942 before a Naval Fire Service began "to take shape."

In 1941, Edward Beals, a civilian fireman with the Toronto Fire Department, was sent by Naval Headquarters to HMC Dockyard Halifax to be its fire

Crash trucks at RCAF Base, Eastern Passage, Nova Scotia

chief. Because of wartime manpower shortages, only 4F (unfit for military service) recruits were initially assigned to his command as firemen. This changed in 1943, when "able-bodied" RCNVR-enlisted men from professional fire departments across the country made up the Naval Fire Service and were given FF (firefighter) status, "effectively preventing individuals from being shanghaied by another branch of the navy." A Naval Dock Yard Fire Hall was built in 1943 and remained in active service until replaced in 1987 (then demolished in 1993). Wartime shipboard fire control also became a priority. By 1944, East Coast personnel were attending a U.S. damage control school in Philadelphia for instruction, then returning to Halifax and training on derelict vessel hulls or at McNabs Island. (A similar program on the West Coast was established at Esquimalt.) Municipal fire departments were understaffed in many cases because of the drain of civilian firemen into the military fire service. According to E.J. Evans, "The expansion from a nucleus of 4F civilians in 1942 to the Naval Fire Service status in 1944 was nothing short of extraordinary. The R.C.N. was indeed fortunate to have been able to recruit heavily from the ranks of the civilian population in towns and cities across the country." Not to be forgotten are the Canadian Corps of Firefighters who served overseas. At the request of British officials in 1942, 422 civilian firemen were recruited from 107 municipalities across Canada. Four hundred and six shipped overseas as civilians and, after four weeks training, were posted to blitz-torn London, Southampton, Portsmouth, Plymouth, and Bristol. Some were involved in the Normandy landings and subsequent special operations. In recognition of wartime service, a Canadian Firefighters 1942-45 discharge badge was struck by an order in council, and changes were made in 1946 so that mothers or widows of firemen "whose death occurred either during their service or subsequent to such service but attributable thereto" became eligible for the Memorial Cross.

Apparatus & Equipment
c.1912-1950

Halifax Air Raid Precautions personnel practice emergency rescue, 1943

With international tensions on the rise in Europe during the mid-1930s, the Canadian government began formulating a secret civil defense plan in the event of war breaking out. Under the auspices of the Canadian Defense Committee, six interdepartmental committees were officially established by an order in council in March 1938 "for the provision of adequate protection for the civilian population." One of the six committees was Air Raid Precautions (ARP) which was to deal with dangers incurred from air attacks. The initial step taken by the federal government was to compile *Air Raid Precautions, General Information for the Civil Authorities,* a Canadian equivalent of the 1934 British Handbook of Passive Air Defence. Intended as an instructional manual for provincial and municipal authorities, it covered a wide array of ARP services in the event of emergency, including directives and duties of auxiliary firemen, auxiliary public utility workers, first aiders, stretcher bearers, ambulance drivers and air raid wardens. When war clouds broke over Poland in August 1939, the wheels were immediately put in motion to initiate ARP units in Nova Scotia, New Brunswick, British Columbia, and Quebec. An umbrella Nova Scotia ARP committee was established on August 29, 1939, with local units operational in Halifax and Sydney shortly thereafter.

As the war progressed, smaller ARP units were organized in a number of coastal towns. By the end of 1941, Ottawa had made two hundred portable pumps and more than a million feet of fire hose available to provincial ARP authorities. In 1942-43, five million dollars worth of equipment—much of it for firefighting—was distributed. Emphasis on ARP grew with increased fears from the Japanese attack on Pearl Harbour, the U-boat war along the eastern seaboard, and German advances in rocketry science. Seven hundred and seventy-five communities across Canada during World War Two would organize some form of ARP protection involving 280,000 mostly volunteer workers.

THE
SMOKE-EATERS

Civil defense was a massive undertaking. As can be expected when three levels of government are called upon to work together, there was no shortage of bickering and glitches. Disbursement of money and equipment were on-going issues, especially during the early war years. Halifax Fire Chief John Churchill had the unenviable task of running not only a wartime city fire department but also co-ordinating the ARP auxiliary firemen. By July 1942, Halifax ARP had been issued twenty-two 150 gpm pumpers. Chief Churchill claimed that it would have been better to have half that number with double the pumping capacity. Pumps were not equipped with universal couplings, leaving Halifax to re-thread all its intake connections. ARP pumps had three-way outlets but no shut-off valves, which meant that each time an additional hose was connected, the pump had to be turned off. When the first lot of pumps were delivered to Halifax in July, they came mounted on iron sleigh runners that had to be replaced by trailer wheels. Government-issue fire hose was reported to be of "extremely poor quality" and

ARP Group D-2 receive new fire truck, Halifax

was continually breaking. Each ARP unit was issued an eighty-nine-cent flashlight for lighting. Axes, ladders, spanners to tighten hose connections, black-out lights for trucks, and hydrant wrenches were all sorely lacking. Faced with shortages, auxiliary firemen fell back on "public spirited citizens" for help. The Brookfield Construction Company built hydrant wrenches and keys at no charge. Canvassing door-to-door for ladders and trucks produced limited results. Two auxiliary firemen bought a truck for their unit from personal savings. Featured in this photo is J.L. Trainor of Trainor Auto Service as he presented the keys for a new truck (on loan until war's end) to Captain Gerald Johnson of the fourteen-member Group D-2, stationed at a converted garage between Henry and Cedar streets. Fire Chief John Churchill (R) and Mayor O.R. Crowell, director of Civilian Defense (far left) look on. ARP firemen are, back row (L-R): F. Kline, H. Bassett, G. Martin, H. Tobin, K. DeMone; front row (L-R): F. Kelly, J. Keddy, B. Williams.

Apparatus & Equipment
c.1912-1950

Pictou Women's Bucket Brigade

Looking more like a bicycle pump than fire apparatus, stirrup pumps are used by ARP volunteers to spray water from buckets during practice drills. Nearly eight hundred of these pumps were issued to ARP units in Halifax during World War Two. Except during wartime, when most everyone was pressed into duty, fire-fighting was a male domain until the late 1900s, when women first entered the ranks in Nova Scotia.* A short-lived exception is the Women's Bucket Brigade of Pictou. In 1872, the Royal Oaks Hotel on the corner of Water and Coleraine streets in Pictou caught fire. The town's two hand engines—the *Phoenix* and *Volunteer*—were no match for the raging inferno and were placed at draft along Pictou Harbour to pump water uphill to waiting firemen forming bucket lines. Historian Roland Sherwood provides this account: "As the fire roared out of control, the firemen became weary with filling buckets and dumping the contents on the blazing building. Suddenly a large group of town women pushed the firemen aside and took over the task of filling the water buckets and making a bucket line....The system was slow but it was effective, and by the time the assisting fire department from New Glasgow had arrived, the Pictou women had the fire under control. The flames were extinguished but the hotel was such a ruin that it had to be demolished." On two other occasions the Pictou women formed their bucket brigade. Such intrusions apparently bruised the male psyche and at the St. Lawrence Hotel fire on November 7, 1881, matters came to a head. "While the women's bucket brigade was much in evidence," writes Sherwood, "this time the local firemen were unable to stand aside and so they pushed into the ranks to assist. The women protested and sought to keep them from helping but their efforts were in vain. From that time onwards, the women were not allowed to form an exclusive female bucket brigade." Women still took their place with bucket in hand alongside the men until 1905, when they were finally "pushed out of service" and the Pictou Volunteer Fire Brigade became "a strictly all-male unit."

* Dartmouth is believed to have had Nova Scotia's first paid female firefighter in June 1991—Debbie McLeod. Halifax hired its first female firefighter a year later.

Wartime training on the North West Arm, Halifax

When the tide of battle began to change in favour of the Allied forces in late 1943, the chance of enemy air attacks on Canada—real or perceived—lessened to the point where Civil Defense across the country, including ARP, was scaled back significantly. At Halifax, however, equipment actually improved in November 1944, when six (of a scheduled eight) one and one-half ton pumper trucks were delivered to the city by federal authorities. These were to be "located strategically in Halifax" and manned by selected groups of auxiliary firemen who received specialized training in "water relay" techniques. With the exception of Halifax and units in British Columbia, all federal assistance to ARP ceased after March 31, 1945, but the six thousand ARP workers in Halifax remained on alert until war's end. While fortunately never called upon to implement emergency procedures in the face of enemy aerial bombardment, ARP auxiliary firemen provided valuable assistance fighting fires, including the Bedford Magazine Explosion of 1945.

With the dismantling of Canada's Civil Defense in 1945, all government-issued equipment was ordered to be turned over to War Assets Corporation. Ottawa then made it available to cities, towns, and municipalities across the country for firefighting purposes. More than five hundred communities in New Brunswick, Prince Edward Island, and British Columbia reportedly owe their beginnings of organized fire protection to recycled ARP equipment and returning war-trained firefighting veterans. Similar provisions were afforded Nova Scotia towns and villages, which were given first option on purchasing surplus fire apparatus. Approximately forty 450-gpm motorized trailer-mounted pumpers, and an unknown but significant number of smaller 150- and 75-gpm pumps were distributed throughout the province. Rather than disband at war's end, some ARP units remained intact to form the nucleus of peacetime fire departments. One of these was the Fairview Fire Protective Association, pictured here as an ARP unit with Fire Chief Leo Nelson kneeling at right holding a fire axe. One Wajax two-cylinder pump, three small rolls of hose, a stretcher and first-aid kit, a couple of axes, scoops, and shovels had been the extent of their wartime issue. Under Nelson, who became Fairview's first fire chief, the post-war ARP group "were tireless in their efforts," holding various fund raisers to build a new $1,500 fire hall and to construct a reservoir dam for a water-relay system. All this was achieved using volunteer labour. By 1946, the Fairview Fire Protective Association had managed to add a siren, small fire truck, hose, a 150-gpm trailer pump and one 85-horse power trailer pump. "With a force of twenty-seven trained volunteers," proclaimed the May 31 issue of the *Halifax Mail*, "Fairview residents may well feel that they have a fine, firefighting force, which, will, in due time, with public support making necessary expansion possible, be able to cope with any emergency."

Fairview Fire Protective Association c.1946

THE
SMOKE-EATERS

On February 22, 1888, Kentville organized a Volunteer Fire & Protective Company comprised of two divisions: a hose and ladder company and a salvage or protective company. Early equipment consisted of two hose reels, a hand-drawn salvage wagon, a ladder truck, and one horse. In 1923, Town council was asked to acquire additional horses and to add running boards to the ladder truck so firemen could ride instead of hoofing it on foot, as they were reportedly too tired to work once they arrived at a fire. By 1925, the department had added a

Kentville Volunteer Fire Department, 1950

motorized Bickle pumper (nicknamed "Lion") and a chemical truck. In 1927, fifty-four volunteers were on the force, with an average of thirty-seven responding to fire alarms. Apparatus and equipment were continually upgraded over the years, with an ambulance corps added in 1941 and an auxiliary fire department organized in 1949 to protect the hospital and the Nova Scotia Sanitarium, both located on the opposite side of the Cornwallis River but still within Kentville town limits.

Kentville has always been one of the most active fire prevention departments in Canada; between 1935 and 1950, the town won five national awards and six regional Fire Prevention Shields. In 1947 and 1949, the National Fire Protection Association awarded Kentville the prestigious National Fire Award, emblematic of "the best" incorporated town in Canada with a population between five and ten thousand people. With Fire Chief Bev Wade at the helm, Kentville firemen were deserving of the accolades they received. In 1935, the town initiated the first system of home fire inspections in Canada. By the early 1940s, a fire-safety education program had been introduced to local schools. In 1949, Kentville was the first in Nova Scotia to pass the "Town Planning Act" requiring all new buildings to meet specific fire regulations and codes. Also that year firemen inspected every structure within the town. Little wonder that Kentville had one of the lowest fire insurance rates in the province.

Apparatus & Equipment
c.1912-1950

Windsor Fire Department apparatus, c.1950

An interesting array of apparatus covering more than forty years of Windsor firefighting, including the town's first 1919 motorized pumper, far right, and two World War Two ARP pumpers, centre. Windsor's original fire company—comprised of "active, energetic men to the number of twenty thereabouts"—was established on January 12, 1881. For the first two years, it was known as the Avon Fire Company, but in 1883 the name was changed to the Windsor Fire Department. That same year, the first water mains and fire hydrants were installed. Equipment was typical of the times—a hose reel, horse-drawn ladder truck, and possibly a hand fire engine. From the outset, the department was organized into two divisions—Division No. 1 was assigned to Windsor proper (circa 1950 apparatus pictured to left of steps), while Division No. 2 was stationed at Curry's Corner on the fringes of town (apparatus to right). Town council appointed the fire chief until 1948, after which he was elected by the firemen. In 1898, the Windsor Fire Department was comprised of thirty-eight members (twenty-four in Division No. 1 and fourteen in Division No. 2); in

THE
SMOKE-EATERS

1918, numbers had increased to forty-three and twenty-three, respectively. Ralph Holmes is credited with building Windsor's first motorized ladder truck in 1927 using a Cadillac chassis purchased for fifty-five dollars from Customs. In 1942, the Windsor Fire Department established a Ways & Means Committee responsible for fundraising activities; the first of these was a Giant Bingo combined with street dance and hot dog sales. Firemen responded to eighty alarms in 1948-49, one of the more interesting being a fire at Maple Leaf Bakery at 3:05 a.m. on April 24, 1948. From the time a night watchman first spotted the blaze a mile from the bakery and called in the alarm, it was a comedy of mishaps. The siren mounted on the fire station roof stuck open, then two of the trucks failed to start. When firemen finally reached the scene, there was a shortage of hydrant wrenches, hose was laid the wrong way, and water pressure failed. From this, it must be assumed that the building was a loss.

Apparatus & Equipment
c.1912-1950

In 1951, Kentville firemen were the focus of a National Film Board documentary (later distributed by Columbia Pictures) as they battled mock fires and demonstrated assorted types of apparatus and equipment. To add to Kentville's growing fame, Canadian magazine *Maclean's* printed a two-page article that year featuring "Chief Wade and his award-winning smoke-eaters." Kentville continued its innovative example in the early 1950s. The Maritimes' first training school for firemen was held at Kentville in June 1950 under the auspices of Chief Bev Wade. One hundred and sixty-four firemen from fifteen areas in western Nova Scotia attended. Better training was necessitated following an incident a year earlier when "an enthusiastic group" of firemen from an unnamed volunteer department had broken out all the first-floor windows of a home, only to find the fire was in an adjacent building on the property. In 1950, discussions were held between the Provincial Fire Marshall and Annapolis Valley fire departments on the establishment of a regional mutual aid organization. With Chief Wade the driving force, the Association of Volunteer Fire Officers and Firemen was soon established, taking in communities from Mount Uniacke to Yarmouth. The name was later changed to Western Nova Scotia Firemen's Association, then to Western Nova Scotia Firefighters' Association. Aside from the obvious advantages of providing assistance in times of crisis, the association mustered a collective voice to pressure hose manufacturers into standardizing coupling threads so that hose from various fire departments was interchangeable. Kentville achieved the pinnacle of recognition in 1952 when it was declared not only the Class D winner (pop. 5,000–10,000) in the International 1952 Fire Prevention Week Contest sponsored by the National Fire Protection Association, but also the Grand Award Winner in all of Canada, beating out such cities as Ottawa, Calgary, and Hull. (Memphis, Tennessee, won top prize for the United States.)

Kentville firemen go Hollywood, 1951

Kentville's Bev Wade was one of North America's most respected fire chiefs. His first experience with firefighting came at the tender age of eleven when appointed the fire department's mascot. At sixteen, he became an "active member" in the hose reel company and was elected fire chief in 1946, a position he held for twelve years. During World War Two, Wade served two years as an instructor at the RCN fire-training school in Esquimalt, British Columbia. In 1947 he attended the International Association of Fire Chiefs' meeting in New York. A

Kentville Fire Chief Bev Wade instructs firemen in techniques of mutual aid, 1950

year later, he addressed the Canadian Fire Insurance Underwriters in Saint John, the Maritime Fire Chiefs convention in Fredericton, and the 75th Annual Conference of International Association of Fire Chiefs in Miami, the latter being a special honour indeed since he was the only Canadian invited to attend.

Chief Wade's accomplishments were legion: president of Western Nova Scotia Firefighters' Association; founder of Western Nova Scotia Mutual Aid System; president of Nova Scotia Chief Officers' Association; president of Canadian Association of Fire Chiefs; president of the forty-nation International Association of Fire Chiefs; member of National Research Council Fire Codes Committee; recipient of honourary commission from Louisiana State Militia for contributions made to North American firefighting; honorary deputy sheriff of Dodge City; honorary chief of numerous fire departments world-wide, including Tokyo, Japan. Upon leaving the Kentville Fire Department in 1958, Wade founded the New Minas Volunteer Fire Department. In addition to his passion for firefighting, Wade operated several successful grocery outlets, served as town councillor, and was heavily involved with civic projects. He was also a noted athlete, being inducted into the Nova Scotia Sports Hall of Fame in 1927 as Maritime 100- and 200-metre sprint champion. Chief Wade died unexpectedly in 1975 at the age of sixty-four while attending the International Association of Fire Chiefs' annual convention in Las Vegas. Two thousand people from across North America attended his funeral in Kentville.

Glace Bay had North America's first respirators

The first breathing apparatus were developed in Britain, France, and Belgium in the early 1800s to protect miners from noxious fumes. Draegermen of No. 2 and No. 6 Collieries at Glace Bay pose in 1909 with their Draeger equipment (named for the manufacturer Draegerwerke, Germany). James M. Cameron writes in his book *The Pictonian Colliers*: "North America's first self-contained breathing apparatus was placed in Glace Bay, Nova Scotia, to serve the area collieries in 1906, some six months before the U.S. Bureau of Mines at Washington procured and tested self-contained breathing apparatus designed for coal mines." It is difficult to say what fire department pioneered the use of

respirators in Nova Scotia. One of the earliest on record was Bridgewater, two firemen there wearing them for the first time on February 1, 1916, at the Orpheum Theatre fire. Chemical, salvage, and supply wagons of the Halifax Fire Department were carrying "smoke protectors" in 1916 that one source described as resembling World War One gas masks. The following advertisement appeared in a 1931 LaFrance Fire Engine & Foamite Limited catalogue "Modern Firefighting Equipment"; the cost of mask and canister described was twenty-dollars, with a replacement canister priced at three dollars.

LaFrance Fire Department Masks are specially adapted for firefighting service and have gained a well-earned reputation among fire departments. For over ten years they have proved their efficiency. The canister used with this mask...will take care of acid gases, organic vapors, ammonia, smoke and practically any poisonous gas, smoke or fume when carbon monoxide is not present.

In 1938, the Amherst fire department owned eight "smoke helmets" that may have been Draeger Oxygen Helmets Type RL 26 or No. 1. Around 1946, the Halifax Civic Safety Committee purchased fifty gas masks from War Assets Corporation for the city fire department; Kentville first used respirators in 1947. Halifax Fire Chief Fred MacGillivray announced in 1950 that self-contained breathing apparatus were being introduced to city firemen. These were in all probability a variation of the Scott Aviation "AirPac" which had been developed during World War Two for high-altitude flying and which were later adapted for firefighting.

The majority of Nova Scotia's 314 fire departments got their start following World War Two by using the resources at hand. River John converted a surplus World War Two jeep and truck into serviceable fire apparatus for its tiny community. When Bridgewater installed electric flashing sirens on their equipment in 1946, fire departments of neighbouring LaHave, Riverport, and Chelsea purchased the antiquated hand-cranked sirens for their vehicles. Four years later, LaHave acquired Bridgewater's vintage 1920s ladder truck for $825. Kentville outfitted an army jeep and ARP trailer pump for responding to outlying districts in times of crisis. And Kingston demonstrated the spirit and resourcefulness typical of volunteer fire departments everywhere. E. Blaikie, owner and president of Valley Creamery, was the catalyst for organizing Kingston town fire protection. The story goes that he called a meeting of interested persons in 1944, where he summarily appointed Shorty Stronach chief, Manning Armstrong deputy chief, then turned to the rest of the group and told them they were firemen. An inventory of early equipment consisted of five- and ten-gallon creamery buckets and a converted farmer's sprayer—a wagon with wooden tank and gasoline engine to pump the water, towed behind a member's vehicle. Subsequent additions included a war surplus ARP 500-gpm trailer pump pulled by an army truck affectionately dubbed "Gravel Gertie," which carried five thousand feet of 2 1/2 inch fire hose. In 1947, the department purchased a 1946 500-gpm LaFrance pumper for $5,500 and became involved in a mutual aid program covering communities from Canning to Annapolis Royal. The Stronach brothers of Kingston must hold some sort of Canadian family record for collective years of fire service: Ken (45 years), Carl (45), Murray (48), Shorty (27), Vaughn (25), and Vernon (2 years volunteer service plus twenty-two paid years with Bedford Fire Dept.)—providing a total of 192 years of fire protection to their community.

Converted army jeep and truck, River John Fire Department, c.1950

Chapter 3

Smoke-Eaters

Veteran Halifax smoke-eaters

At the time of this circa 1955 photo, the dwindling ranks of the Halifax Veteran Firemen's Association still counted men whose fire service dated to the smoke-eater days. Familiar names of yesteryear included Captain Tom Strachan, Captain John Brooks, Billy Wells, Patrick Morialty, J. Whalen, J. Mann, W. Bowser, E. Ryan, F. Condon, J. Barnaby, L. Cahill, J. Sullivan, J. Doherty, and J. Fultz. By 1961, only five veterans attended the March 12 meeting. They maintained their spirit, however, the principal piece of business then being to secure a liquor and beer permit for their new club at 587 Barrington Street. Kentville organized a "veteran corps" in 1925, which was summoned to active duty in 1940 to assist with fire protection for the town due to wartime manpower shortages.

Bill Graham, Canada's longest-serving volunteer fireman

Two Nova Scotian firefighters share a distinction no other Canadian can claim," wrote the *Hants Journal* in 1994. "Bill Graham of Windsor and A. J. (Paddy) Cormier, a lifelong Pictou resident, have served their community fire departments longer than anyone else in the country, according to the Chancellery Office in Ottawa." In recognition, both men were presented the fourth bar to their Fire Service Exemplary Medals, a "highly unusual" accomplishment since few applications for more than forty years service have ever been received by the Chancellery Office. Paddy Cormier joined the Pictou Volunteer Fire Department in 1927 and remained an active member until he retired in 1991 at the age of eighty-four. Bill Graham, just seventeen when he signed on with the Windsor Volunteer Fire Department in 1931, was still going strong at eighty. For sixty-three years, except for overseas military service during World War Two, he responded to every alarm—dressed in a tie! In 1994, past the age of scaling ladders, he was placed in charge of traffic control at fires. On February 14, 1991, Graham received his fourth bar from the governor-general of Canada, and on September 30, 1994, accepted congratulations from Canadian Prime Minister Jean Chrétien.

Union Protection Company smoke-eater, Halifax, 1888

"Smoke-eaters" and "leather lungs" were terms used when referring to firemen "who seemed to be able to breathe the smoke without having to come out for air." Legend contends that smoke-eaters grew long beards so the whiskers could be soaked in water, then clinched between the teeth to act as a filter. Reference has also been found to a watered sponge substituting for facial hair. Another trick was for a hoseman to place his face close to where the water stream left the nozzle as there tended to be a small pocket of fresh air trapped in this area. Firemen took great pride in their ability to "eat smoke." In December 1858, William H. Kelly of the Union Engine Company braved smoke and flame to save a young girl

At left is Robert Barnhill, Truro's first fire chief, 1868. The firefighter at right is unidentified.

from a burning building at Bigby's Corner. Suffering no apparent ill effects at the time, Kelly attended a ceremony in February 1859 when he and John Leach, who assisted with the rescue, were presented with engraved silver watches and chains for "their noble and intrepid conduct." Kelly's condition worsened, however, and on September 19, 1859, he was buried in Camp Hill Cemetery, the victim of an insidious respiratory disease brought on, it was believed, by his heroic efforts of ten months earlier. Even with the availability of respirators in the early 1900s, firemen generally spurned them from a sense of stubborn pride and long-standing tradition. This may have cost Halifax hoseman William Gorman his life. Having survived severe injuries on October 17, 1921, after falling through a burning roof, Gorman's luck ran out on Valentine's Day 1926, when he became trapped in a smoke-filled room while fighting a fire at Ben's Bakery; he died in hospital three hours after being rescued. Deputy Chief Billy Howell was a renowned smoke-eater who retired in 1944 after fifty-two years with the Halifax Fire Department. A tribute made reference to his "remarkable record for being able to stand a tremendous amount of smoke, in fact he was practically in-human when it came to take this sort of punishment which has left its mark on his health." Billy Howell died four years later on September 11, 1948.

Smoke-Eaters

Hosemen of the Union Engine Company and a fire warden pose before the burned-out shell of St. Joseph's Orphanage, Halifax, July 1881

Firemen were governed by constitutions that carried sanctions for insubordination and breach of rules. As early as 1795, the Halifax Union Engine Company "exercised an oversight on the morals of its members [for swearing], not in the Company meetings but elsewhere, and they were promptly fined various sums ranging from five to twenty shillings." Twenty-one members of the Truro Fire Brigade were expelled on May 2, 1872, "for refusing to obey orders of the Captain," while another was banished for not attending drills or paying his fines. In 1886, a Truro fireman was discharged for "disorderly conduct while in a

THE
SMOKE-EATERS

fireman's uniform." Eleven Glace Bay members were dismissed in 1903 for poor attendance, while twelve others escaped with warnings. The following offenses and fines taken from the Bridgewater Fire Company's 1913 By-laws were representative of the times:

Sec.1. Members for being absent at Roll Call at regular or special meetings shall pay a fine of 10c.; absent the evening, 25c.; absent at Roll Call at the hour appointed for practice, 10c.; not attending the Roll Call after returning from practice, an addition of 15c.; after a fire, 25c.; sickness or absence from the fire, exempting only when satisfactorily explained to the Company. For leaving the room without permission of the Chairman, or not coming to order when called on to do so, 25c.; for leaving the apparatus while on duty without leave from the proper officer, 25c.; gambling in the Fire Station, for first offence, $2.00, and for the second to be dealt with by the Company; for disobedience to the orders of the officer in command; wilfully damaging anything pertaining to the Apparatus or Fire Stations; altering, defacing or damaging the Roll of Members, or any other property of the Company, or for taking the same from the Fire Station without consent of the officer in charge, $2.00, and for a repetition of these offences he may be dealt with by the Company.

Sec.2. If an officer or member on duty shall render himself incapable from the use of liquor, or shall visit the Fire Station in a state of intoxication, use or allow any to be used in the Fire Station, he shall for the first offence be fined $2.00 and for the second offence be dealt with by the Company.

Sec.3. Any member who may in any way interfere with the officer in command, or give counter orders, shall be fined $1.00 for each offence.

Sec.4. For neglect of duty on the part of an officer or member, or for disobedience of orders of an officer or Chairman, for which a specified penalty is not herein provided, he shall incur and pay a fine of not less than 10c., or not more than 50c., at the discretion of the Company.

Sec.5. Any member spitting on the floor shall pay a fine of 25c. for each offence.

Smoke-Eaters

Fines were not to be taken lightly. In November 1869, the Truro Fire Brigade's secretary notified firemen that if fines remained outstanding for one week, the matter would be turned over to the Stipendiary Magistrate. When accused with a breach of rules, a fireman was generally afforded ten minutes to argue his case before the company. On one memorable occasion at Halifax, it was moved, seconded, and agreed upon by a vote of twenty-six to four "that a Mr. Frost was only one minute late at cleaning the engine in consequence of having a foot too

Unidentified Halifax Union Engine Company executive, late 1800s

large for his boot." This anatomical stroke of luck entitled Frost to have the charge rescinded. Following the William Stairs, Son & Morrow fire in August 1893, it was reported that some Halifax firemen "who were near the fire but did not work, will be arraigned at a meeting and perhaps expelled from the Company, as were two men after the John Street fire." Union Engine Company fireman Edward Coy was fined in 1907 for being absent from duty at a three-alarm fire. Coy explained that he was being married at the time and was subsequently "excused on this account but the fine of $3 imposed by the rules could not be remitted." Halifax firemen, it seems, even took their sports seriously—to the point of levying fines. On February 18, 1840, it was ordered "that a medal awarded by this Company some time previously to Mr. Robert Frost, for his activity in running a sack race, be worn by him at each and every festival of the Company under a penalty of 2 shillings 6 d." One of the more amusing fines arose from an incident on October 16, 1838: "Several dogs, without leave, ballot or beans intruded into the Union Hall this evening, where they commenced hostilities to the great annoyance of the Company and it was unanimously agreed that a fine of 1s 3d be extracted from the owner of any dog or dogs found in the room while the business of the Company is transacting."

THE
SMOKE-EATERS

Firemen had a penchant for strong drink, and newspaper accounts often made subtle references to the frequent imbibing. "The evening was spent as firemen know best how to do. Great good feeling characterized this firemen's feast and all who participated were 'merry and wise'." To instill a semblance of sobriety, fire brigade by-laws addressed over-indulgence. The Halifax Union Engine Company executive in 1835 instructed its members at monthly meetings that "No liquor was allowed to be brought in the room till the business of the

Sydney firemen on parade, c.1900

Company was over." The Union Protection Company took similar steps in 1861, as there was "objection to the use of liquor by firemen at their meetings and a resolution was passed opposing consumption of intoxicants before the business was disposed." Rule VI, Section II of the Tatamagouche Hook & Ladder Company stated that "Any member appearing at a drill or at any meeting of the Company, or at an entertainment given by the Company, or at a fire in a state of intoxication, shall be fined ($1.00) One Dollar or expelled, as the Company see fit." In the Sydney Volunteer Fire Department, "should any member attend a fire or any public demonstration of the Department, and become there at intoxicated, disorderly or otherwise disagreeable the officer in charge shall, or any member may, report the same at the next regular meeting of the Department, when the member so charged may be excused, fined, or resignation requested as a majority may decide." Fines were the norm, with few men actually expelled for drinking. In 1893, a Halifax steam fire engineer was arrested for drunk and disorderly conduct. It was recommended he be suspended for two months, but in the end an apology sufficed. This incident resulted in a resolution being unanimously passed "that in future any paid official of the fire department whether on or off duty, who gets intoxicated and the charge is proven, immediately be discharged."

Early fire companies were very much fraternal orders. At Halifax in March 1837, records show it was "further understood that any member exposing the business of the evening to any person not a member of the Company shall be expelled from the Company." This gag order was later repealed in 1845. A real hulla-baloo erupted in 1838, when a Union Engine Company member was expelled for snitching. The unnamed, ostracized individual reputedly "informed against persons selling liquor without license and other-wise ungratefully used several persons in the community who had tried to befriend him."

As the company considered it "a duty of the first importance to keep themselves as a body respectable," they agreed unani-mously to the fol-lowing resolution:

Yarmouth firemen with an array of apparatus

(L-R) ladder cart, hose reel, hand engine, hose cart, Amoskeag steam fire engine

Whereas this Company entertains the highest respect for the law and the authorities and feel satisfied that the taxes imposed by law ought to be paid and exacted by those whose duty it is to collect them but at the same time they can-not consistently with their own feelings and out of respect to the community allow a Public Informer to remain among them and hold such an individual in the utmost contempt. Therefore Resolved, That ____, a Public Informer who is a tradesman and a member of this Company be held by us as a body with the greatest contempt and he be forthwith expelled.

The Honourable J.B. Uniacke wrote a letter on behalf of the accused, but the resolution "was immediately acted upon," and the issue resolved. In April 1898, a Truro councillor claimed that the majority of firemen had been drunk at a recent fire. The accusation caused much ado among firemen, and a special closed meet-ing was held to address the matter. The charge was read before the brigade, with members sworn to secrecy in their deliberations. As the roll was called, each fire-man denied the allegation. "It was unanimously decided to stand by each other in the matter," and a rebuttal was forwarded to town council requesting specific details and names in regards to the charge. "A full and complete investigation and an expression of confidence" was demanded of council. It would seem the councillor in question had been misinformed regarding intoxicated firemen as he "promptly withdrew the charge and apologised," with council passing a resolu-tion of confidence in the brigade.

George Craig was a well known nineteenth-century Dartmouth businessman, fireman, and photographer who took great delight in doctoring images, as he did with this staged firemen's rescue, complete with exterior smoke damage. Such comic relief underscored the reality that a fireman's lot was a dangerous one, something not lost on the people they served. It was customary for appreciative citizens to make cash donations to their fire department. Following a December 31, 1905, blaze that razed Gunn's Opera House in Truro, a number of contributions were sent to the brigade for "commendable work in connection with this fire. Frost & Wood $5, Black & Co. $10, F. Cantwell $25, W.D. Ross $15, Mrs. Connor $5, E. Phillips & Co. $50, A.T. Dalrymple $25, Angus & Pollock $10, Mrs. White $5, Levy Bros., Hamilton, Ont. $50 for jewelry samples protected." In September 1908, the Government of Nova Scotia presented five hundred dollars to Truro firemen "for excellent services rendered" in connection with a fire at the Agricultural College. The long-established tradition of fire insurance companies giving cash bonuses continued into the 1900s. In January 1904, the Truro Fire Brigade received twenty dollars from the Halifax Fire Insurance Company and twenty-five dollars from Acadia Insurance Company, for which firemen "voted hearty thanks." Cards of appreciation published in local newspapers were also popular, although not as lucrative for firemen. William Jenkins of Halifax took out the following:

Dartmouth firemen stage a rescue, c.1890

> The subscriber begs to return his sincere thanks to his friends and the Union Protection Company, for their timely assistance in saving his Furniture from destruction by Fire on Tuesday morning last. Also to the Volunteer Engine and Axe Companies for their praiseworthy exertions arresting its progress.

At Pugwash, *The Night Blooming Cereus* of November 24, 1869, carried this public notice:

> The Hon. H.G. Pineo begs to return his sincere thanks to those who so nobly exerted themselves in his behalf on the occasion of the late fire and by their almost superhuman exertions succeeded in saving his dwelling from the devouring element.

Smoke-Eaters

The uniform featured in this photo was typical of the bib style worn by fire brigades in the late 1800s. Such regalia had no practical firefighting purpose but was intended for special occasions, such as parades, banquets, dances, and photo shoots. The earliest reference found to a fireman's uniform in Nova Scotia dates to January 17, 1860, at Halifax, when "the officers of the Company were appointed a committee to devise a uniform for members and directed to report at a special meeting to be held April 24. On that occasion the following was adopted—red shirt, black pants, cap according to pattern and black belt. It was resolved that the front of each member's fire cap be ornamented with a gilt crossed branch." Rules dictated that a new member "furnish himself with a fire cap, such as shall be approved by the Company. In default thereof he shall pay a fine of $1." Shirts and pants were no doubt fitted by local tailors, while caps were provided by William Ross, "the well known Granville St. hatter" and W.F. Knight, a saddler who also made firemen's belts. Fire caps predate the first known uniforms in Halifax, as lieutenants were instructed in 1835 to have Lieut. painted on the front of their cap instead of Union. In May 1856, W.F. Knight presented the Union Engine Company with a cap "to be worn by the Captain when on duty." Peter Henderson of Division No. 2 was given "a very handsome" fire cap by the business firm of E. Albro & Company in February 1859 to replace one that "all but burned off his head" while fighting a fire in the city business district. It was compulsory for Halifax firemen to wear their fire caps "at the working of the engines in April and October for cleaning and putting the engines in good order." Each man's cap was then inspected by their division lieutenant, and "the owner of any cap not found clean and in good order" was fined one shilling.

Union Engine Company dress uniform, Halifax c.1895

THE
SMOKE-EATERS

Dress uniforms were a fashion statement, with firemen sometimes given preference to wear the style and colour of their choosing. This no doubt developed an *esprit de corps* among divisions, with engine, hose, axe, and ladder men vying to make a favourable impression when out in public. In 1868, Halifax firemen on parade wore scarlet tops trimmed in blue, with the officers of each division sporting "elegant silk scarves." On another occasion, firemen wore a solid coloured uniform to a picnic, which struck a "lively appearance, the brilliant red uniforms of the men contrasted pleasingly with the light dresses of the lasses." For the Grand Firemen's Tournament of 1886 in Halifax, some Union Engine Company members wore a "decidedly handsome" blue serge uniform with silver buttons, while others dressed in more traditional red, which "looked very pretty." This fireman's embroidered lapels with tie, cummerbund, and watch fob stand in sharp contrast to the relatively plain design featured in the previous photos, which may indicate that the unidentified gentleman held a position above the general rank and file, possibly that of company captain. As a point of interest, the leader of an early fire brigade or company was usually denoted with the rank of captain. This gradually changed during the era of steam engines to chief engineer, then to chief by the early 1900s.

Note the ornamental horn on the table. Fires were chaotic scenes, and to be heard above the cacophonous din, officers shouted directives to their men through a brass speaking trumpet. On one memorable occasion, Halifax fireman Patrick Connors took command at the Grafton Street Methodist Church fire by occupying a position atop the pump organ. In addition to their practicality, trumpets were also highly prized for ceremonial trophies. Specially engraved silver trumpets were awarded for various events at firemen's tournaments, and several are displayed today in museum and fire hall showcases throughout Nova Scotia.

Early fireman's uniform, Halifax c.1880

Bridgewater firemen received their first uniforms in 1884

The uniforms were black flannel waist jackets and white trousers. Caps were added in 1886 at a cost of $1.25 each.

Truro's fire brigade was ordered to turn out in their inaugural dress uniform on May 24, 1874, with each member to be outfitted at personal expense. Similar to that of Halifax, the Truro uniform included a cap made locally by C. Kent, a red flannel shirt with hook-and-eye fasteners and breast pocket, waist belt, and dark pants, with shirt and pants trimmed with blue silk ribbon. A black leather belt with narrow red edging and stamped with the company name completed the ensemble. Special events sometimes called for an entirely new wardrobe. In July 1885, Truro firemen competed at a tournament in Saint John, New Brunswick, wearing blue shirts and navy blue pants, with belts and caps. For the twelve Truro firemen going to a Sydney tournament in 1905, "it was necessary for the delegation to be properly uniformed, and caps and buttons were rounded up and a committee appointed to pick out cloth for suits required from samples. It was decided that the coats be made double-breasted. Those not going to Sydney can have them the way they like." New Glasgow's Engine Company in 1883 wore blue, pull-over thigh-length wool tops, two-inch-wide ornamental white belts, and leather and metal helmets. The belt buckle and helmet badge were inscribed with the word "Lulan," for the brigade's steam fire engine. Firemen provided dark trousers and footwear "to their own taste." The five companies comprising the New Glasgow force each contributed one hundred dollars, with the town adding $750 to help defray expenses. A new "ceremonial uniform" was introduced in 1928—blue, four-pocket jacket with metal buttons and peak cap. The Kentville Volunteer Fire and Protection Company's first uniform included a cream-coloured shirt trimmed in blue, with a blue shield bearing the initials KFD, black pants and belt, a "regulation" cap and badge completing the outfit. In 1927, the department spent $2,500 on fifty-four "snappy new uniforms" to be worn only for "dress occasions."

Dartmouth Union Engine Company firemen and *Lady Dufferin*

Dartmouth firemen circa 1885 wore ceremonial dress: a thin, wool pull-over tunic with red body; white collars, lapels, and cuffs; braided gold trim; and four brass buttons down the front. As can be seen from this photo, colour schemes varied, some choosing to wear white tunics with dark lapels and collars. Dartmouth fireman George Craig owned one of each, indicating perhaps that firemen had "home & away" tops. A fire helmet's frontal piece was traditionally emblazoned with a company logo or division number. Some were very ornate; a copper, die-cast lion reclines on the peak of George Craig's 1895 helmet. Firefighting memorabilia today are hot items—a New Glasgow fireman's helmet from 1877 sold in December 2001 at an internet auction for $2,966.24.

This account of Dartmouth firemen appeared in an 1880 October issue of the *Halifax Evening Mail*:

> The half yearly inspection of the Dartmouth Fire Company took place this afternoon and we learn that the working of the engines and apparatus gave the most unbounded satisfaction. The Company has recently been furnished with a quantity of a new quality of patent suction hose, imported from the United States, which gives entire satisfaction. The work performed by the old hand engine, No. 2, purchased from the Corporation of Halifax, in the year 1822, quite surprised many of the spectators. The Dartmouth boys, who are noted for their muscular power, took hold with a will, and broke her down until they threw a stream almost equal to our city steamers, and proved to the entire satisfaction of the fire authorities that everything is secure in the hands of the Dartmouth boys. The late Benjamin Elliott, father of the present J.B. Elliott, joined the Dartmouth Company in 1822 and served an apprenticeship of 36 years—and died one of the oldest firemen in the Province of Nova Scotia.

Smoke-Eaters

The Dartmouth Axe & Ladder Company running team posed in dress uniform for a photo at the Yarmouth Firemen's Tournament, held July 23-30, 1911. Their uniform design, with slight variances, was widely adopted by fire departments in the early 1900s. Log book entries provide insight to a fireman's daily routine. Listed here are un-edited 1924 excerpts from Halifax's Morris Street Engine House, when it was staffed by paid, full-time firemen:

Dartmouth Axe & Ladder Company firemen, 1911

Back row (L-R):
2nd Lieut. A. Patterson,
W. Chipman, A. Bonang,
Marshal J. Baker,
R. Walsh.
Front row (L-R):
D. Patterson, Treasurer
M. Murphy, Captain H.
Young, C. Short, Chief
DeFries, Y.F.D.,
A. Emery.

Jan. 1   spare team shaude; 48 bales hay came.

Jan. 7   spare team halling durt to dump from seller.

Jan. 10   used 11 harde wood slats to fix horses stalls.

Jan. 16   out tonight flooding rink at College St. school; brought hose from Quinpool Road to dry.

Feb. 5   the waggon horses out to get exercised, can't take them out much, can't keep them sharp.

Feb. 12   got shoe nailed on little brown horse today; men out all day shovelling snow.

Mar. 1   had three teams out for childrens slay ride.

Mar. 8   horse walked on F. Condon's foot.

Mar. 9   F. Condon reported sick at 9 am.

Mar. 24   there was 18 ton of coal came today; the team took cabnet to Bedford Row that the carpenter made today.

Mar. 25   the chemical horses took lumber and tools to Grafton St. for carpenter.

Apr. 1   had horse out in cart halling ashes today.

Apr. 9   got 9 fetther pillows and 1pair blankets.

Apr. 24   lumber for ladders came from mill today; sent 40 feet of harde wood boards to Quinpool Road; got 100 watt light for carpenter to work by.

June 18   Chief's Convention opened at Technical College today; the Chiefs went to McNabs Island for hodge podge.

July 1   had white face horse into Dr. Jakement for the day, he had colic.

Aug. 19   filled 5 extinguishers for Blind School; Mr. O'Connell's picnic at Gardens today, had men over there to keep order; took bords and three plank to Quinpool Road to fix stalls today.

Aug. 28   took 50 feet bords from Quinpool Road to Grafton St. to fix floor in barn.

Sept. 12   all hose tested today.

Sept. 17   men went to Dartmouth for tug of war.

A.W. Sturmy, Union Protection Company, Halifax

While the majority of fire departments were volunteer, it was not uncommon for a paid caretaker to live at the engine house. In some instances, accommodations were provided for his family to stay with him. Departments without a caretaker customarily left a key to the building at the nearest residence. Records of the Union Engine Company circa 1856 show a Mr. Sturmy being "keeper of the engine house." This may possibly have been the gentleman portrayed here as it

was only five years later the firemen resigned en masse and organized the Union Protection Company, as depicted on his helmet. At Truro on November 2, 1868, "the necessity of having a steward whose duties were defined as providing refreshments after fires and keeping engine house and hose in good order at the company's expense was passed unanimously." Later on, Scott Henry and his wife served as Central Engine House caretakers for many years. On December 17, 1900, they were presented with chairs "as a token of the appreciation of the firemen for kind service rendered in past year." Mrs. Henry was "remembered annually by Christmas presentations by the members." New Glasgow hired a caretaker in 1878 for the winter months to maintain stove heat, so water in the steam engine boiler wouldn't freeze; by 1883 he was being paid forty dollars. Rule 23 from the Bridgewater Fire Company's by-laws of 1913 shows that the responsibilities of their caretaker went far beyond keeping the building warm:

A Janitor shall be appointed for the Central Station at a salary to be governed by the Company. His duty shall be to keep the space in front of the Station clean and free from snow, take care of the Station, and see that the meeting room is prepared for each meeting. Whenever the apparatus has been used he shall clean the same, grease the wheels of the engine and hose reels from time to time, and keep them clean and in running order; see that the apparatus is in the proper place and ready for use, and whenever anything is out of order to report the same to the officer in charge without delay; look after the fire and see that the stove is kept well filled; ring the bell at all regular meetings 15 minutes before time, for 3 minutes; he shall keep the station in a neat and respectable condition, and he shall be under the orders of the officer in charge of the Station, if he is not doing his duty, he may be dismissed and another appointed by said officer.

William J. Beck, a native of Pictou, Nova Scotia, moved to Antigonish in the 1850s where he became a successful merchant and later "took an active interest" in establishing fire protection for the town. Unlike some who feigned interest in firefighting to escape forced militia duty, Beck apparently embraced the responsibility, rising to the rank of major. Antigonish purchased a hand engine in 1864 and organized its first fire brigade, the Rescue Fire Company. Little is known about the company's early years until 1892, when a new constitution allowed for a fire brigade comprised of two hose companies of ten men each and a hook-and-ladder company of seven men. In February 1876, *The Casket* announced that "The Fire Company of Antigonish had a cheerful sleigh ride and dinner yesterday. They went to Marshy Hope to enjoy dinner there." In July 1882, it was reported,

Major William J. Beck, Nova Scotia Militia, Antigonish

The members of the Antigonish Fire Engine Company [performed] exercises and parade on Friday last and looked remarkably well in their new uniform of hats and jackets recently procured at considerable expense. The company seems to be in first-rate order under the efficient management of Capt. Somers. [Martin Somers retired in 1883 having served with the brigade since its inception, the last seven of those years as its captain].

The hand engine, preserved today in the Antigonish Heritage Museum, resembles the *Honeyman Tub* used by Truro. This stands to reason, as Truro officials consulted with Antigonish before buying equipment and forming their own fire brigade in 1868. Antigonish's fire engine arrived without suction hose and, as luck would have it, a barn caught on fire soon after delivery. Undeterred, firemen pressed the engine into service, supplying it with water from puncheons kept filled by bucket brigades from Brierly Brook. Cisterns made of hemlock staves were later built in various parts of the town for emergency purposes. The hand engine was retired in 1893, with the installation of a piped water works. In 1916, Antigonish had a volunteer force of thirty-one men equipped with three hose carts, 1,500 feet of hose, and a hook-and-ladder cart "which gives it an efficient fire protection."

Rufus Keating Memorial, Camp Hill Cemetery, Halifax

Rufus Keating had the dubious distinction of being the last volunteer Halifax fireman killed in the line of duty before the re-organization in 1894 of the Union Engine Company into the Halifax Fire Department. Keating, 32, suffered grotesque injuries while fighting the Wm. Stairs, Son & Morrow fire on August 21, 1893. A long ladder supporting five firemen slid sideways along the building throwing Keating to the ground where he was impaled under the chin by an iron gate spike. He miraculously survived, but died in January 1894 from complications associated with the fall. It was determined "the immediate cause of death was the cutting of the chords of the neck, resulting in what may be termed a slow process of strangulation." The Keating monument was unveiled on November 25, 1894. A little-known tale surrounds Camp Hill Cemetery and another firemen's memorial. In December 1859, members of the Union Engine Company asked the mayor and council for a grant of sixteen lots in Camp Hill Cemetery "for the purpose of erecting a firemen's monument in which to inter members of the Company who might die." The mayor was more than generous, giving the firemen thirty lots. Nothing much was done for nine years, until the Union Engine Company held a three-day centenary celebration. On August 8, 1868, the ringing of bells and waving of flags signalled the start of "one of the most brilliant fetes ever given by a public body in Halifax," which included the always-popular firemen's procession through city streets accompanied by marching bands. "The parade went to Camp Hill Cemetery where the cornerstone of the firemen's monument was laid. The mound then was described as about eight feet in height and handsomely laid out in terraces. The plans called for the erection of a pillar of stone thirty-six feet high. In the cornerstone a handsome mahogany box was placed, containing the usual documents and mementos and was sealed in place." Unexplainably, the project was apparently never finished, as no towering monument, nor a cornerstone for that matter, can be found today.

Truro Fire Chief "Bis" Stewart

N. Bismark Stewart was both fire chief and entrepreneur, whose business interests on Inglis Street in Truro included a tobacco store, billiards hall, bowling alley, and fishing tackle shop. "Bis," as he was commonly known, joined the Truro Fire Brigade on February 15, 1892. He rose to the rank of first lieutenant by September 1896 and chief on December 15, 1902. Upon his promotion, Stewart became Truro's first fire chief, as all others before him had carried the title of captain. He was elected to twenty consecutive one-year terms, during the course of which "the Brigade made notable progress under his leadership." One noteworthy change made under Chief Stewart limited the distance from the engine house that town horses could be employed for work detail unrelated to fire duty. Before a horse could be taken beyond the established boundaries, provisions first had to be made to pull fire apparatus should an alarm sound in its absence. As a token of appreciation and respect for services rendered, Stewart's men presented him with a pair of buffalo robes in 1910, following a New Year's concert at the engine house. A humorous story involves Bis Stewart and a fire at the D.H. Smith building opposite the YMCA. Apparently the chief was returning from a funeral dressed in his Sunday best—complete with a silk top hat—when he came upon his men actively engaged in fighting the aforementioned blaze. Without a second thought, he entered the burning building and took command of the situation, still bedecked in his "topper." Word of his firefighting apparel soon spread across the province. For sometime thereafter, when reporting details of a fire, various members of the press corps would end their coverage with "None of the firemen wore plug hats."

At right, members of the Truro Fire Brigade flank their hose truck Darley which doubled on this occasion as a hearse for Chief Bis Stewart's cortège. Honouring a "brother" fireman with an elaborate funeral is still a tradition, dating back to the hand engine days. On June 19, 1832, the Halifax Union Engine Company "resolved that on the death of a member the surviving members attend his funeral in a body and wear crape as a mark of respect to his memory." Further to this, company records show that on March 19, 1844, "a question was raised respecting members who may be attending a funeral at the time that an alarm of fire is given and it was agreed that persons in the following situations shall be exempt from fires—relatives of the deceased, pall bearers and hearse or wagon drivers." On October 21, 1845, the Union Engine Company voted the sum of seven pounds to pay for the funeral and related expenses of departed member Joseph Hutt. It was common practice for firemen to be "assisted during illness, also by fraternal attention and otherwise when necessary." In 1841, the sum of $18.65 was collected and given to the widow of Halifax fireman James Thompson "as she and her son were in very indigent circumstances" after the boy was injured when run over by a fire engine. It was agreed upon in 1845, that the Union Engine Company would donate fifty pounds and all entry fees "to assist members who may be injured while at their duty." In July 1845, an additional thirty-eight pounds "was subscribed by the members of the Company and paid to the Mayor for the relief of the suffers by the fire at Quebec." On June 25, 1846, thirty pounds from company funds and "what may be collected by

Fire Chief Bis Stewart's funeral, June 1935

voluntary subscriptions" were donated for "alleviating sufferers by fire at St. John's, Nfld." In July 1874, the Truro Fire Brigade raised two hundred dollars "as the fire enginemen were desirous of assisting our brother engineman" James Smith who lost his house to fire. On February 2, 1882, firemen came to Smith's aid again, approaching town council on his behalf for money after he was seriously injured in the line of duty.

Smoke-Eaters

Capt. John Brooks, Halifax Fire Department, c.1910

Captain John Brooks retired from the Halifax Fire Department on October 1, 1943, after thirty-five years of service. He joined the force as a call man in 1908, became a permanent fireman in 1918, and was promoted to captain of Bedford Row Engine House in 1920. During his days on the call force, Brooks was employed with Robin, Collins, Jones and Whitman at Boak's Coal Wharf, where he saved a number of persons from drowning in Halifax Harbour. "Putting duty before any fear of personal injury, he was hurt many times during his career as a fireman," claimed a newspaper tribute. "Sometimes he went to hospital, other times he insisted on remaining on duty." At a 1933 fire, Brooks crashed through a floor onto a cellar beam. In 1937, he fell off a roof but kept working. On another occasion in 1937, he was injured and remained in hospital seventeen days. In 1939, he cut his leg at Bedford Row while splitting wood and again spent five days in hospital. This accident eventually necessitated the amputation of his leg and retirement in 1943 at the age of sixty-seven. There was very little assistance in the early days for firemen injured in the line of duty. Records show that on October 18, 1842, the Halifax Union Engine Company "unanimously resolved that all the sums remaining in the Treasury, after the incidental expenses of the Company are paid, shall be kept as a sinking fund for the relief of members who may be injured at the time of duty." The *Daily Echo* of July 21, 1894, reported that no Halifax firemen were then currently insured, as city officials believed "if they were to insure them [firemen] they would also have to insure the police and other officials." New Glasgow firemen requested insurance through town council in 1909 for job-related accidents. In 1902, Truro firemen were first covered against general accidents, with the cost of premiums shared between individual members and brigade funds. By 1910, each fireman carried $1,150 accidental death benefit coverage, with "corresponding proportions for loss of limbs etc. and for death or disability of a special list of diseases."

Halifax Fire Chief John Connolly, 1894-1903

John Connolly joined the Union Engine Company circa 1870 as a volunteer, and after twenty-four years of service was promoted to fire chief in 1894, when re-structuring led to the formation of a part-paid, part-call force. He served as chief until 1903, when he was unceremoniously dismissed from office. His problems began in November 1902, when a committee of six aldermen was authorized "to take into consideration the improvements of the Fire Department, its efficiency and economy." For the next five months the local newspapers had a field day reporting the on-going investigation, which developed into a witch-hunt aimed at ousting Connolly. On April 22, 1903, he stood before city council to answer charges of misappropriation of funds, condoning alcohol consumption and gambling among his men, "lack of harmony" within the department, and poor decision-making at recent fires. (For details see *Evening Mail* , March 19 and April 22, 1903; *Daily Echo*, March 31, 1903.) Chief Connolly was able to defend himself on all accounts, but his fate was already sealed. Battle lines were drawn among aldermen, accusations of complicity and patronage met with denials and counter-accusations. One official stated that he had received orders from the mayor "to dismiss Chief Connolly at the first opportunity to take the patronage of the Fire Department away from the Liberals and give it to the Conservatives." This revelation resulted in "deep silence throughout the Council Chambers," followed by lively discussion. When all was said and done, council voted ten to five in favour of dismissal. "Council Trial Was A Farce," proclaimed one headline. On May 1, 1903, an appeal for reinstatement was defeated by a margin of six to five, effectively ending the John Connolly saga and a thirty-three-year career.

Halifax Fire Chief Patrick J. Broderick, 1903–1916

Patrick Broderick became a Halifax fireman circa 1873 and assumed the mantle of chief (at an annual salary of $1,500) when John Connolly was terminated in 1903. Chief Broderick was described as "an experienced and capable officer, a strict disciplinarian." By 1916, Halifax's population of approximately fifty thousand was served by a force of thirty-six full-paid and eighty-six call men posted to eight engine houses—Spring Garden Road, Grafton Street, Bedford Row, Morris Street, West Street, Brunswick Street, Gottingen Street, and Quinpool Road. Within the full paid force were one chief officer, one chief mechanical engineer, two chauffeurs, eighteen drivers, three chemical operators, four hose-and-ladder men, two blacksmiths, and five relief men. The call men included two chief officers, eight captains, nine lieutenants, five engineers, five stokers, and fifty-seven hose-and-ladder men. The department was divided into twelve companies—five engine, two ladder, one combined ladder and chemical, two chemical, and two hose.

Discipline under Broderick was reported to be "fairly good." The chief had powers to suspend a fireman for one week without pay; all other punishments—including a reprimand, dismissal, or fine not exceeding one month's pay—had to go before the Board of Control. Call men could be fined for missing fires or leaving the city without permission. Total fines for 1915 amounted to $366. From 1911 to 1915, eight firemen were dismissed and four suspended "for various causes." The year-end report for 1916 showed that Halifax was experiencing difficulties with some of their call men:

> Engines are placed at hydrants and are supposed to be connected immediately if the fire appears serious but this rule is not always carried out as the call men usually rush to get hold of the nozzle instead of connecting the suction and generally the engineer and stoker are late in responding or fail to respond at all and the engines cannot be used; there have been cases where the operators failed to appear even on third alarms. In such cases the mechanical engineer runs one of the engines and the others are not used.

It was no doubt incidents such as these that led Halifax to switch to a fully paid force in 1918.

THE
SMOKE-EATERS

Halifax Fire Chief Edward Condon, 1916–1917

Patrick Broderick died on December 23, 1916, after a lengthy illness and on January 5, 1917, Halifax City Council voted nine to six in favour of appointing Edward Condon his successor. He was to receive a salary of $1,200 plus free quarters. Politics historically raised its ugly head whenever discussions and decisions evolved around the fire department, and Condon's appointment was no exception. He had served many years as the fire department's chief engineer and on occasion had held the position of acting fire chief. For unexplained reasons, a letter protesting his candidacy was submitted by the Board of Fire Underwriters to council prior to the vote. It caused quite a stir, one alderman wanting to hold off voting in fear that underwriters would raise insurance rates in retaliation to Condon's appointment. Another angrily retorted, "If one-half of the fire underwriters intend to take charge of the civic departments, it might be just as well to let them run the city. If the board of control and the city council are going to run the city, let them do it!" The city comptroller claimed that "if men in the service were not given preference to promotion, it would have a tendency to paralyse the service of the fire department. We have a splendid lot of firemen and I think we will do the right thing by appointing the legitimate successor." The best response perhaps came in the form of a letter to the editor of the *Evening Mail* on January 6, 1917, from J.S. Edward, a former chairman of the Halifax Board of Firewards:

> I do not think…any alderman or controller need lay awake nights worrying over the suggestion that the appointment or non-appointment of a fire chief will in any way affect the insurance rates, for, as far as I have been able to observe the insurance rates are based on certain things that might be called intangible, at least they are not visible to the ordinary mortal. We may talk as we like and do as we like; we may put all sorts of fire ordinances into effect; we may do all in our power to meet the wishes of that mysterious organization commonly known as underwriters, and then after we have done all we can, the insurance rates, like the cost of living, keeps "soaring, soaring, up to the vaulted sky…and if we don't want to "pay up and look pleasant" we can go without insurance and that is all there is to it.

The fervour died down and Condon retained his rightful place as fire chief. He served only one year in office, as he was killed in the line of duty during the Halifax Explosion.

**Halifax Fire Chief
John W. Churchill,
1917–1945**

John Churchill joined the fire department in 1895, becoming chief on December 12, 1917, following Edward Condon's death in the Halifax Explosion. He was born on April 9, 1871, the son of Lieutenant George S. Churchill who founded the North West Arm Fire Department. Chief Churchill's residence at 146 Jubilee Road was on the site of the first fire station in West End Halifax. As a young boy, he wore period fireman's garb and rode on a Union Engine Company float in a parade honouring the appointment of the Marquis of Lorne as governor-general of Canada. Described as "one of the foremost firefighters in the Dominion," he never missed a major fire in fifty years of service and was always at the front. During the Prince George Hotel fire of March 26, 1928, Chief Churchill made his way through four smoke-filled storeys to rescue a hotel domestic trapped on the top floor. With the building a "seething mass of flames" he carried the unconscious woman to safety. While fighting a fire at the Nova Scotia Furniture Company building during his earlier years, Churchill and several colleges cheated death when the roof collapsed under them, plunging the men into the fiery inferno; miraculously, only one fireman was killed. During Churchill's tenure as fire chief, he completed the motorization of the Halifax Fire Department, instituted a fully paid service, and initiated the Fire Prevention Bureau. In 1932 he was instrumental in hosting the 24th Convention of the Dominion Association of Fire Chiefs, a first for Halifax. A year later, Churchill was elected their president; he also served as vice-president of the International Association of Fire Chiefs. During World War Two he headed the auxiliary firefighters branch of the ARP in addition to his other duties. Chief Churchill was "an ardent student in the latest techniques of fighting fires and his foremost hobby was keeping up to date on all new methods of fire control." Under his command, not a single fireman was lost. Chief Churchill died at home after a brief illness on Tuesday September 26, 1945, at the age of seventy-four. He was replaced by Frederick C. MacGillivray, who served as chief from 1945-1962.

Halifax Fire Chief Frederick C. MacGillivray, 1945–1963

Fred MacGillivray was born November 4, 1893, the youngest of thirteen children, and began his career as a Halifax fireman in 1911 as a volunteer on a coal wagon. In 1918, at twenty-three years of age, he became one of the original members of the newly formed permanent force. MacGillivray worked as driver and pump operator on the *Patricia*, making twenty dollars a week, four dollars more than a captain's weekly wage. In 1937, he was promoted to captain, then to captain-inspector in 1943 for city council's "fire escape committee," which that same year became Halifax's first fire prevention division. As captain-inspector he was the division's lone employee, eventually expanding its strength in 1954 to ten men. MacGillivray became chief in 1945 by the narrowest of margins, winning a city council vote seven to six following a highly publicized campaign. Aware perhaps of the politics involved in the city fire department, he took a hard line against city hall interference. In a January 2, 1962, *Mail Star* article, Chief MacGillivray was quoted as saying he "automatically disqualified any applicant recommended by a city council member or other political official. If a man needed an alderman's recommendation to get into the department then he was sure not to be the kind of man who would be the best asset to the staff."

Chief MacGillivray focussed his efforts with "missionary zeal" on fire prevention, fighting public apathy to improve safety in city schools and tenement slums, and to promote sprinkler installation. In 1949, he created the Nova Scotia Firemen's Regional Training School. He was founding president of the firemen's Local 268 in 1926 and as chief held many high posts, both nationally and internationally. A respected administrator, MacGillivray re-organized fire departments at Windsor in 1925 and at Moncton and Sydney in 1959. In fifty years, he missed only twenty-one days of work, eleven in an oxygen tent for exposure to phosgene gas. Unlike his four predecessors, Chief MacGillivray was the first to retire from his post. He died at the age of eighty-four on July 18, 1978.

James Cody, 1910

James Cody joined the Halifax Fire Department in February 1903 as a supernumerary, working "just for the glory of it." In 1905, he moved up to a call man, earning an annual salary of one hundred dollars. When a permanent force was established in 1918, Cody was promoted to captain. By 1920, a Halifax fireman's pay was twenty dollars a week, with one day off in eight. Organized labour movements were afoot, and James Cody stepped to the fore on behalf of firemen. On May 26, 1926, Halifax firemen were granted a charter—Local 268—as unionized members of the International Association of Firefighters in Washington, D.C. International Secretary-Treasurer George J. Richardson greatly assisted Halifax firemen to unionize and was instru-mental in having the Platoon Act legislated onto the provincial statue books. Richardson was branded "an imported agitator from the United States" but was actually a fireman with the Vancouver Fire Department. As secretary of Local 268, James Cody waged a bitter, highly publicized campaign against city council for more pay and shorter working hours. In 1927, firemen won the right to have one day off in three during summer months. On February 1, 1928, the department was placed on a two-platoon system and eighty-four-hour work week; this was later followed by a three-platoon, seventy-two-hour week. (On July 1, 1955, shift work changed to 24 hours on duty, 24 hours off-duty, with one free shift every eight working days). Captain Cody also served on the Board of Trustees of the International Association and championed for the common worker on a number of local fronts. In August 1952, he was presented with a gold emblem button in Washington, D.C. for twenty-five years service to Local 268. Injuries sustained at the 1939 Queen Hotel Fire forced Captain Cody into early retirement, but he was reactivated during World War Two to organize fire protection on Halifax harbour tugs. For his role in saving the burning U.S. Victory ship *Volunteer*, Cody was presented a U.S. Merchant Marine citation at the Pentagon in Washington, D.C.

THE
SMOKE-EATERS

In March 1903, the Halifax press reported that for several years the city had been supplying fuel and lights for the veterans' rooms in Spring Garden Road Engine House. This was in reference to the Veteran Firemen's Association, comprised then of fifty men— "thirty of them real old firemen"—who organized an auxiliary force to be called upon in times of emergency. "We consider the city is deeply indebted to the Veterans for services rendered in the past," stated council, "but a number of them are physically unable to attend fires." In this

"Old Vets," 1920

1920 photo, veterans pose with a float displaying some of the memorabilia collected from more than one hundred and fifty years of service. An article appeared in a Halifax newspaper on July 6, 1929, listing many of the artifacts on display at the veterans' clubhouse—solid silver ceremonial trumpets won at firemen's tournaments, "massive" brass and nickel lanterns that once hung from the sides of horse-drawn fire wagons, and a 150-year-old clock that "had been telling off the hours and minutes for the firemen of Halifax almost since the inception of the Union Engine Company." Oil paintings of famous rescues and fires dating to 1856 covered the old engine house walls. There were many photographs as well, one showing the Union Engine Company delegation that attended Philadelphia Centennial celebrations in September 1876. The author of the piece went on to say that "with the possible exception of the collection in the provincial museum there is perhaps no more extensive display of relics of the early days in Halifax than those on display in the Veteran Firemen's Hall, although little is perhaps known to the public generally of their intrinsic value. It can at least be said that there is no collection in the province associated with the business of firefighting more valuable than those in the possession of the Halifax veteran firemen." The Veteran Firemen's Association eventually moved from Spring Garden Road to hold meetings in buildings on Hollis, Gottingen, Green, and Barrington streets, leaving one to ponder the fate of the treasures they held.

Fire poles were once standard equipment in engine houses, but in recent years they have been phased out because of safety concerns. The three Halifax firemen featured in this January 17, 1953, photo are (from top to bottom): Jackie Joseph, Doug Keeping, and Ken Walker. Poles enabled firemen to quickly descend from their sleeping quarters to the fire apparatus below. The earliest two-storey engine houses are said to have used iron spiral staircases. Chicago fireman David Kenyon of Engine Company 21 is credited with designing the first fire pole; it was built of three-inch-diameter wood, sanded, and oiled. Kenyon was permitted to cut a hole in the engine house floor to demonstrate his invention, but it was his responsibility to close it back in if the chief wasn't pleased with what he saw. Apparently he was, and the first fire pole on record was used in 1878. Charles Allen of Engine Company No. 1 in Worchester, Massachusetts, perfected Kenyon's design when he built the first brass pole in 1880. In 1897, members of the Halifax Union Protection Company used an interesting arrangement in conjunction with the fire pole at their building on Jacob Street. A rope suspended within reach of the pole stretched from the second floor sleeping quarters to the rear of the wagon house on the ground floor where it was attached to a stall door in the stable. When answering an alarm, the driver grabbed the rope and held onto it while descending the fire pole. This opened the stall door, allowing the horses to take their place under the hanging harness at the front of the salvage wagon.

Training was a part of every fire department's routine. Some practiced more than others. Stellarton, circa 1900, averaged twenty a year, while Kentville staged one a week. A humorous entry appeared on the Truro Fire Brigade minutes of April 18, 1870, in regards to working the hand engine: "This day was appointed for drill. The roll being called, 18 persons reported. The Captain ordered that the Company proceed to the well of William McKay. After playing a short time, the weather being unfavorable, orders were given to retrace steps. The members being so near drowned and out of humour, no business was done." Firemen, being mostly volunteers, did not always look favourably upon drills, and attendance was on occasion sparse. A fine of five cents was imposed on truant Liverpool firemen for skipping practice in the late 1800s, but bribery seems to have worked better. A favourite treat of the Liverpool brigade following practices is said to have been banana splits at the local apothecary, where twelve could be purchased for three dollars.

Smoke-Eaters

Demonstration on Grand Parade in front of Halifax City Hall, c.1950

During the months of June and July in the early 1900s, all members of the Halifax Fire Department were drilled one night a week under direction of the district chief. No training facilities were then available, so firemen held practice at various locales, the Exhibition Grounds being one, where they raised and

mounted ladders, carried up hose lines and roof ladders, laid lines from engines, connected lines to engines and "threw" water, practised using freshwater feeds, and changed a burst suction. A competitive drill was staged once a year during the annual inspection. Entrance prerequisites to the Halifax Fire Department in 1903 required the applicant to be temperate, not older than thirty years of age, and in possession of a valid health certificate from the city medical officer. Controversy erupted that year over one thousand dollars compensation requested for the widow of fireman Richard Supple, who had died in the line of duty from what was determined to be "over exertion and exposure to cold." City council voted to pay only five hundred dollars, which was in line with an earlier settlement "under the same conditions." Questions were raised at the time by aldermen as to the physical fitness level of city firemen. It was agreed upon "that steps be taken at once, to have all members of the Halifax Fire Department, from the chief down, undergo an examination as to their physical condition, the services of those who failed to pass the required examination be dispensed with." What the end result of this proposed new policy was is not known but thirteen years later entrance requirements were still not what would be considered stringent. "Candidates for appointment must pass a physical examination by the city medical officer and must not be over 35 years of age; no other qualifications are prescribed."

94

Kentville smoke-eaters munch smoke of a different variety while enjoying a game of cards. Poker, cribbage boards, and pool tables were common recreational fare in engine houses. Andrew "Tobe" Mounce joined the Windsor Fire Department in 1925, and during the course of his fifty years of service became well known for his snooker and pool shot-making abilities. Some believe Tobe's ghost still returns to his old haunts on occasion. The April 11, 1934, *Halifax Mail* claimed the city fire department "boasts a number of fine cueists and Jack Spruin is generally classed as the best player. Captain James Lloyd [winner of the Halifax Civic Billiard League in 1922] is still able to wield a cue expertly it is said. When the boys get time for a little game of cards they drag out the cribbage board and then the fun begins. Tis said too that the Department boasts some mighty good teams and that Hoseman Jim Connolly and Captain Ryan, Bedford Row, would hold their own with any other pair in the City. In fact the boys at the Station figure they could 'take' the recent city champions, George Power and Bill Conway. They may be used to dousing fires but when it comes to cribbage the fire-laddies are 'hot stuff' themselves."

Down time at the Engine House, Kentville, c.1950

The Halifax "fire-laddies" couldn't have been happy when Fred MacGillivray took the fire chief post in 1945 and promptly ordered the pool tables removed. In a retirement tribute for MacGillivray by the *Mail Star*, January 2, 1962, the ex-chief was quoted as saying he had "determined that it was time the fire staff spent their time constructively on classes and maintenance. The familiar cartoon of firemen sitting around a poker table waiting for the bell has no place in Halifax."

95

Firefighting apparel, early 1900s

An exhausted group of Halifax firemen sport the work wear and head gear typically worn by fire departments. Waterproofed greatcoats had outer shells of heavy cotton duck or rubber, with layered liners of rubber and cotton; large metal clasps or hooks served as closures. In many cases, only sou'westers protected the head. C.H. Petch from Ottawa advertised waterproof duty coats and pants for firemen in the 1930s. Petch claimed to be the "sole manufacturer and recognized as the Canadian standard." In 1898, the Parrsboro Fire Brigade purchased twenty-eight rubber coats at four dollars each and twenty-eight caps at seventy-five cents each. Amherst owned forty helmets and rubber coats in 1905 and allocated $61.25 of the fire department's 1908 budget to replace worn suits, coats, and boots. Fire helmets were originally fashioned from treated leather. The first—designed in 1740 by Jacob Turck, a New York gunsmith—had a narrow brim and high crown. In 1828, Henry T. Gratacap made an improved helmet with curved sides and an elongated rear brim, which kept water and sparks off the neck and deflected heat from the face when the helmet was reversed. The American-style helmet, featured here and in previous photos, became the standard for decades. Leather fire helmets used by New Glasgow firemen in 1877 were made by Cairns and Brother of New York City. Halifax firemen may have also worn Cairns helmets, as the *Acadian Recorder* in August 1886 reported that Division No. 2 of the Union Axe Company had recently received "a handsome lot of hats made by a firm in New York through the agency of Mr. C.S. Lane." Some fire departments went helmetless well into the 1900s, one being Bridgewater, which—although its first fire service was organized in 1876—didn't begin using head protection until 1941.

THE
SMOKE-EATERS

Halifax began a change-over in 1933 from the American fire helmet to a British design, which the fire department continued to employ until post-World War Two. The following account appeared in the *Halifax Mail* of August 8, 1933. "Awaited for the past few months, the English-made firefighter's headgear which may supplement the American-style hat now the vogue among local smoke-eaters have finally arrived and will make their appearance at your very next neighbourhood fire….The new helmet is said to be about the best thing in the firefighting business. It is made entirely of leather and is lighter and more serviceable than the type now in use here. Moreover, it provides much better protection for the firemen's face. In addition it can be adjusted to suit the weather, whether for summer or winter wear. Similar helmets are worn by the splendidly equipped firemen of Liverpool England and Glasgow, Scotland. Twelve such helmets were purchased by the Halifax Fire Department, on recommendation of Chief Churchill and if found serviceable as the chief is confident, it is quite probable that they will supplement the old entirely. Only the ten Captains have been issued with the new headgear which is conspicuous by its bright red color." The British helmet doesn't appear to have caught on with other fire departments, and Halifax firemen returned to American designs in the 1950s. Some later models made of metal or fibreglass were produced as far away as the E.D. Bullard Company of San Francisco.

Halifax firemen bedecked in British helmets, 1945

Smoke-Eaters

A jury-rigged water tower using a hose attached to an aerial ladder allowed firemen to deluge fires in tall buildings from the safety of ground level. Ladder work could be especially dangerous, as already attested to by the grisly account of Rufus Keating's death. A fire at the home of Lawrence Gourley on Duke Street was reported as one "long to be remembered. The night was a piercing cold one. The thermometer had dropped below zero and the firemen were frozen to the ladders and had to be cut off." Hoseman John Spruin was one of those men; he

Labour Temple Fire, Halifax, January 2, 1945

remembered it as "a lovely fight while it lasted. It was so cold that the water became frozen almost immediately after it had left the branch….The ruins were covered with ice resembling a miniature Niagara." Ice was only one factor that firemen had to contend with when working from ladders. At the Pickford & Black waterfront fire on September 19, 1904, "the firemen were on ladders pouring streams in the second storey windows and at times the men were shut out from view by the dense volumes of black smoke which rose slowly skyward. The building was filled with oils, tar and other combustible material, making great food for the flames." And these men were working without breathing apparatus. Halifax smoke-eater Ray Beck drew the attention of onlookers during the course of the $300,000 Morris Tea Fire of March 27, 1927. *The Evening Mail* described the incident:

> Many prominent citizens watched the blaze and were loud in their praise of the excellent work of Chief Churchill and his men. One of the worst jobs was that of hoseman R. Beck of Bedford Row engine house who was mounted on the aerial guiding the hose. During the lengthy period he was on this work he had to hold on to the ladder and at the same time control the hose. An *Evening Mail* reporter in conversation with Alderman Daw, a member of the Fireward, drew attention to the difficulties under which Beck was working. The Alderman at once agreed and said that a man in Beck's position should have his hands free and that he should be strapped to the ladder for this purpose.

Upon being told later of the alderman's proposal, Mrs. Beck purportedly scoffed, "Now they're going to strap them to the ladders! What next?"

THE
SMOKE-EATERS

Windsor Street Fire, Halifax, 1952

A fireman's work was far from over when the last of the smoke had cleared. There was the drudgery of cleaning and storing equipment, and polishing apparatus for the next alarm. Thousands of feet of fire hose might have to be rolled, which— according to this ode from the Glace Bay Fire Department— could be a proverbial pain in the dead of winter.

Rolling Frozen Hose

Of all the tasks in a fireman's life,
The polishing, scrubbing, washing and strife,
Like cleaning the windows and polishing brass,
Rolling hard frozen hose is a pain in the ass.

The temperature's zero; the snow is quite deep
And its four hours ago since you woke from
    your sleep,
And you've lost all the feeling in most of your toes
And that's when you start in to roll frozen hose.

Your fingers are numb from knuckle to tip
And your nose is so runny, it drips on your lip.
You're tired and hungry like nobody knows;
And that's when you start in to roll frozen hose.

You're coated with ice from helmet to toe,
And you hear yourself crack everytime you
    bend low
Then someone says, "Hey Bud", you've frozen
    your nose
And that's when you start in to roll frozen hose.

You start in to roll it the best you can
But it never rolls straight…it goes on a cant
But roll it you do, through rubble and glass,
Rolling hard frozen hose is a pain in the ass.

And when you are finished on this earth below
And you go to that place where district chiefs go
You won't hear harps tinkle and no trumpet blows
You can bet your sweet ass; there'll be no
    frozen hose.

Smoke-Eaters

Firefighting records are replete with accounts of mutual aid between communities in times of crisis. This steam fire engine, hose wagon, and group of firemen from Yarmouth travelled eighty miles by rail in 1921 to fight a fire at Annapolis Royal which swept the town's business district (See Chapter 6). Pictou and New Glasgow sent steam fire engines to Stellarton in November 1880 to help fight a coal mine fire at the Foord Pit, which killed forty-four miners and twenty-nine horses. Halifax and Dartmouth firemen ferried across the harbour on many

Mutual aid

occasions providing mutual aid. Trains were often the quickest means of long-distance response in the early days, and Halifax sent a steam fire engine by rail to help combat the Great Windsor Fire of 1897. In 1912, Bedford citizens held a fire at bay using buckets and water-soaked blankets spread over threatened roof tops until a steamer arrived by flatcar from Halifax. The provincial capital again sent a steam fire engine by train in August 1928 to Ingramport; on this occasion, "a great fire" destroyed the general store, warehouse, two barns, seven houses, cookhouse, and lumber yard belonging to Lewis Miller & Company. The loss of the mill, which was never rebuilt because of depressed lumber prices at the time, was a severe economic blow to the community, throwing two hundred men out of work. An interesting tale of mutual aid involved the towns of Pictou and Truro. In 1872, Pictou wired an urgent message to Truro, forty-three miles distant, requesting immediate assistance in fighting a conflagration that would eventually raze twenty-seven buildings. Being a major railway terminus, Truro responded with a special train carrying a hand fire engine and thirty men. En route, the relief train overtook a section man and handcar on the tracks. With time ticking, the engineer opened the throttle wide rather than slowing down, smashing into the handcar and driving it one hundred feet from the tracks. Fortunately, the section man jumped clear before impact, leaving him shaken but otherwise unscathed.

THE
SMOKE-EATERS

There were several categories of smoke-eaters outside the traditional firefighting service. Railways often employed their own fire crews. These unidentified C.N. firemen who posed with a depot master look better suited to a fishing schooner on the Grand Banks than a rail yard. In 1922, a mutual aid agreement was reached between Dominion Atlantic Railway firemen at the Kentville terminal and town firemen. The Richmond sugar refinery at Halifax and the Woodside sugar refinery outside Dartmouth both organized fire departments in the late

**C.N. Railway
fire crew**

1800s to protect factory and company housing interests. Rhodes Curry of Amherst, a large industrial contracting and manufacturing firm, had its own twenty-six-member fire department and station on the corner of Albion and Pleasant streets in the early 1900s. The Dominion Coal Company in Glace Bay had several colliery fire brigades; it was John Leaman, an experienced colliery fireman, who was consulted, then elected Glace Bay's fire chief, when the town organized its first fire department in 1901. There was also the forestry service. Railways and portable sawmills were two of the biggest culprits for setting forest fires outside of arsonists. The first fire laws were passed in 1883, giving the Department of Crown Lands "some little authority" over wanton acts of negligence on the part of lumbering and rail operations. In 1904, legislation was passed requiring paid watchmen at portable mills and appointment of the first chief fire rangers in each municipality. The Forest and Game Act was amended in 1922 to address the need for better firefighting equipment such as motorized and backpack pumps. In 1927, the Nova Scotia Government took over the costs of firefighting from municipalities; that year, there were fifty-one steel or wooden fire towers and observation posts in the province. By 1930, the Department of Lands and Forests owned only twenty-four motor pumps, twenty-eight thousand feet of hose, and 187 hand pumps for the whole province. In 1934, volunteer firefighters were paid 18 3/4 cents an hour; from 1931-1945, 4,895 fires burned 251,183 acres.

Smoke-Eaters

A specialized category of firefighting are the draegermen and mine fires. Coal has played an integral role in Nova Scotia's history since first discovered in 1798 at Stellarton. From 1832-1957 there were forty-eight "large-scale" mine fires in Pictou County. Estimates put the death toll during that period at 246 miners from explosion alone; a conservative estimate for total fatalities in Pictou mines from 1807-1972 is 650 miners. Stellarton firemen fought mine fires in 1894 and 1906. To address the issue of coal mine fires and rescue in Pictou County, the

Acadia Rescue Corps, Stellarton, 1925

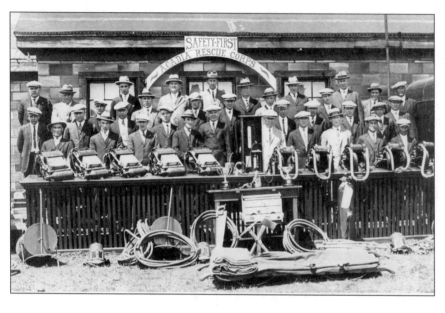

Acadia Coal Company followed Glace Bay's lead of 1909 and purchased six Draeger self-contained breathing units in 1911, opening the first rescue station at Stellarton. The "mine commandos" had little time to wait before putting their skills and equipment to the test. In November 1913 they were called in to assist at the Albion Mine Fire. With draegermen at the stand-by and New Glasgow's *Lulan* pumping water, un-protected firemen fought the blaze underground for two weeks using four shifts a day. The heat was so intense that men laid on their sides to aim hoses as there was more air nearer the ground; water was sprayed from behind over the lead hosemen to give some measure of cooling relief. In the coal mines of Springhill, Cumberland County, 429 miners have died since 1827, 121 of these in the explosion of 1891. The coal mines of Glace Bay, Cape Breton Island have their own story to tell. In Ron Caplan's *Cape Breton Lives*, veteran draegerman Gordon Whalen had this to say:

> A fire in a mine isn't like a fire anywhere else in the world. A fire in a building, the outside world is probably only through a door or a window to you, if you're caught in that building. Or blow a hole in the wall. But the outside world's maybe 5 or 6 miles away from the guy caught in a mining fire. Different thing altogether. You have very little carbon monoxide from a fire on the surface…but in the mines, she's loaded with CO because the fire's in a con-fined space. So the fire's got to be handled very differently. You may not get within 1500 feet of a fire in a mine on account of the heat that's generated—it's like in a tube….You can get on the intake side, where it's getting its air from, you can get pretty close to the fire on that side. But on the return side, where the fire is tending, you might not get within 2 or 3 thousand feet…so the only thing you can do with a fire like that is seal it off. You rarely can fight a fire directly in a mine if it's spread, if it's of any dimensions. You can fight small fires. Once a fire gets beyond control, the only thing you can do then is either flood it or seal it off, to cut the oxygen off.

There is, unfortunately, little information on the role of Blacks in early fire-fighting for Nova Scotia. As many volunteer brigades were comprised of prominent citizens in a community, and as membership was often pursuant to majority ballot by existing members, chances are that few Blacks were allowed the opportunity. When Truro took steps toward organized fire protection in 1860, a leading proponent was George Jones, a Black resident and the town's first barber. The initial meeting of concerned citizens was held in his shop, from which a Bucket and Ladder Company was established. Walter 'Cut' Brown became a volunteer fireman at an early age with the Dartmouth Union Engine Company circa 1919. According to Brown, however, he was given only demeaning "go-for" jobs and little respect by firemen. As can be seen in this photo, Black men and women took an active role in civil defense at Halifax during World War

Back row: (L-R): *Gus Backus, F. Berry, Walter Johnson, A. Bramah, W.R. Johnson, Fred Jackson, Edward Killum, A. Jackson*
Middle row: Miss J. *Brooks, A. Sampson, Miss P. Adams, F. Talbot, Miss. A Bundy, T. Jackson, ?*
Front row: (L-R): *A. Simmond, C. Smith, T. Allison, A. Davis*

103

Two. This was one of the few avenues open to serve their country as the regular forces did not accept Blacks, at least not in the early years of the war.

In 1996, the former cities of Halifax and Dartmouth, the town of Bedford, and Halifax County were amalgamated into the super city of Halifax Regional Municipality. The Halifax Regional Fire and Emergency Service was established to encompass sixty-three fire stations and protect 343,000 residents. The Upper Hammonds Plains Volunteer Fire Department was then designated Station 51 and, although beyond the time period of this book, is deserving of special mention. The community was settled by five hundred Blacks following the War of 1812 and suffered over a century of racism and segregation. After numerous fires and little support from some neighbouring fire departments, thirteen residents founded the Upper Hammonds Plains Volunteer Fire Department in May 1966, followed by incorporation on June 25, 1976. This was a significant achievement as Upper Hammonds Plains was the first, and to the best of information remains the only, all-Black incorporated fire department in Canada. (See *Halifax Herald*, January 31, 1999, for details).

**Elroy Hill,
Nova Scotia's first
professional Black
firefighter**

Elroy Hill, shown here at the age of seventy-three, was raised in a family of sixteen in the village of Bear River, Nova Scotia. As member of the Bear River Volunteer Fire Department in the early 1950s, Hill received firefighter training at nearby HMCS Cornwallis, the largest recruit basic training facility in the British Empire. Fire departments from Bear River, Digby, and Annapolis Royal routinely attended sessions provided by Department of National Defense (DND) firefighters. In 1954, he filled out an application to join the DND fire service but with no openings at the time he moved to Saint John, New Brunswick to seek work. While there, Hill received word that a position was available at Camp Aldershot, an army training base in Kentville. He returned to Nova Scotia and was employed as a firefighter until the camp closed in 1959, at which time he transferred to HMC Dockyard in Halifax, where he continued his firefighting career until retirement in 1981. During the years in Halifax he and his wife Joan lived in Kentville and he commuted the seventy miles to work, a chore made somewhat easier by the fact that with the long hours and different shifts he ended up working fourteen days a month. Starting annual salary was by his estimate three thousand dollars. One hundred and eighteen civilian firefighters were required to handle the responsibility of four rotating shifts in fire stations at the Dockyard, Stadacona, NAD, Bedford Magazine, and onboard the naval fire boat. Specialized training in shipboard, structural, and crash fires was ongoing at York Redoubt and RCAF Shearwater. While aware of racism, Hill was fortunate in that for all his years of work, it never was a problem for him. Up to retirement Hill remained the only Black making his living as a firefighter. In an interview conducted in 1991 by the Halifax *Chronicle-Herald*'s Joel Jacobson, Hill said, "I never thought that much about being the first Black professional firefighter. I was after the job and the money." A noted athlete in his youth, Hill still maintains a 99 bowling average in the seniors' league and sings in the church choir. "You get to meet so many people being involved in the community."

THE
SMOKE-EATERS

Chapter 4

Engine Houses

Central Fire Station, Wolfville

Wolfville firemen pose circa 1912 in front of a fire station on Central Avenue. This photo illustrates the add-on wings that were typically built when a department increased its inventory of firefighting apparatus. After years of procrastination and more than one scare from a near-disastrous fire, Wolfville finally took steps in 1890 to organize a fire service. On October 14, the Wolfville Fire and Protection Company officially began serving the town and surrounding districts. Early hose reels and horse-drawn apparatus began to give way to mechanization in 1924, when ten thousand dollars was allocated to purchase a 1923 LaFrance pumper. By the 1940s, membership stood at sixty, which town council considered "too many for a manageable group." The company was re-organized into a smaller twenty-man force and re-named the Wolfville Volunteer Fire Department, with council assuming control of the selection process for new members.

This 1853 photo of the Grand Parade Engine House* on Argyle Street was taken by Halifax photographer Daniel J. Smith and is thought to be one of the two earliest street scenes in Canada. St. Paul's Church, the oldest Protestant church in the country, is prominent in the immediate background. On October 6, 1836—after six years of lobbying the Board of Firewards and Court of Quarter Sessions by the Union Engine Company—work finally began on a new engine house at the Grand Parade, pictured here. Completed in January 1837 at

Grand Parade Engine House, Halifax, 1853

a cost of approximately four hundred pounds, the building measured forty-five feet by thirty feet. Its first two floors housed the Union Engine Company's hand engines and hose, as well as the ladders and equipment of the Axe Fire Company. The upper storey was an exclusive firemen's club, furnished and carpeted at members' expense and much noted as a Halifax social centre for banquets and gala events. The cupola was added in 1844 to house a 417-pound fire bell donated by the Sun Fire Company. A ninety-five-foot flag pole in front of the engine house doors was erected circa 1853. In May 1860, a Dr. Cogswell presented firemen with a Nova Scotia flag; "on motion it was ordered that the doctor's flag be hoisted on the Engine House staff every Sunday for the future." The doctor later donated a much larger provincial flag as a replacement, at which time "it was resolved that this new flag be not hoisted on wet Sundays." Grand Parade Engine House lasted until the early 1870s, when it was replaced by a new structure on the southeast corner of Brunswick and George streets.

* *Buildings used to store early hand and steam fire apparatus were generally called engine houses; the name was gradually changed during the motorized age to fire station or fire hall.

THE
SMOKE-EATERS

Brunswick Street Engine House, Halifax

Brunswick Street Engine House was for many years the "centre of the whole department," its caretaker Joseph Murphy described as "the leading spirit of the department." Brunswick Street was the only three-storey engine house in Halifax, all others being two storeys. The annual civic report for 1916 listed it being staffed by five full-time firemen and ten call men, with two being the fewest number on duty at any given time. Each engine house was responsible for various repairs within the fire department. At Morris Street, apparatus was overhauled and painted. Spare parts for the motorized pumper *Patricia* were kept there, and a harness shop was maintained on the second floor. Carpentry work was assigned to West Street; in a small room at Grafton Street "one of the company was skilled at making rope bridles, canvas bags, etc." All machine repairs and bench work was done on the second floor of Brunswick Street in a shop equipped with hand tools, electric power, 14-inch engine lathe, grinder, and hand hose expander. The walls of a meeting room on this level were "adorned with paintings, commemorative of the great fires and gallant achievement of the firemen of Halifax." On the third floor were recreational rooms where "no pains were spared to contribute to the enjoyment of the men." A blacksmith shop in the street-level basement handled horse-shoeing and assorted smithy work. On December 13, 1933, Fire Chief John Churchill ordered a hasty evacuation of Brunswick Street Station because the building was deemed "unfit to live in and could collapse at any time."

Union Engine Company Division #6, Queen Street Engine House, Halifax, c.1880

Queen Street operated from 1877 until circa 1907, when a new engine house opened on Morris Street. Privately owned today, it is one of the few buildings remaining from the smoke-eater era. Halifax firemen were big on pomp and circumstance. A classic example was October 4, 1854, when they staged two "processions" in one day. On August 20 of that year, "a disastrous fire occurred at Government House which did considerable damage and was only controlled and extinguished by the most strenuous exertions on the part of the brave firemen."

The lieutenant-governor, Sir John Gaspard LeMarchant, sent a letter of appreciation to the firemen "in recognition of their gallantry and coolness in the presence of great danger." For their part, the firemen "determined that an address in acknowledgment of his letter be prepared," and at 9 a.m. on October 4, they marched through city streets led by the band and pipes of the 72nd Highlanders to His Excellency's temporary residence in the dockyard. With barely time to catch their wind from that excursion, the firemen regrouped and joined a large afternoon procession "in the presence of an immense concourse of spectators" to mark the opening at the Provincial Building of the first Industrial Exhibition ever staged in Nova Scotia. "Where all looked well and played their several parts effectively, it would almost appear invidious to particularize but we cannot forbear mentioning the splendid display made by the Engine and Axe Fire Companies," wrote the *Nova Scotian*. "The six city Fire Engines [all hand engines then] and ladder waggon, together with the carriages attached, were decorated with flowers, silk flags and other ornaments, which challenged the admiration of every beholder." It was later written that "the 'fireboys' must have been thoroughly tired out after their two marches and all the excitement of the day; but had a fire broken out that night, which happily none did, it cannot be doubted that they would have been as ever 'prompt to the rescue' and have done noble work in fighting the flames."

Morris Street Engine House opened on the corner of Robie and Morris streets circa 1907. Firemen assigned here were nicknamed "Collegians," no doubt in reference to their close proximity to Dalhousie and Saint Mary's universities. An interesting point regarding Morris Street Engine House is that it was designed by a fireman, William Fidler (1845-1919). Fidler was a carpenter by trade in the early 1870s, who joined with Josiah Jordan in 1877 to form Jordan & Fidler, Builders. Jordan died in 1887, but Fidler maintained the building and contracting business until 1895, when he joined the fire department. Halifax was just then moving towards chemical fire engines, and Fidler started off as a chem-ical operator, moved to engineer, and eventually became superintendent of the city's three chemical apparatus. He proved invaluable to the fire department with his construction background, acting as consultant on repairs to existing engine houses and designing new buildings at West Street (1896) and Morris Street. A popular anecdote associated with Morris Street was its Blue Bonnet. The Halifax *Mail Star*, December 27, 1963,carried this account:

Morris Street Engine House, Halifax

In the rear of the street-level floor, stalls stabled the half-dozen, always shiny and perfectly conditioned horses. These horses required daily exercise and to provide this, the station was equipped, in winter, with a huge sleigh. It consisted of a six-by-ten foot, box-type body, mounted on two runners with a two-horse hitch. This was the Blue Bonnet. To ride in the Blue Bonnet was the ambition of nearly every school boy or girl, that at some time attended Morris Street, Tower Road or College Street schools. The high walls of the box sleigh made the vehicle perfectly safe and under the watchful eye of the driver there was never an accident recorded against the famed old sleigh. Loaded with fifteen or twenty happy youngsters, the Blue Bonnet made limited trips as far south as Inglis Street, east to Tower Road and west to Seymour Street—never too far from the station but it was a real "tour" to the occupants....What became of the Blue Bonnet? Like the old fire horses, she just disappeared from the scene. When last recognized the old sleigh was pushed aside in the West Street Station. The once brilliantly painted blue sideboards had lost their coloring. It was written off as surplus. But to many who resided in the south end of the city during their early years, the Blue Bonnet and No. 3 Fire Station remain a pleasant memory.

Spring Garden Road Engine House, Halifax

Division #5 firemen pose with decorated hose reel cart and Smith hand engine at Spring Garden Road during the 1886 Grand Firemen's Tournament. Located in Grafton Park at the corner of Spring Garden Road and Brunswick Street, the engine house's firefighting days ended circa 1920. It was recommended in the mid-1890s that the engine house be closed, but as late as 1916 it was still operational as a hose company, manned by two paid and nine call men equipped with a single wagon and horse, six hundred feet of hose, and one three-gallon fire extinguisher.

As mentioned, the days of the volunteer Halifax firemen ended in 1894 after one hundred and forty years when the Union Engine and Axe companies were re-structured into a part-paid, part-call force known thereafter as the Halifax Fire Department. The *Daily Echo* of December 8, 1894, posted twenty-eight revised "ordinances and regulations for the government of the department" with the following estimated cost breakdown:

Chief Engineer [Fire Chief]	$800.00	Light & Fuel	800.00
Electrician	700.00	Rent	400.00
Pipeman & Operator of		Feed	2,300.00
Chemical Engine	600.00	Incidentals & Repairs	2,000.00
Four Engine Men For Steamers	800.00	Veterinary Surgeon	115.00
Sixteen Drivers ($443 ea.)	7,088.00	Telephone	300.00
Pipeman & Operator For Second		Fourteen Hose & Truckmen	
Chemical Engine	600.00	($416 ea)	5,824.00
Maintenance Of Fire Alarm	600.00	Sixty-two Call Men	
Salvage Corps [independent of fire		($60 ea.)	3,720.00
department but received grant]	600.00	**TOTAL:**	**$27,247.00**

West Street Fire Station, Halifax Carnival Week 1922

The *Evening Post* carried the following headline in 1932: "Veteran Returns To Firefighters Ranks." The veteran was Colonel, one of the famed "Gray Ghosts" of West Street Fire Station and lone surviving member of the Halifax fire horse corps. When the last of the horses were retired or assigned to other duties in 1929, Colonel and his partner Major had been relegated to work detail at the City Prison Farm, where Major soon died. Colonel continued plodding along until the call came that his services were once again required with the Halifax Fire Department. Paired with a city works horse, Colonel was temporarily re-activated to pull an old ladder truck (wagon) while the motorized version from Morris Street Station underwent repairs necessitated by a recent accident. "The horses responded to the alarm for the fire at Garden Crest apartments on Saturday morning and the sight of them in action on the streets of Halifax caused much comment," reported the *Evening Post*. "Old Colonel according to Fire Chief Churchill seemed to glory in the thrill and excitement of the moment, realizing that once again he lived the life of a firefighter. Remembering well the splendid service which Colonel and his fore-fathers rendered in the fire department, Halifax citizens glory with him in his comeback."

By the early years of World War Two, operational fire stations in Halifax had been reduced to four, with forty-four firemen on duty at any given time (Bedford Row, 17; Morris Street, 13; West Street, 9; Quinpool Road, 5). An inspection carried out by the mayor, deputy mayor, and several aldermen to determine the state of city fire apparatus showed "the resourcefulness and originality of Halifax firemen" in the face of wartime conditions.

Quinpool Road Fire Station No. 5, Halifax

One piece of apparatus was almost entirely rebuilt by the firemen. Others showed where more than one repair job was done with the exactness and completion of a garage job. All the ladders are made by the firemen. Conversion of what was once a hay loft at the Quinpool Road station into formidable living quarters was carried out by the firemen. Installation of shower baths and toilet facilities, painting, the laying of new concrete floors—all carried out in addition to their regular duties.

Such jack-of-all skills was a common trait with firemen everywhere, who usually made do with what they had. When Halifax first went to a part-paid, part-call force in 1894, city officials were interested in recruiting tradesmen as firemen for just such reasons.

In 1946, an issue arose over beds in Halifax fire stations. Officials in Regina, Saskatchewan were then proposing that all beds there be removed because a report warned "being aroused from a warm bed might have a bad effect on the hearts of firemen." Halifax Fire Chief Fred MacGillivray scoffed at such a notion. "I've been on the job 28 years and have been called out of bed on many occasions during that time to answer a fire call. But it never hurt my heart and I don't know of any cases where it hurt other firemen." One hundred and thirty Halifax firemen worked twelve-hour shifts in 1946, with twenty-four hours off every sixth day when changing over. For this reason alone, beds were essential, MacGillivray said, not to mention the possibility that firemen might be needed in emergency situations for several days at a time and required sleep. A similar bed controversy had been raised years earlier in Halifax but was overruled at the time. This latest one was squashed as well.

THE
SMOKE-EATERS

**Bedford Row
Fire Station No. 4,
Halifax**

Bedford Row Fire Station opened circa 1906 and was headquarters for the Halifax Fire Department until the station closed in October 1964. Today it serves as a downtown eatery. The second floor was equipped with locker facilities for twelve men, private rooms for the fire chief and chief engineer, a work shop, a harness room, and a hay loft. Two brass poles provided quick access to the fire apparatus on the Bedford Row level; a secondary stairway led from the hay loft to the stables. There were stalls for ten horses and a ventilation system to keep the ever-present stable smells from permeating the building, with manure and straw removed from a ground-level door on Prince Street. There was a sixty-foot heated tower for drying hose. Fire apparatus included, left to right, a 75-foot Horton aerial ladder truck, chief's buggy, hose wagon, the steam engine *Alexandra*, and a chemical engine (not pictured). A gala firemen's ball in 1906 marked the grand opening of Bedford Row, with one hundred and twenty-five couples in attendance. Dignitaries included the mayor, fire commissioners, city clerk, chief of police, representatives from the various branches of the Halifax and Dartmouth Fire Departments, and Chief Bis Stewart from the Truro Fire Brigade. A grand march was held at 9 p.m. followed by a twenty-two number "dance list"; great pains had been taken to adapt the fire station for the occasion. "The big apparatus room was for the time being transformed into a ball room and the walls and ceiling were fairly covered with bunting, flags, shields and decorative paraphernalia."

Lunenburg Central Engine House c. 1900

Lunenburg purchased a tub engine in 1819 and established its first fire company a year later. This initial venture lasted until April 19, 1838, when thirty-two volunteers formed the Lunenburg Crown Fire Company. There was a restructuring again in 1876, at which time the name was changed to the United Fire Company. When a new Central Engine House (pictured here) was completed in 1889 to replace an earlier building, it was reported that "the whole establishment reflects the highest credit on the Lunenburg firemen, and all who aided them in the work." Note the tall rectangular structure to the rear of building. Fire hose was hung here to dry so that mould and mildew wouldn't rot it during prolonged periods of storage. Hose towers were relatively common, and as they were usually heated to enhance the drying process, problems did arise. The following incident, which occurred at Grand Parade Engine House in 1861, must have proved especially embarrassing for those involved:

> Yesterday morning about nine o'clock, an alarm of fire was given in consequence of the discovery being made that the Engine House, corner of Grand Parade, was on fire. It appears that an apparatus for drying the hose after being used at fires, erected on the hot air principle, was sometime since put into the building and it was being used to dry the hose after the fire of Tuesday morning when the fire at the Engine House originated. There cannot be a doubt but there was either very great defects in the drying apparatus itself, or neglect on the part of those whose duty it was to look after the building and hose while the furnace was in full blast, otherwise the fire could not have made so much progress before an alarm was given. The building is covered by insurance in the "Halifax Fire Insurance Office" and the only actual loss the city has met with, as far as we can ascertain, is that of seven lengths of hose worth $50 each or in all $350.

Further to this incident, the *Morning Chronicle* of March 4, 1868, carried the following comments:

> We hear the old complaints of hose bursting….At the fire of Mr. Carey's store on Sunday night the largest portion of the water appeared to be on the street where it was not required. It is of the utmost importance that the Fire Department should be brought into an efficient state. The firemen may work as hard as they can but if the hose cannot be relied on, their labor is almost altogether lost. We think the great trouble with the hose is the want of a proper drying house. This will of course cost money but unless it is provided the money now spent on the Fire Department is thrown away.

Shelburne Engine House

In 1873, Shelburne organized the Union Fire Engine Company No. 3 (No. 1 and No. 2 probably dated to 1785; see Chapter 1). A hand engine was acquired and, in 1874, the engine house pictured here was built on King Street. In 1891, a Ronald steam fire engine was purchased and the engine house moved to Water Street, at which time a hose drying tower, a belfry, and attached storage sheds for the company's three fire engines were added. The engine house burned on October 14, 1948, after which a brick building was erected on the same site.

Ringing church bells or running through the settlement yelling at the top of one's lungs were the earliest means of sounding a fire alarm. In later years, a factory steam whistle would often serve the purpose, sometimes blowing a series of blasts to give the fire's location. Engine houses generally had a belfry and fire bell, with the rope hanging outside the building so that passersby could summon help. A bell's resonance was important; in 1867, the Halifax Union Protection Company imported a new fire bell "of first class character as regards power and tone." The Tatamagouche Hook and Ladder Company received a quote from Black & Company of Halifax in 1902 that a "suitable" fire bell could be purchased for thirty cents a pound. Bells were expensive as they often weighed hundreds of pounds. New Glasgow purchased a one-ton bell with a two-year guarantee in 1902 for "eleven pence ha'penny" a pound. This did not include a striker, which cost an additional three hundred dollars; another $160 was charged for moving the bell from the railroad car to a tower on the Customs House. In the event of fire at Truro, a general alarm was sounded by driving an Inter-Colonial Railway shunter back and forth in the yard while blowing its steam whistle. With the arrival of the telephone and party lines, the operator sometimes initiated the alarm. At St. Margarets Bay, for example, three long rings alerted residents to answer the telephone to find the fire's location.

From its founding in 1750 until the early 1800s, Dartmouth was largely dependent upon Halifax for firefighting equipment in times of emergency. This arrangement proved to be slow and unreliable as a ferry was the only direct link between the harbour towns. On one occasion, No. 1 engine, hose reel, and "a large number of volunteers" from Halifax gathered at the ferry wharf to render assistance but "after waiting in vain for the steamer a considerable time" the men were ordered back to the engine house. Dartmouth finally organized its own

volunteer Union Engine Company on September 21, 1822, comprised of Captain William Allen and nine men. Arrangements were also made for a board of fire wards, the procurement of a tub engine from Halifax, and the building of a small engine house at Queen Street on the present site of the Dartmouth Main Post Office. An axe and ladder company was added in 1865, and a salvage branch, the Union Protection Company, was formed in 1876; its members built a hall opposite the engine house. A more spacious fire station on King Street (pictured here) later replaced the Queen Street site. In 1878, a new steel fire bell weighing 870 pounds was placed in its tower. By 1888, Dartmouth had thirty telephones in use, one of which was installed principally for fire calls in the police chief's residence above the town lock-up near the fire station. Dartmouth purchased its first motorized fire apparatus in the summer of 1919—a triple combination—and hired two full-time firemen to stay at the station for still alarms (telephone calls). After 1919, the fire bell—which had been used exclusively for ninety-seven years—was sounded only for general alarms. The Dartmouth Fire Department was formerly organized on June 22, 1932. In 1950, a new $110,000 fire station was built on the site of the old King Street station and manned, at that time, by eight permanent firemen, forty volunteers, and twenty Union Protection members.

Yarmouth's first engine house (circa 1838) was a barn near Argyle and Main streets. It was replaced in 1840 by a new building, the St. George Company No. 1 Engine House in the south end of Yarmouth. A second engine house, Milton Engine Company No. 2, was built the same year at the north end of town on Water Street. In 1857, Central Engine House was erected at the village core; this was replaced by a brick structure at First and Alma streets in 1896-97. Ironically, both St. George and Milton engine houses were destroyed by fire

Milton Fire Engine House, Yarmouth c.1880

circa 1859; Milton's was claimed to be so decrepit at the time that firemen "used a lot of brain work to keep the water pumped off the fire." Two identical replacements were built in 1860—St. George at Tooker and East streets, and Milton (pictured here) near the present-day baseball field. St. George Engine House burned for a second time in 1899 and was then replaced by a brick building (next page), which closed in 1975 and later burned in 1991. On May 29, 1878, Yarmouth took possession of its first steam fire engine, a 5,400 pound Amoskeag with a rated pumping capacity of 600 gpm; the engine and the new steamer company organized to run it, were called *Neptune*. In early 1880, a second steamer arrived; the Silsby was also rated at 600 gpm and was named the *Naiad*. Firefighters, it seems, have always exhibited a competitive nature when it comes to apparatus. The *Naiad* crew at Milton wanted their engine to upstage the *Neptune*, so they raised sufficient money to have their engine nickel plated instead of the more commonly used bronze.

The wheels of progress often worked slowly in the firefighting world. Telephones, for example, were installed at Yarmouth engine houses in 1922, a mere twelve years after firemen first petitioned town council. At New Glasgow, firemen asked in 1893 to have electric lights hooked up in the engine house. Nine years later they got their wish—six lights at an operating cost of six dollars a year. Little wonder that firemen and town officials seemed to be at never-ending loggerheads.

St. George Company No. 1 Fire Engine House, Yarmouth, c.1899

When Yarmouth purchased two American-built steam fire engines, the Ronald Company from Ontario wrote a letter to the local newspapers chastising the town for not buying Canadian. Yarmouth answered with a retort that they would "buy what they wanted from where they wanted."

Yarmouth was fortunate in that its fire protection coverage was well spaced with three engine houses. Because most fire companies operated from one engine house, provisions were often made for small buildings in strategic parts of town for storage of hose reels. This allowed for faster response times, especially with the advent of hydrants, because fire crews didn't have to run great distances with the hose. It also made reels accessible should fire cut off a section of the town. In 1861, Halifax had six engine houses and an equal number of hose reel stations. Truro's hose reels were "located at points of vantage in districts distant from the Central Engine House." After each fire, men were assigned to remain at the reel house to dry and put away the hose. A length of hose was strung along one wall, then a fire was built using four-foot maple logs in a large open fire place. When that piece of hose dried, it was taken down, stored inside, and another hung in its place, a process which took hours to complete.

New Glasgow erected three hose houses circa 1888, each costing $126 to build and measuring fifteen feet by twenty feet. In 1895, the town built a fifth hose house for $157.50. Stellarton spent $2,143 in 1893 for a reel, hose, ladders, and materials to erect a hose building. On the matter of construction costs, Parrsboro accepted W.C. Hatfield's tender in 1898 to erect a new engine house for $1,136; the price was conditional upon Hatfield agreeing to paint the lower part of the finished building for fourteen dollars.

Central Engine House, Truro, c.1889

With the opening of the Nova Scotian Railway between Truro and Halifax in 1858, it was imperative that Truro consider some means of town fire protection because of sparks spewing from wood-burning locomotives. On February 13, 1860, a public meeting was held at George Jones' barbershop, at which time a "bucket and ladder company" was formed. However, the frequency of destructive fires continued unabated, as did the rise in fire insurance premiums. Eight years later, some of the "more heavily taxed citizens" petitioned the Court of Special Sessions in Colchester County for money to buy a fire engine and build an engine house. On October 24, 1868, the fifty-member Truro Fire Brigade was officially established to take charge of a newly acquired Boston-made hand fire engine (the *Honeyman Tub*; see Chapter 1); shortly thereafter, a two-storey engine house was built on Lorne Street (a new Central Engine House on Young Street, pictured here, replaced it in 1889). In 1876, a $27,000 water works system was completed: ten thousand feet of cast iron piping and a brick pump house that fed water to hydrants from the Salmon River. Early records show that special provisions sometimes had to be made for extenuating circumstances. On October 17, 1870, the captain ordered the fire engine be taken to the courthouse "in order to give the members the privilege of attending the school meeting." There were times also when the issue of meddlesome citizens had to be addressed. Following a fire "of some magnitude" in July 1887, the brigade secretary was instructed "to give notice through the press that, in future, the public be requested not to interfere by giving orders during fires." On March 17, 1902, the secretary again served notice in the local newspaper for the general public to refrain from riding the apparatus to and from fires. It has been said that the Truro Fire Brigade had the enviable record (and good luck) for fifty-six years of never allowing a fire to spread from one building to another. This streak ended in 1924, when a blaze in Davison Block on Prince Street scorched a nearby barn.

Engine Houses

New Central Fire Station, Truro, 1899

Central Engine House was only ten years old when this new brick fire station next door on Young Street was "formally occupied" on November 20, 1899. Four hundred dollars was spent decorating the station, described as "admirably adapted to the uses of the Fire Department, having all appliances necessary for the quickest possible dispatch of the hose wagon, engine and ladder truck." Ample space was allotted for entertaining, with a large firemen's hall, ladies' room, and smoking room. In 1908, the firemen's hall "was renovated, handsomely decorated and finished with a polished hardwood floor at expense of Brigade." Furnishings included desks for the chief and secretary, a piano in one corner, an extension dining table at the centre, and hardwood settees along the walls. "In another part of the building a full outfit of napery, china, delft cutlery and table silverware is kept. Extra tables, the whole sufficient to provide a hundred covers, are also on hand." A dance was held to celebrate the recently completed alterations. This in itself was a noteworthy event, as meeting minutes for April 20, 1908, mentioned how the fire station had become a "bachelor's retreat for nine long years." Fireman Arthur Christie proposed "an entertainment of some kind in the hall in the near future to include the ladies whom we have not entertained since we left the old hall."

No. 1 Fire Station, Church Street, Amherst, 1921

The vehicle featured at the centre of this 1921 Amherst fire department photo was a 1908 Rambler, claimed to be the Maritimes first motorized chemical engine. (This differed from Halifax's *Patricia* in that it only performed one duty compared to a triple combination apparatus.) Left of the chemical is a horse-drawn ladder truck and circa 1914 Chevrolet hose car. A Waterous steam fire engine and World War One-era Buick salvage car are to the right; the steamer was replaced circa 1927 by the town's first motorized pumper. At one time Amherst had three fire stations—No. 1 on Church Street (opened 1889), No. 2 on LaPlanche Street (facing photo), and No. 3 on the corner of Albion and Pleasant streets (Rhodes, Curry firemen). The Amherst Fire Company was organized in 1883, six years before town incorporation, and was comprised of volunteers from the Citizen's Band, Robb's Foundry, and a small brigade of firemen (six in all), who had been using a tiny hand engine prior to this time to provide some measure of limited fire protection. The fire company's first by-laws were adopted in 1890, and four years later its name was changed to the Amherst Fire Department. The first steam fire engine was purchased in 1890 for twelve hundred dollars; the town eventually owned two, an Amoskeag and a Waterous. In 1915, a Salvage Corps was organized and a McLaughlin Fire Police and Salvage truck added for $1,615. In 1938, Fire Chief Alex C. Neil boasted that "This department is now thoroughly equipped in every respect and second to none in this province." A humorous anecdote involves Dr. C.W. Bliss, Amherst's fire chief in 1894. According to his recollections, not a single house burned while he was in charge of the department. His innovative methods gave new meaning to the "surround and drown" theory of dousing fires. According to a straight-faced Chief Bliss, the first order of business when his firemen arrived at the scene was to stuff cotton-battan into all the cracks around window and door frames and key holes. Having completely sealed the building, a hole was then cut in the roof and firemen with hoses "filled 'er up with water."

*Engine
Houses*

Volunteer firemen have traditionally received a nominal payment from the town or municipality which even today is referred to as a "clothing allowance." In 1900, the Amherst Fire Department had a volunteer force of fifty men. In 1920, the fire chief was paid a yearly stipend of $150, with firemen receiving an honorarium of seventy dollars a year; by 1942, this had been increased to ninety dollars. In lieu of money, the earliest fire brigades were often exempted from paying a poll tax or from performing statutory road work. In 1877, New

No. 2 Fire Station, LaPlanche Street, Amherst

Glasgow compensated its firemen two dollars a year. By 1882, firemen deemed this to be "unsatisfactory" and it was raised to six dollars, providing a man produced a certificate to the town clerk signed by the captain and company secretary vouching that he had been a fireman for at least one year. Circa 1885, it was decided that New Glasgow firemen who had served at least sixteen years were entitled to a six-dollar-a-year pension for life. This was subsequently repealed in 1911, although those then receiving the pension were protected by a grandfather clause. The last of the pensioners, "Big" John Fraser, died in 1955. In 1916, firemen were paid twenty dollars annually plus fifty cents an hour for actual fire duty; the bonus was not given for false alarms, "which resulted in night turn outs sometimes being skimpy until a second alarm sounded." In 1922, fifty cents an hour became standard for all alarms; this was later increased to one dollar an hour. The chief then was paid $120 per annum, with the assistant chief receiving fifty dollars plus hourly pay while fighting fires. Parrsboro organized a fifteen-man fire brigade in 1889, and each member received a grant of one dollar a year, raised to five dollars in 1891. Town council agreed that year to also pay two dollars to the "first team that gets to fire-wagon at the time of a fire and ready to take the wagon to and from the fire." In April 1898, council took steps to reduce the annual grant while firemen threatened to resign en masse if it wasn't increased to ten dollars. The town accepted their resignation and organized a new twenty-eight man department comprised mostly of the members who had quit.

Windsor Fire Station, c.1919

Windsor firemen pose in front of the combination fire station and town hall built in 1900 on the corner of Gerrish and Grey streets. Earlier engine houses were located on Stannus Street in 1881 and Gerrish and Victoria streets in 1897. Featured in the foreground is the department's first piece of motorized equipment, a 1919 White Pumper with a forty-five gallon chemical tank and pneumatic tires purchased for $13,000. Firemen called it the *Avon* in honour of the town's original fire department, the Avon Fire Company. Horse-drawn apparatus

included a hose wagon, a Ronald steam fire engine, and a ladder truck. Windsor Town Council hired a caretaker for the fire station in 1902 and gave orders for the firemen's social rooms to be locked every evening at 10:30 P.M.; on Sundays they were to be shut down completely. A curfew was imposed following complaints from residents of late night rowdiness in and around the station house. Firemen were not only notorious partiers but were also stubborn, and on this occasion refused to obey the edict. This, of course, did not ingratiate them with town officials, and the department was relieved of its duties. The Fire Committee was instructed to round up forty replacements, but before proceedings could begin, the fire wardens intervened, differences were resolved, and the firemen reinstated. Town council and the fire department again locked horns in 1926. On this occasion, firemen had made plans to hold games of chance at a Windsor festival as a fund raiser. Local clergy were horror struck and, at their behest, the constabulary were instructed to shut it down. In response, the entire fire department resigned. For the short term, fire wardens and councillors were pressed into fire duty until Fred MacGillivray was sent from the Halifax Fire Department as a mediator and to restructure the Windsor fire department. It was not uncommon for fiercely independent-minded firemen to square off with an equally stubborn town hall. Only one year after organizing in 1893, Stellarton's firemen resigned, recanted, and re-organized. In 1905 they again reorganized, and in 1933 were dismissed and reorganized for a third time.

Engine Houses

Glace Bay built its first engine house in December 1901, paying Hugh Cameron $160 to erect a building thirty feet long, fifteen feet wide, and ten feet high to hold fire apparatus as well as equipment for the street works department. This was a marked improvement over earlier accommodations, which had firemen storing hose reels in two privately owned barns. In September 1903, the fire department moved to the new town hall, pictured here nearing completion. The "apparatus room" was located at the front of the building (note the double doors

Glace Bay Engine House & Town Hall

at far left), with stalls for two horses in the rear and a firemen's recreational room on the second floor. Stalls were an unnecessary addition as horses were hired on an as-needed basis and shared among departments to save money, which often left firemen shortchanged when an alarm came in. After many complaints from the fire chief, town council addressed the problem by supplying two sets of harness, so firemen could commandeer horses from unsuspecting passersby. People must have soon tired of giving up their mode of transportation and detoured past the engine house, as it was reported on January 9, 1905, that not a single horse could be found to pull apparatus in response to a fire alarm. Following this fiasco, livery stable owner Louis Petrie generously offered the service of his horses at any time to the fire department. The town finally built a large barn at the rear of town hall in 1908 and purchased several horses. As they were still shared among various departments, this did little to alleviate firemen's woes until the first motorized apparatus, an American LaFrance triple combination, arrived in 1918. James A. Calder was then hired as chemical operator and engine house caretaker, the department's first—and for the next twenty years its only—paid fireman. In January 1938, the fire department moved to a new building on Main Street, and Fred Calder became the second paid member of the force as an assistant operator and caretaker.

Chapter 5

Firemen's Sports & Leisure

Firemen's tournament, Halifax 1892

Members of the Union Engine Company hose reel race team posed for this 1892 photo at the Halifax Polo Grounds, after defeating competitors from the Maritime Provinces and United States. Nova Scotia was a hotbed for firemen's tournaments during the late nineteenth and early twentieth centuries. Halifax played host on numerous occasions, while towns such as Yarmouth, Lunenburg, Kentville, Windsor, Dartmouth, Pictou, Oxford, Sydney, Truro, and Amherst all staged large twenty-team Maritime tournaments or smaller three- and four-team competitions as part of Natal Day or Home Coming Week festivities. Amherst firemen were some of the keenest, competing almost yearly from 1885 to 1948, with the exception of two World Wars, when tournaments were cancelled.

LaFrance Trophy Winners

The Dartmouth Fire Department staged a firemen's tournament in September 1923 on the sports field of the Dartmouth Amateur Athletic Association, with teams competing from Halifax, Windsor, Kentville, Stellarton, Glace Bay, and Dartmouth.

Pictured are delegates of the Halifax Fire Department, winners of the three-hundred-yard hose reel race for the LaFrance Trophy in a time of fifty seconds; Halifax also won the fifty-yard ladder race in fifteen seconds.

The *Acadian Recorder* reported that "Halifax made a splendid showing in the firemen's sports....They not only carried off the chief event of the day, the hose reel race, but won first and second places in every other event except the hose coupling....The handsome trophy of LaFrance Fire Engine Co., presented for annual competition last year, was brought from Glace Bay and presented to the H.F.D. as winners this year...Glace Bay came with identically the same ten men who captured the hose reel race last year and their splendid run was marred in their coupling which doubtless lost them the event. They however, proved to be good sports as did all the visitors and locals as well." The Glace Bay team consisted of John McDonald, George Weir, Hibbert Debison, Stanley Scott, Joe Debison, Charlie Weeks, John McMullen, John Weir, Hector McDonald, and Davie Nolan. In 1922, they won the LaFrance trophy by claiming seven first-place finishes and two second-places out of ten events, setting a record time of forty-nine seconds in the three-hundred-yard hose reel race.

Four of the men pictured here—James Doherty, Harry Whalen, George Sheppard, and Harold Fraser—teamed together as the "Flying Firemen" and for several years were the fastest fire department relay foursome in the Maritime Provinces.

Standing (L-R):
H. Beaton, F. Condon, R. Rapell, Geo. Shepherd, James Doherty, Capt. E.S. Graves, C. MacKay, H. Fraser
Seated (L-R):
G. Norman, Chief J.W. Churchill, Alderman W.I. O'Toole, Deputy Chief W. Howley
Front: (L-R):
J. Whalen, H. Whalen.

THE
SMOKE-EATERS

Halifax delegation at Saint John, New Brunswick Firemen's Tournament, 1910

Firemen often attended tournaments outside the province. Charlottetown (Prince Edward Island) and St. Stephen, Chatham, Sussex, Moncton, Fredericton, and Saint John (New Brunswick) were all popular destinations. An occasional team even ventured as far as Bangor, Maine to compete. Travelling by train or steamer, firemen often took a decorated hose reel with them for the traditional opening-day street parade and the closing evening torchlight procession. At a Bangor tournament in 1892, Halifax firemen won an engraved silver trumpet as first prize for "being the finest looking body of men in the parade, which was one of the important features of the tourney." A firemen's tournament hosted by Saint John in August 1893 to celebrate the visit of Canada's Governor General Lord Aberdeen attracted fire brigades from New Brunswick, Nova Scotia, and Maine for a $250 purse. Amherst firemen walked off with top prize in the prestigious hose reel race, besting nine other teams by first running a sprint of three hundred yards, then laying two hundred feet of hose, in a time of one minute flat. These tournaments were so popular that town council or a private business often donated money to help defray travel costs for their firemen. Truro was particularly supportive of its fire brigade. Town officials there donated sixty dollars in 1883 for a ten-man team to compete at Saint John's centenary celebrations. In July 1888, Truro firemen received $125 to attend a summer carnival at Halifax, and in 1906 were given two hundred dollars for travel expenses to Charlottetown and Fredericton. The Intercolonial Railway showed its appreciation for the fire protection afforded ICR property in Truro by giving free passes or reduced fares to brigade members attending tournaments.

The Grand Firemen's Tournament hosted by the Halifax Union Engine Company in August 1886 was one of the largest ever staged in the Maritime provinces. Halifax was abuzz with excitement, and newspapers carried detailed accounts surrounding the big event. Below are selected excerpts from the *Acadian Recorder*, August 3-9, 1886:

Special rates are being given from all points on the ICR and W&A.R. [Railways]. An excursion steamer is to run from Yarmouth and intermediate points. Edward Gerrard has the monopoly of the refreshments at the Polo Grounds. Harry Teas is making elaborate preparations for the banquet in the Exhibition Building. One table the whole length of the main floor, runs along the west side of the centre space, and from it 19 other tables run at right angles. The Mayor will preside and the Aldermen will probably be vice-chairmen. There are 18 tables and 18 aldermen-very appropriate. Late Saturday night and early this morning, men and women were busy in the Exhibition Building preparing for the banquet; several thousands of plates were washed; over a thousand tumblers ditto. Tables will be laid today. The Mayor has made arrangements so that D. Henry Starr will be at his office Monday, Tuesday and Wednesday till ten p.m. so that strangers in town can obtain lodging should hotel accomodations be scarce. The Mayor has a list of persons willing to take boarders and lodgers at moderate rates. Cabmen can drive straight to the Mayor's office and find lodgings for visitors at once. Meals and refreshments can be had at all hours at City Restaurant, 102 Granville St. Upwards of 500 people were on the Polo Grounds last evening watching the different teams training. The tug-of-war team are doing splendid work, and will give a good account of their muscle next week. The silk flag presented to the tournament committee by P.&J. O'Mullin will be awarded to the team winning the tug-of-war. W.D. O'Donnell will photograph the procession from the Academy of Music balcony and will also if possible take a view of the banquet in the afternoon. D. Henry Starr was busy this morning making out a list of over 40 persons willing to take from one to a dozen boarders. The rush will commence when the trains come tonight. The Carroll brought 375 passengers and it is said refused 200. Another steamer will arrive tonight or tomorrow with over 300 who paid $5 each for the charter of the boat and $5 for their week's board on board. The Lunenburg firemen will arrive tonight by the City of St. John. The Bangor, Amherst, Truro, Moncton, Charlottetown, and New Glasgow teams are expected by the Intercolonial [Railway] this evening and the Portland and Yarmouth delegates by the Windsor and Annapolis [Railway]. The St. John, St. Stephen and Woodstock delegates are coming by a special train which is expected about midnight. The Chelsea firemen arrived by the Carroll and are registered at the Globe Hotel. They brought with them a two-horse carriage which was taken to the Central Engine House and will appear in the parade tomorrow drawn by two gray horses from Greene's stables, Dartmouth. The St. John men will put up at the Queen; Portland at Sandford's; Windsoreans at Boutiller's, Bedford Row; Charlottetown boys at Colonial; Amherst's team at Sandford's. The Lunenburg team will have quarters on the steamer "St. John", the Americans will register at the Queen and Halifax. Wm. Ross the well-known Granville St. hatter has supplied No. 1 'Salamander' and No. 5 and 6 Divisions with caps to wear during the tournament.

Union Protection Company Hall, Barrington Street, Halifax, 1886 Tournament

"All the engine house fronts will be elaborately decorated with evergreens and transparencies, at which the various artists to town have been at work for weeks past. Those on the Central represent fire scenes—the rescue of women and children from burning buildings. On the U. A. C. [Union Axe Company] building will be two transparencies representing the Poor House fire of 1882 and the Queen Building fire. All these transparencies are the work of J. J. Henderson. The U.P.C. [Union Protection Company] are painting the front of their hall and raising a frame work to be decorated with flowers and evergreens. On the U.P.C. Hall will be placed three large and handsome transparencies prepared by George T. Smithers. One will represent a Union fireman of 1768, dressed in old fashioned costume, with heavy hooded hat and top boots. Another represents the modern U.P.C. man of 1886, rushing down a burning stairway with a child in his arms. From the centre window on this floor will be shown a transparency of an old-fashioned fire engine. The other engine houses will be decorated but not as elaborately."

Dartmouth Hose Reel Race Team, c.1886

GRAND FIREMEN'S TOURNAMENT
To Be Held In
HALIFAX
AUGUST 10TH, 11TH, AND 12TH, 1886
Under The Auspices of the UNION ENGINE COMPANY

PROGRAMME

1. Half-mile hose cart race—1st prize, $300 and Silver Trumpet; 2nd, $150.
2. Salvage corps team race, for teams of 10 men, distance 1/4 mile—1st prize, $100; 2nd, $50.
3. Flat race, open to hosemen only, distance 100 yards—1st prize $25; 2nd, $10.
4. Hook and ladder team race, teams of 10 men to run 300 yards with hand truck, remove ladder from truck, raise and mount, time to be taken when man grasps top rung—1st prize, $100; 2nd, $50.
5. Grand tug-of-war for teams of 10 men—prize, $100.
6. Flat race, open to members of salvage corps only, distance 100 yards—1st prize, $25 ; 2nd, $10.
7. Quarter-mile flat race—1st prize, $30; 2nd, $20; 3rd, $10.
8. Flat race for hook and ladder men only, distance 100 yards—1st prize, $25; 2nd, $10.
9. Three hundred yards hose reel race—1st prize, $100; 2nd, $50.
10. Half-mile flat race—1st. prize, $50; 2nd, $30; 3rd, $20.
11. Consolation race, distance quarter mile, open to all competitors who have taken no place in any of the events—1st prize, $20; 2nd, $15; 3rd, $10.

THE
SMOKE-EATERS

**Hose Reel Team
in action**

RULES

Grand Firemen's Tournament
Halifax
August 10TH, 11TH, And 12TH, 1886
Under The Auspices of the UNION ENGINE COMPANY

1.   Races to be run dry; single on time. Cart to carry 250 feet of hose
     (five lengths).
2.   Lay 200 feet of hose, break coupling, put on branch pipe; when the pipe
     is on to satisfaction of pipe-man it is to be thrown down, and the time
     taken when it strikes the ground. The judges will at once examine the
     coupling, and for every quarter turn that can be given the pipe, one half
     second shall be added to the running time.
3.   Hose to be used will be that of the Halifax regulation service, in lengths
     of 50 feet.
4.   Twelve men only allowed to run on hose reel, and no coaching to be done.
5.   The branch pipe to be regulation size and to be carried on the reel.
6.   None but regularly organized companies shall be allowed to compete,
     and no person will be allowed to run with any company who is not a
     legitimate member of the same, and vouched for by the captain of the
     team or company.
7.   Each Department represented will be entitled to one judge to act in
     connection with the judges appointed by the U.E. Company.
8.   The hose cart to be used in the races will be furnished by the Department.
9.   All contestants to compete in running costume.
10. In order to avoid dispute all competitors must take part in the processions.

The *Acadian Recorder* advised residents "To cut this out and paste it in your hat."

Tuesday: Grand Procession of firemen in uniforms with apparatus through the principle streets.

Wednesday: Sports on the Polo Grounds to be taken in by the visiting teams….In the Evening a grand concert in the Public Gardens with two or more bands, the grounds lighted by electricity, dancing in the rink and other attractions.

Thursday: Conclusion of the sports and firemen's torchlight procession through the principal streets.

The Procession will be formed on the North Common Tuesday morning at 9 o'clock in the following manner:

U.E.C. Division 6 firemen & float at Queen Street Engine House, 1886

Grand Marshall Robert McKenzie
Carriage containing Marshal Cotter and Detective Power
Squad of Police
63rd Band
Mayor and his Guests
Corporation
Ex. Chairman, Board of Fire Wards
Board of Fire Wards
Engines and Apparatus
Fire King Steamer No. 2 of Chelsea, Mass. and Company of 25 men
St. John, N.B.—20 men and Hose Carriage
Charlottetown Delegation—30 men
Portland, N.B.—14 men and Hose Carriage
St. Stephen, N.B.—18 men
Bangor, Maine —20 men
Bangor Artillery Band
Carriages containing Officers of Companies— Portland, Woodstock, Yarmouth, Amherst, Lunenburg, Truro, Windsor
Captain Webby of Halifax Axe Company
Woodstock Delegation—8 men
Lunenburg—30 men
Yarmouth—25 men and Hose Carriage
Truro—20 men
Windsor—10 men and Hose Carriage
Amherst—12 men and Hose Carriage
Carriages containing Officers of DartmouthUnion Engine Company and Guests
Dartmouth Engine Company Engine, Hose Carriage and 38 men
Haverhill, Mass.—4 delegates

THE
SMOKE-EATERS

Union Engine Company hose reel Alert decorated for 1886 firemen's procession

Great Barrington, Mass.—2 delegates
Lunenburg Band
Salvage Corps
Carriage containing Officers of St. John, Charlottetown and Dartmouth Salvage Corps with Captain of U.P.C. of Halifax
Dartmouth Union Protection Company with Salvage Wagon and 20 men
Charlottetown Delegation—10 men
Halifax Union Protection Company with Wagon and 30 men
St. Patrick's Band
Hook and Ladder Companies
Charlottetown Delegation—10 men
St. John Delegation
New Glasgow Hook and Ladder Company
Halifax Union Axe Company with Ladder Truck and 38 men
Hibernian Fife & Drum Band
Carriage containing Chairman, Board of Fire Wards, Captain of Fire King Steamer No. 2 of Chelsea, Chief Largie of Charlottetown and Alderman Allen of St. John
Carriage containing Ex-Captains and Honorary Members
Captain's Carriage containing Captain, Secretary,
Engineer Blake of St. John, Chief John Ryder of St. Stephen
Company Officer's Carriage containing Financial Secretary, Treasurer and other Guests
Company Men and Apparatus
66th Fife & Drum Corps

The Torchlight Procession on Thursday evening will form in the same manner at 7 o'clock. The following will be the Route of Procession on both occasions: Starting down Cogswell Street, south by Brunswick, up Sackville to South Park to Spring Garden Road; thence to Pleasant, south to South, down to Hollis; north to George, up to Granville; thence to Buckingham up to Argyle; thence to Jacob up to Brunswick; thence to Cornwallis up to Gottingen; thence to North down to Brunswick; south by Brunswick to Cornwallis, down to Water; South by Granville to Water; thence to George, up George to Barrington, south by Barrington to Morris; out Morris to Tower Road. Counter March. Dismiss.

Yarmouth firemen pose with decorated hose reel in front of a muraled Central Engine House on Brunswick St., 1886

"The procession was a magnificent affair," wrote the *Acadian Recorder*, "and eclipsed anything of the kind ever attempted in the Maritime Provinces, with the handsome uniforms, the gaily decorated hose carriages, the superb steam engines, and the fine looking lot of men. The visiting firemen all looked well and their presence lent great interest to the procession. Our American visitors added greatly to this result, the American flag carried by the Chelsea men occupying a prominent place. The St. John delegation made a splendid appearance and looked decidedly neat. The various other divisions appeared in the regular firemen suit and all looked exceedingly well. Chief Largie of Charlottetown was a notable figure in the turnout, his large brass helmet attracting great attention. The Dartmouth men looked superb and as usual the U.P.C.'s were remarkable for their neatness....Space prevents us from mentioning all, but every one in the procession did his best and at least may be satisfied that they made a turn out which was a credit to each and every one of them. A pleasant feature of the procession was the music which was excellent. The visiting bands attracted great attention and their music received much praise."

THE
SMOKE-EATERS

Windsor Hose Reel Team, 1886 Champions

Members of the victorious Windsor hose reel race team who captured the $300 purse and engraved silver trumpet (listed in no particular order): Harry Pemberton, Victor Curry, Edward Cox, Robert Fox, William Warr, Nathaniel Dill, Thomas Purdy, E. Murphy, Everet Redden, Fred Lavers, John MacDonald, John Murphy, Samual Curry, and George Lavers.

"Thousands of persons visited the Polo Grounds during the progress of the sports making a larger crowd than has ever hitherto been seen before. A great number came in carriages and the sight presented a grand one, every plot of vantage being fully occupied. In fact the crowd was so large that it was difficult for the majority to have anything more than a passing glimpse at the competitors....The great interest, of course, centered on the hose reel race which was won by Windsor [followed in order by St. Stephen, Yarmouth, Halifax, Charlottetown, Dartmouth, Saint John, Portland, and Bangor]. The Halifax men claim to have made the fastest time to the post but the coupler made a mistake in connecting the branch. The Windsor team ran in good style and Thos. Purdy did wonderfully quick work, as by his rapidity at coupling they won the prize....Protests were entered against Windsor and Halifax for coaching but the judges did not entertain them."

Firemen's ladder arch at corner of Cunard and Gottingen streets welcomes Prince of Wales to Halifax, August 19, 1919

Street arches like the two featured in these photographs were commonly erected by firemen to celebrate special events. One of the earliest was reported in the Halifax newspapers on May 18, 1860, when the Union Engine Company planned an expenditure of $480—a grand sum for the times—to erect a Firemen's Arch Tower and to illuminate their engine house in honour of the arrival of the Prince of Wales. "At the regular Monthly Meeting of the Union Engine Company on Tuesday evening last, it was unanimously resolved that the members hold themselves and their apparatus in readiness to take part in the expected pageant on the arrival of His Royal Highness the Prince of Wales in Halifax.... The Firemen, as usual, are thus the first public body in Halifax to come forward when duty calls, whether to prevent a conflagration, celebrate a victory, or to receive a Prince. It is understood to be the fixed determination of the "Union Volunteers" to even eclipse themselves on the forthcoming reception of the heir apparent to the British Throne, when he comes hither to inspect this fair portion of his inheritance. It is earnestly to be hoped that the example thus promptly and loyally set by the Halifax Firemen will not be lost upon all other Societies in this city and that it may induce them at once to go and do likewise." The *Morning Journal* carried the following when His Royal Highness arrived on July 30, 1860: "Those of the Fire Company vied with all others in taste and elegance. The Fire Companies were stationed at the Dockyard gate, their engines beautifully decorated, and the firemen in their uniforms....On the upper

Dartmouth Axe Company Arch, 1911

side of the Parade Ground, the Firemen's Tower rose conspicuously to a great height having the figure of a fireman, in full uniform, on the top. In the evening the firemen's monument was lighted with torches, the flag staff on the Union Engine Company's House supported a pyramid of colored lanterns. In the several beautiful illuminations, the Company excelled."

Welcoming the "Hose Reel Champions of the World" home

Ladder arch welcomes "Champions of the World" home to Windsor

Windsor was justifiably proud of their victorious firemen and gave them a heroes' welcome upon returning home. Unfortunately, in the Great Windsor Fire of 1897 that swept away much of the town, the engine house fell victim as did company records, books, and trophies—including the "coveted" 1886 Grand Firemen's Tournament trumpet.

The tradition of firemen's tournaments continues today, with Firefighter Combat Challenge Teams competing in a variety of modern events including hose hoist, forcible entry, stair climb, and victim rescue. Re-enactments of "engine trials" or "musters" are also popular in many American states. These involve teams of men working hand engines in competition to see which machine can shoot a stream of water the greatest distance. The first such muster is claimed to have been held on July 4, 1849, in Bath, Maine, nine years before Halifax firemen staged their inaugural engine trial at Her Majesty's Dockyard (see Introduction). In 1890, the New England States Veteran Firemen's League was organized to standardize muster rules, many of which are still followed today in New England and New York.

THE
SMOKE-EATERS

Union Protection Hall decorated for Queen Victoria's Jubilee, 1887

Canadians have an affinity with the British monarchy dating back more than two centuries. This was especially evident during the reign of Queen Victoria when firemen took every opportunity to demonstrate their devotion. At a meeting of the Union Engine Company held on June 19, 1838, a letter from the Honourable J.B. Uniacke requested that the company walk in procession on June 28 to celebrate Victoria's coronation. After some discussion, it was "agreed that as most of the members of the Company belong to other societies who intend walking on that day, they must decline the honor of walking together as engine men." It was decided upon instead "to illuminate the Engine Hall on the evening of that day, and the funds of the Company were voted to be expended in doing this." In 1841, the following resolution was passed by the Halifax Union Engine Company marking the birth of Edward VII:

Whereas every other society and institution is celebrating the birth of an heir apparent to the British Throne, and as the Union Engine Company yields to no other society or company in its attachment to the British Empire, or love to our Most Gracious Queen, therefore resolved that the engine house be decorated with colors, and that, by permission of the fire wardens, the hall be illuminated on the evening of the 23rd. Inst. in honor of the birth of the Duke of Cornwall, each member to pay 1s.3d. towards the expenses, and that the hall be open for the amusement of the public.

Upon the marriage of the Prince of Wales in 1863, the firemen staged a public celebration "that won admiration on all sides. On this occasion Halifax was illuminated at night and the cottage of the poor man vied with the mansion of the rich in honoring the nuptials of the young and beloved royalties." A newspaper article in 1897 reported that, in the Union Protection Company Hall on Barrington Street,

A pair of large pictures with heavy gilded frames of Queen Victoria and the Prince Consort occupy the place of honor at the head of the meeting room. These portraits were given the company in acknowledgment of the splendid reception the Prince of Wales received from the fire department [in 1860] as he emerged from the dockyard gate. His Royal Highness was so impressed with the firemen's welcome that upon his return to Great Britain the episode was made mention of and Her Majesty ever ready to acknowledge such instances of loyalty caused the pictures of herself and Prince Albert to be forwarded to the Halifax department. The portraits were conveyed to the company's hall under escort of guard of honor.

Firemen's Sports & Leisure

A parade today would be incomplete without a fire truck, a tradition which began in the mid-1800s, when any festive occasion was reason enough for firemen to hit the streets. At a meeting of the Union Engine Company in Halifax on May 15, 1849, "the Company decided to march in a body in the procession at the centenary celebration of the settlement of Halifax. This event was celebrated on the 8th of June. It will be observed that in this procession the Fire Company, as the oldest organization in the city, headed all the other societies. This place of precedence it has always claimed and maintained on all occasions of public demonstra-

Firemen on parade at Glace Bay, early 1900s

tions since that time." The Truro Fire Brigade organized a torchlight procession for September 13, 1882, to mark 121 years of the town's settlement. On June 8, 1887, the Yarmouth Fire Department marched through Main and Parade streets under triple arches for Queen Victoria's Jubilee. One hundred years after the Union Engine Company's first procession, Glace Bay firemen won accolades at a Fredericton firemen's tournament in 1949, when they were presented not only with first prize in the firemen's parade but also the keys to the city. A fire department occasionally formed a marching band, although these were generally short-lived ventures. The oldest band in the Maritimes is claimed to be the Bridgewater Fire Department Band, organized in 1952. There had been a Citizen's Band in the town for many years prior to this, but it folded because of financial woes, and the fire department was asked to fill the void. As most of the instruments and uniforms were well worn, they were sold for $500 and new equipment purchased— twenty-eight horns and one snare drum—for $5,200. New band uniforms were an additional $2,000. With little experience but lots of dedicated practice, and the odd Citizen's Band veteran interspersed among them, the Bridgewater firemen quickly became a headline attraction in parades throughout the province, and in 1958 it was the only Nova Scotia band chosen to play before Princess Margaret on her visit to Halifax.

THE
SMOKE-EATERS

Alexander "Tommy" Strachan, captain of No. 4 Engine Company, Halifax, 1910

Tommy Strachan joined the Halifax Fire Department in 1894 and served twenty-three years before leaving with the rank of captain. Under Strachan, Engine Company No. 4 became noted as the "social leaders" of the fire department and community, organizing a variety of popular soirées. It was a long and storied tradition dating to the early 1800s. The first record of the Union Engine Company celebrating its anniversary was August 8, 1827, when firemen and several "respectable" guests crossed the harbour to Dartmouth and dined at Edward Warren's Mill Bank House on Victoria Road. "After the cloth being raised, a number of loyal and patriotic toasts were drank, songs were sung, etc. when about half-past nine p.m. the company broke up, in good order, to return to their homes. From this may be traced the practice of going out of town to enjoy themselves on festive occasions." The first fireman's ball was held February 25, 1829, at Mason's Hall, where the company also convened its monthly meetings. Dancing began at 8:30 p.m. and continued until 4:30 the next morning. It was deemed to have been "very successful and to have pleased all concerned." Women were not permitted to attend the Union Engine Company's annual August 8 anniversary fête until 1839, when "it was finally agreed that the members of the Company, with their male and female guests have an excursion in the steamboat and land at Mr. Flowers at the North West Arm. As this was a new method and the first time that ladies were to participate in the festivities of the day, the officers of the Company were appointed as managers. Each manager was allowed, if he desired, to take an extra female. No children allowed under 12 years of age and the expenses to be paid out of the funds." On August 12, 1840, the annual fireman's picnic was held with "ladies also to be there to enliven the scene. Members of the Company allowed one extra female only by paying five shillings. One gentleman and lady guest to each member. Stewards to be free of expenses for their trouble."

Firemen's Sports & Leisure

Junior "firemen" dressed for annual Union Engine Company picnic, Halifax c.1890

The earliest firemen's picnic on record in Nova Scotia was the inaugural "hodge-podge frolic" staged by the Halifax Union Engine Company on August 28, 1833. These "frolics" became one of the most talked-about social events of the summer. It is interesting to note that, while the Axe Fire Company was organized at Halifax in 1813, and worked in conjunction with the Union Engine Company providing city fire protection, it was 1843 before axemen were invited to attend a company picnic, at which time "tickets for its members [Axe Company] were made the same as for those of the U.E. Co." Professional jealousy, perhaps. In 1845, the local newspapers proclaimed "a rage for picnics has taken possession of the inhabitants of Halifax" especially among the various societies and fraternities. (Selected accounts of Union Engine Company outings and picnics are included in Appendix 3.)

THE
SMOKE-EATERS

Annual Outing. Truro Fire Brigade   July 2nd 1924

Truro Fire Brigade annual outing, July 2, 1924

Truro firemen held their first picnic in August 1873 at Savage's Island, after which a bill of two dollars for violin music "was ordered paid." In July 1875, a picnic was held on the Marshall grounds at North River. The Colchester Cornet Band charged twenty-three dollars for music on that occasion; later meeting minutes show "a bill from Mr. Marshall for loss of his grass crop and for damage to his fences was presented and paid." The annual outing of the Truro Fire Brigade featured here would appear to have included a skit, as evidenced by several costumed participants. Truro firemen were certainly one of the most sociable groups among the early fire brigades. On July 11, 1876, brigade members held their annual picnic at Curtis Mills, North River, and the town council was invited to attend. Firemen cancelled their traditional outing in 1881 to "patronize" a July tea social in Harmony. In 1884, ladies were invited to a supper held at Maitland House to commemorate the brigade's sixteenth anniversary; a twentieth-anniversary bash followed in January 1888 at Chisholm's Opera Hall. In June 1894, firemen organized a ball that generated "exceptional interest and was largely attended by the townsfolk." Windsor firemen presented the Truro Fire Brigade with a silver water pitcher in October 1903 for an undisclosed special occasion; Amherst firemen attended a "house warming" at the newly furnished Central Engine House in March 1906; and, in May 1908, the brigade was "at home" to ladies and other guests. With firemen travelling the social circuit sometimes far from home, it makes one wonder who, if anyone, was left to mind the store in the event of a fire breaking out.

....

Firemen's Sports & Leisure

Firemen's sleigh rides were gala events

Sections of country roads often remained unbroken for days after a heavy snowfall. About every Dartmouth organization like the firemen…took advantage of favorable weather to hold their annual sleigh drive to the usual roadhouses. In midwinter, it was almost a daily sight to see a parade of four, six or eight-horse sleigh-loads of merrymakers hurrahing through town with bells jingling and a band playing in the large leading sleigh. All the sleighs were bedecked with patriotic flags and festooned with gay bunting which blended beautifully with the bright colors of the plumes on the horses' heads, bobbing along the whitened streets in the crisp morning sunlight….This custom of holding convivial gatherings at inns continued for some years. (John Martin: *The History of Dartmouth*)

Sleigh rides were the winter equivalent of summer picnics. The Halifax Union Engine Company held the first of its celebrated sleigh rides on February 20, 1849. These were "the feature events of the winters for years and years; they are always successful, always enjoyable and at each of these annual gatherings are people who are with them at every festivity, and this is because those who go once always want to go again because the [firemen] are jolly fellows and make their guests feel perfectly at home." They may have been a little too jolly on February 20, 1860, when fire destroyed Thomas Mitchell's Chebucto Iron Foundry and Robert Lawson's brewery. Reports claim the men "did their best" to fight the blaze but the revellers had just returned to Halifax at midnight by torchlight from their annual sleigh ride. Response time, as well as the firemen's senses no doubt, were somewhat slowed, having spent several hours wining and dining at Butler's Hotel where "they amused themselves in divers ways, with some deriving more pleasure than others."

In April 1830, Halifax firemen first adopted plans for holding a supper on their quarterly meeting nights. Many fire brigades staged similar "meet and eat" get-togethers. Corn suppers were especially popular, as attested to by this photo of ARP firemen enjoying a wartime feast with Mayor O.R. Crowell (centre, facing).

Corn suppers played a significant role in the Tatamagouche Hook & Ladder Company, which experienced troubles from the time of its organization in 1902 until it faded away in 1906. Thirty-six members originally signed up, but after an initial flurry of interest, numbers dropped to fourteen or fifteen attending meetings on a regular basis. On July 23, 1902, the captain offered to "set up the corn" if the entire company turned out to the next practice. How this incentive worked out was never recorded. What is known, however, is that corn was the central item of business on many occasions at Tatamagouche, with committees specifically appointed "to see that the corn was furnished." For minor infractions such as interrupting the speaker or leaving the room without permission, the offender faced a fine requiring that he supply corn for all members at the next scheduled meeting. Minutes for January 5, 1903, record that a consensus could not be reached for purchasing new fire apparatus, but it was unanimously approved to hold a practice and corn supper "on first good moon light night." Hosting banquets for neighbouring brigades were also regular events. In 1873, Truro firemen embarked on an "excursion" to Pictou and later reciprocated by hosting a "sociable supper" for the Pictou Hook, Ladder & Engine Company. And firemen were often the guests of appreciative, influential citizenry. In July 1895, for example, the entire Truro Fire Brigade was invited to the farm of J.C. Black "to partake of strawberries and cream by the side of the strawberry patch. The visitors enjoyed themselves very much. On several other occasions Mr. Black furnished a barrel of corn for the annual corn boil of the Brigade." In November 1907, the prominent Stanfield industrial family of Truro treated the fire brigade to an oyster supper that was "annually repeated under the same auspices."

Halifax firemen's hockey team, c. 1944

Firemen's hockey can be traced to at least 1899, when the officers and men of the Halifax Union Protection Company faced off in two games. The officers won game one in overtime with a score of 5 to 4. Game two was also tied 4 to 4 after regulation time, but as "both [teams] were exhausted from the night's play, it was decided to adjourn. The teams having received many pointers from the recent Montreal games showed great improvement and fast skating was a feature. At half time an interesting exhibition of fancy skating was given by a Hollis Street bookkeeper who showed remarkable proficiency but was interfered with by some skaters who should learn to skate before they go on the ice a second time." Hockey stirred popular rivalries throughout the province. In February 1907, Amherst firemen "entertained" the Parrsboro Fire Department in a "keen" game of shinny. Wolfville and Kentville fire brigades faced off in 1928 at University Rink in Wolfville, with Kentville skating away victorious. The Bridgewater Fyr Fyters (named for a manufacturer of firefighting equipment) iced a championship hockey team in the South Shore League during the early 1950s. Rumour has it that Halifax firemen played some spirited games against city policemen which may explain the eye bandage in this photo. In the 1880s, Union Engine Company officials promoted the merits of playing baseball in the Halifax newspapers: "The fire companies in many of the large American cities have regularly organized baseball clubs. The material for three or four good clubs is among our own men and the game is both healthful and invigorating. Organize your clubs at once and be prepared for the coming season." (See Appendix 3)

Front row (L-R): Berkley Smith, Earl Fox, Gerald Curran, Jim Hayes, Harold Jollimore
Back row (L-R): Frank Lewis, Tom Mulcahy, Jack Fitzgerald, Doug Publicover, Gerald Brundige, unidentified.

THE
SMOKE-EATERS

Halifax Fire Department 1600-pound Tug-of-war Team, 1920

Seated (L-R): J. Cody, A. Skinner, Wm. Howley, __ Muise, Wm. Lownds
Standing (L-R): E. Graves, T. Powell, Wm. Knanian, J. Brooks, A. Lynch, and C. McKay.

On October 18, 1920, Halifax firemen won the tug-of-war event at a sports day hosted by the Dartmouth Amateur Athletic Association. Tug-of-war competitions among firemen in Nova Scotia date to at least 1880, when the Union Protection Company staged its annual sports day on August 10 at McNabs Island. Separate from the traditional firemen's tournaments, sports day featured a variety of athletic events-tug-of-war between divisions of ten or more men; pairs quoit match; cricket ball throw; quarter mile race; hop, step, and jump; potato race; two-mile running race; two-mile Labrador whaler race; 100-yard swimming match; double pairs oar flat race; single pair oar race; best and best boats-two miles. There was also something called a ten-minute "go-as-you-please" match in full firemen's uniform, consisting of fire cap, coat, bag, and belt. Prize money was derived from entry fees and awarded to first and second places in each event. Mr. N.C. Duff also donated a prize for "a special Scotch contest to be named by himself." On July 1, 1904, a firemen's tug-of-war team from Truro visited Windsor, "and in company with many members participated in sports of the Avonian Athletic Club."

Standing third from right in this photo is Captain John Brooks, known as "one of the greatest 'scratch men'" on Halifax tug-of-war teams. For many years he was a member of the perennial firemen's champion Coal Heavers team. Brooks was claimed to be the smallest man in the Halifax Fire Department, weighing barely 140 pounds, but made up for it when competing with "lightening speed and cleverness."

Firemen's Sports & Leisure

Dartmouth Fire Department float in support of wartime thrift stamps, c.1918

Firemen are noted for fundraising, be it to purchase equipment and apparatus or in support of benevolent projects and charities. Dartmouth firemen encouraged citizens to purchase Thrift Stamps in aid of Canada's war effort. In World War One, more than $1 billion was raised in Canada by selling Victory Bonds. House wives and children were encouraged to purchase 25-cent stamps at post offices and banks, sixteen of which could then be exchanged for a four-dollar War Savings Stamp. Twenty of these, when converted to a War Savings Certificate, returned one hundred dollars at maturity. The Halifax *Evening Mail* in August 1880 carried this account of an eighteenth-century Union Engine Company fundraiser:

THE
SMOKE-EATERS

In 1796 the Company decided to endeavor to aid its funds by investing in lottery tickets. Accordingly $48 were expended in purchasing tickets to a lottery that was drawn 29th October. The Company drew one prize of $300 and three of $6 each. Thus encouraged they again tempted fortune....On these occasions they invested $48, $54 and $32 respectively but as they only drew $30, $28 and $6 on these trials, netting a loss of $70 it appears that they decided to "try the fickle jade no more" for we find no further record of their "making haste to be rich" in this way again.

Truro firemen during the early 1900s staged "an entertainment for the benefit of the Company's funds" which turned into an annual event. On January 1, 1905, a concert was held in the academy, raising $225.53 for the brigade's Insurance Premium Fund. In 1945, the Halifax Fire Department presented a minstrel and vaudeville show Meet Your Fire Department, whose proceeds were donated to St. Joseph's Home & School Association "to carry on its activities." A similar act was staged during the war years as a spoof on Hitler; monies from Der Furher were split between firemen and the Home & School Associations at the schools they performed. Bear River, in later years, had its Singing Firemen, a male chorus of eighteen who, along with wives and children, supported fire departments in tiny hamlets throughout the area by singing and performing skits before packed auditoriums.

In August 1926, *The Still Alarm* played at the Orpheus Theatre in Halifax for three days. William Russell, "the valiant fireman," and Helene Chadwick, "the beautiful sophisticated woman of the world," starred in the movie which was billed as "a gripping romance of smoke, flame and heart aches." A special prologue was presented by Halifax firemen on the Orpheus stage prior to the daily movie showings. As can be seen from this photo, the skit props were elaborate. Tickets in aid of the City Firefighters Association were sold in advance for a chance to win a new car, the draw being held at the Orpheus on the last evening. The *Acadian Recorder* reported that six thousand people took in the three-day event. In one morning alone, five hundred children from St. Joseph's Orphanage, St. Patrick's Home Industrial School, Jost Mission, and the Protestant Orphanage were the guests of the "fire ladies" for a special screening. A motorcade of automobiles provided by charitable Haligonians conveyed children to and from the theatre.

The Still Alarm, 1926

Firemen have long depended upon their Fire Department Ladies Auxiliary for support. The first Firemen's Auxiliary in the world is claimed to have been established by Mrs. Dora Quill of Capitol Heights, Maryland, on December 1, 1920. While that may be so, Truro women held a "tea meeting" on March 15, 1886, at the YMCA Hall "to aid the funds" of the fire brigade. This proved to be a "splendid success due to the prompt and generous manner in which the ladies of the town responded to the requests of the committees." One of the biggest events for a ladies auxiliary (and for firemen) is the Cherry Festival, an annual summer attraction since 1893 for the village of Bear River. Although settled shortly after the American Revolutionary War, Bear River didn't organize a fire brigade until 1931, at which time firemen were authorized to take over the widely popular summerfest for fundraising purposes. Featuring parades, water sports, games of chance, sumptuous meals, and cherries, of course, the festival remains an important source of revenue for the Bear River volunteer firemen.

THE
SMOKE-EATERS

Chapter 6

Great Fires & Disasters

Aftermath of Brunswick Street explosion

Firemen sift through rubble at 214 Brunswick Street, Halifax, following an explosion of suspicious origin on October 11, 1934, which killed seven people. Halifax's enviable fire record of the mid-1800s crumbled during a sixty-year period between 1890 and 1950. The "Great Waterfront Fire" of October 1, 1891—fuelled by massive stores of petroleum oil—was described as the "most disastrous in thirty years," burning shops, offices, warehouses, and wharves "like matchwood." On February 27, 1895, the grain elevator fire at Deep Water Terminus caused an estimated one million dollars in damages. Eighteen insurance companies lost $200,000 in the Pickford & Black waterfront fire of September 19, 1904. The March 5, 1944, Pier 21 fire accounted for another two hundred thousand dollars in damages. There was also the toll in human lives, upon which no value can be placed.

Poor House fire of November 6, 1882, Halifax

This picture was taken two years after thirty-one people died on November 6, 1882, in what is known as the Poor House Fire. The burned-out shell at the corner of South and Robie streets stood as mute testament to the greatest loss of human life attributed to fire in the city's history. A similarly designed Poor House or Poor Asylum reopened on the same site in 1886 and "remained a prominent part of the Halifax landscape" until it was torn down in 1972. The following early-1900s account of the fire was based upon a graphic and gruesome report, appearing in the November 7, 1882 issue of *The Citizen and Evening Chronicle*:

About twelve o'clock on the night of November 6th, 1882 while all the inmates were sleeping, fire broke out in the basement of the poor's asylum on South Street. The smoke spreading through the building into the dormitories caused the utmost terror among the five hundred inmates of the institution. An alarm was sounded from Box 5, Carleton Street....Old women and children were seen at the windows, shrieking to be rescued, and as they were breaking the glass, it was feared they would throw themselves out. At this junction a sturdy axeman dashed at the door leading from the wing into the yard, and with a few vigorous blows knocked it in. The stairway was crowded and out came a procession—old grey-headed, feeble men and women. All were screaming and as they smelt the fresh air they ejaculated their thanks. Then it became known that in the upper wards of that wing were all the most helpless of the inmates. Some of the firemen, an alderman, a clergyman and a fireward, who were among the early arrivals, hastened upstairs and willing hands were soon getting the blind, the halt and the lame down the long, winding stairs. The work was slow but finally the wing was emptied. Meantime the flames in the basement spread to the base of the long air shaft, or elevator, reaching to the top of the main building. The draft swept the flames upward with a tremendous roar and in a few minutes, the heaviest part of the conflagration was in the top of the building. A room just under the eves was used as a hospital and in it were seventy patients, most of them perfectly helpless. The fire was fiercely burning bright in the hospital, and above it the heat cracked the roof until molten lead poured down in streams of brilliant fire and slates flew on every side in a deadly shower, rendering any near approach to the building almost certain death. An attempt was made to raise the ladders but they were too short and after a fireman had been knocked off by the falling bricks and it was seen that ladders even would be swept away, the attempt was stopped. Far above the roar of the flames and cracking of bursting slates were heard the cries of wretched patients in the hospital who were roasting to death. Some were seen to dash themselves against the windows and cling to the sashes. A woman was seen to drag herself to a window and forcing her body half out till she could breathe the cool air, remained in that position until her head was burned off....Even until the present day that night's catastrophe is remembered with horror by those who witnessed it.

Main Street after Great Liverpool Fire of 1895

Liverpool was settled in 1759 by New Englanders and within two years could already boast of being the boom town of North America. Much of its wealth and fame, in time, was derived from the spoils of privateering. It was a pity that captains Cobb and Barss, and salty compatriots didn't invest some of their plunder into firefighting equipment. Liverpool of 1865 was still without an organized fire brigade but did own a solitary hand fire engine. It proved of little value on September 15 of that year, when a "Great Conflagration" started in the Royal Mail coach barn and swept away fourteen buildings and two churches, resulting in fifty thousand dollars in damages. The invariable cry then went up to form a hook-and-ladder company, as well as a protection company, because "no one can tell the amount of property secreted by those who come to fires merely to plunder." This was followed in typical fashion by a post-recovery lull in enthusiasm. It was three years before a second hand engine was purchased in 1868, an engine house built, and Liverpool's first volunteer fire department organized. Not until 1884—when fire destroyed the Masonic Temple—was a protection and salvage company finally established. In 1892, the town purchased a steam fire engine, but on September 8, 1895, nearly thirty years to the day when the "consuming flame" last visited, fire again laid waste to the town. Liverpool suffered the greatest losses in its history—sixty-six buildings, including nineteen businesses, valued in excess of $130,000. The adage that things happen in threes rang true on April 1, 1914, when the town was again ravaged by flame, this time sustaining damages of $88,000. A Mr. Snaddon, having his store and wharf burned for the third time, was reportedly "fed up with losing his livelihood."

Windsor looking from Windmill Hill before Great Fire of 1897

The photo above, and the next two, were all taken from Windmill Hill and show the remarkable transformation of Windsor from one of prosperity to desolation to rejuvenation—all within the span of three years. The Halifax Explosion excepted, the Great Windsor Fire of 1897 ranks as the single worst town disaster in Nova Scotia's history. Estimated damage stood at $2 million dollars, with only $600,000 insurance coverage. All major factories were razed and every church devoured, with the exception of Christ Church, which many believed owed its salvation to the rector who remained inside praying while the fire raged around. Four-fifths of the town core—approximately five hundred buildings—were destroyed and two thousand people left homeless. The conflagration's red glow was visible in the night sky seventy miles away; embers were wind-borne forty miles. The heat was so intense that it buckled and twisted the Dominion Atlantic Railway tracks, halting rail travel for several days. Even today, how the fire began remains a great mystery. Some have attributed it to "rum guzzlers" said to have kicked over a lantern in an alley shanty during the throes of a drunken brawl. The most widely circulated account (never substantiated) was claimed to be arson. George Fletcher, an ostracized Windsor Black man, became the prime suspect as the blaze is said to have originated in his establishment. The story goes that Fletcher was a heavy drinker who also allowed drinking in his restaurant, in contravention of the temperance Scott Act. He had recently been served papers in regards to this and was quoted as saying on the night of the fire, "I will see Temperance women burned in hell before long!" Of course one must consider the source of this revelation, given in an official police statement from his co-accused; John McIntyre had moved to Windsor five years earlier from Yarmouth, where a woman in that town had tried to end his days by placing strychnine in a milk can. Known as the "Spoolman Dude," McIntyre allegedly set fire to his building using a paraffin-oil soaked mattress in hopes of collecting

Windsor after Great Fire of October 17, 1897

insurance after Fletcher torched his restaurant. Many believed it was one guilty man trying to pin the entire rap on his partner. Both men certainly behaved suspiciously, leaving Windsor for Halifax during the ensuing hysteria, then returning two days later. The local tabloids referred to McIntyre in reports only as "a well to-do man," saying he was known to sport gold rings, gold-headed canes, and "frequently donned the beaver." While McIntyre was sent in shackles to Kentville's jail until a hearing, Fletcher was locked in the old Windsor blockhouse. In no time, he squeezed his way through an ancient cannon aperture to freedom but was soon apprehended in nearby St. Croix and returned to the blockhouse with hands tied. But what of the fire?

The first issue of the *Hants Journal* published after October 17, 1897, carried the following account:

> Early Sunday morning, about 1/2 past 2 o'clock the town was aroused by the ringing of the fire bell and the whistle of the electric light station. The fire company was early on hand and for nearly an hour held the fire in check. It was thought for a while that the fire was practically under control but about four o'clock, what proved to be the most severe gale experienced in Hants County for twenty years sprang up and the fate of the Town was sealed.
> The fire started on Water Street and spread out from this point like a leaf or fan. It went north to King Street and south to Albert and marched east on these streets to the point where they converge near the Church of England. Everything within the triangle, having its base upon Water street and its apex at the Episcopal Church was burned. The fire did not altogether stop at the Church. It burned a number of dwellings and tenements along O'Brien Street north-easterly and a lot of buildings east on King Street. A block of dwellings to the south of King Street were also consumed. It goes out King and O'Brien Streets and the Wentworth Road as far as the houses extend, then following

along O'Brien Road again across to Edgehill, down Chapel Lane, up Elm Street, along Albert Street to Ferry Hill, down this hill and along the water front to Water Street to its starting point [an area two miles long and one-half mile wide]. It traversed a region which until a few days ago was covered with happy homes and prosperous places of business but now is valueless except for what bare devastated ground might bring....How did this awful calamity come upon so fair a town? Windsor had no adequate firefighting apparatus. A wooden town of 4000 inhabitants and not a steam fire engine; a volunteer fire

Windsor two years after Great Fire of 1897

department nominally numbering 60 men with only two or three faulty reels of hose; circumstances like these made complete destruction inevitable.

[A Ronald steamer was finally purchased in 1899]. Captain Smith's firemen got to work with all speed that could be expected. They did not live in the atmosphere of the fool's paradise breathed by the Town Council. They knew that they had not the material for fighting any kind of fire. It is well they did not fully realize how weak they were or what a terrible night was before them, or their brave hearts may have failed at the very start. As it was they got to work with a will...[Kentville, Wolfville and Hantsport fire departments responded to pleas for help, as did Halifax which outfitted a special train with men, a steam fire engine, three horses and eight hundred feet of hose]. The terrors of the awful scene are indescribable. The flames pent up within residences burst through the heavily glazed windows with a roar like exploding cannon and the crackling of the fire, fanned to fury by the gale, made a fearsome sound never to be forgotten. The street was impassable to all but the most daring. The hurricane swept down from the north-east carrying before it clouds of dust and small gravel, masses of burning embers and volumes of smoke....The heat makes one calloused to fear in the midst of a battle with bullets flying as thick as hail and something like the same sensation overcame the people in this bitter hour of peril and loss. Just nothing seemed to make one accustomed to the bewilderment of that scene of wind, dust, fire and smoke making day as murkey as night."

THE
SMOKE-EATERS

By daylight, the fire had either been contained or burned itself out and, miraculously, not a single life had been lost. During the night, relief stations were set up at the old fort, the railway station, and the Dufferin Hotel. Military supplies and tents arrived from Halifax for the homeless, accompanied by an armed guard, the Royal Berkshire Regiment, with orders to shoot looters on sight. Bank vaults were also placed under armed military watch. "The thieves that were so troublesome during the day disappeared when the Regulars

First house built after Great Windsor Fire

arrived…. About 20 men did duty at different parts of the Town. Shots were heard…fired in rapid succession. It was subsequently ascertained that the men who had been fired at had come to the Town on the Halifax train. The men dropped their booty and were not pursued." When the relief train left for Halifax in the morning carrying the firemen and equipment, many destitute, homeless people stowed away on board, hoping to find relief of their own in the capitol city. When the train stopped to throw them off, dozens more took their place as the tracks were strewn with refugees pulling carts and wagons. One man was half a mile from Windsor when a bed in his wagon ignited and burned what few worldly possessions he had remaining.

Relief poured in from across Canada and the New England States. Halifax, Saint John, New York, Victoria, Toronto, and small communities throughout Nova Scotia all contributed food, clothing, and money. Boston staged a benefit concert at the Bijou Opera House. Windsor businessmen returned to work immediately in makeshift digs, one man hanging out his shingle on an empty baggage rail car. Within one year of the fire, 150 new buildings had been erected. The *Halifax Herald* had this to say on July 29, 1899: "Windsor justifies her continued existence, and, though business may be dull now, in the time of reaction, she has rebuilt more beautiful and more imposing and more substantial than ever. Her population is great and her people are busy employed as of yore. Her future is sure. Windsor is all right."

Great Fires & Disasters

Durham Street, Pugwash, before fire of 1898

According to James Smith in *The History of Pugwash*, "Surely few Canadian communities have recorded a history of so many disastrous fires as has Pugwash. Flames swept the centre of the village in 1877, 1890, 1898, twice in 1901, again in 1928 and lastly in 1929." Time and time again newspaper accounts proclaimed that "The heart of the village is in ruins." And each time the postscript was the same—"Like the phoenix, Pugwash rose again from the ashes. New buildings were erected and stood until history repeated itself." No less than six times did Pugwash suffer major losses during a three-year period between 1926 and 1929. Three fires occurred in less than two months in 1928, prompting Pugwash native and noted industrialist Cyrus Eaton to send financial aid from his home in Pittsburgh. The last fire of note occurred on May 12, 1929 when thirty-five buildings were consumed, resulting in $125,000 damages. Still, it was not until after a conflagration on November 10, 1901, destroyed twenty-five buildings that Pugwash finally purchased its first fire engine and organized a fire department.

The *Amherst Daily News* of March 19, 1903, reported that "the new fire engine proved its value in saving property….The firemen, under the direction of J.G. Johnson, assistant chief, managed their first attempt at using a fire engine with tact, laying one thousand feet of hose in a very short time."

Twenty-nine buildings were destroyed in Pugwash fire of July 25, 1898

The burned-out brick shell of W.H. Brown's store on the corner of Water (foreground) and Durham streets is all that remains after the conflagration which swept Pugwash during the early morning hours of July 25, 1898. The *Amherst Daily News* on July 26 gave the following account:

As the dread call of fire went forth and the flames were seen gushing through the sides and roof of the warehouse at the rear of the W.H. Brown three-storey brick block and the American House there went forth a shudder of alarm among the men and women, girls and boys fast assembling on the scene. At a glance the very serious nature of the outbreak was all too apparent and not a moment was lost in getting to work in the endeavour to quench the flames. There was further assistance soon at hand, the captains and sailors from the various ships in the harbor soon came ashore and for their valuable assistance and daring deeds in helping to save property they have the deep gratitude of all interested. Mention should also be made of the visitors, many of whom were Amherstonians who fought side by side with the toilers against the fiery element.

In but a few brief moments the flames started out against the brick block on the one side and the American House on the other and soon both these buildings were in the hands of the fire, the flames leaping high into the air and throwing forth showers of sparks. All this property was owned by W.H. Brown. The brick building comprised a general store and a dwelling house overhead occupied by Mr. Brown and was valued at $15,000 including contents. The hotel was valued at $2,000 including contents. The warehouse and contents was valued at $1,000. On this loss there was only $3,500 insurance. There was a gentle breeze at the time of the outbreak from the south-east. As the fiery element increased its deadly grip on the three buildings the sparks increased in size until large embers were wafted by the breeze right on to the other buildings joining the fast becoming conflagration.

**William McLean
House on Victoria
Street miraculously
survived
conflagration**

At this time a telegraphic message was sent to Amherst and Pictou for urgent aid from their respective fire departments. To these appeals immediate responses were given and a steamer and men sent forth from each place. Both departments arrived there almost simultaneously at about 4 o'clock. In the meantime the conflagration rapidly increased, building after building following with great rapidity in the general devastation. On the opposite side of the street, buildings became afire but happily most of them were saved with little damage, wet blankets, etc. having been placed upon. Sparks alighted on the Episcopal, Methodist and Roman Catholic Churches but fortunately the small blazes as they appeared were put out, Rev. Robert Williams very heroically working on his church. The fire continued on its headlong way, all near by buildings coming in closer contact with the flying embers, yielding like tinder until twenty-nine buildings—eighteen houses and eleven barns and outbuildings—were either reduced to ashes or fast becoming so, making seventeen families homeless. Later in the afternoon the breeze dropped and the fire ceased to spread. On the arrival of the two fire departments both steamers were got to work and the then smouldering ruins were worked upon with great energy by the united forces.

A singular happening was the saving without even a scorch by Joseph Hayward of the house owned and occupied by Wm. McLean [pictured here], one of Pugwash's oldest residences. Out of the block this house alone remains intact, although the barn at the rear of it was burned to the ground. The Pictou fire department, as soon as all danger was over, returned on their special train. The Amherst department remained on duty until about 3 o'clock this morning quenching the smouldering mounds. R.H. Bell, who had charge of the [Amherst] fire engine stuck to his post manfully through the long hours of the night only leaving it for a short time to get some supper. Joseph McLaughlin of Pugwash, while heroically at work sustained severe burns to his face and legs.

W.H. Brown building (left). Chimneys at right are all that remains from a building housing two stores and three apartments. Photo taken from Durham Street.

The site now presents a desolate spectacle with its standing chimneys, also its three towering walls, all that are left of the handsome brick building. Sad it is that among some of the victims are those who lose their own modest dwellings without insurance to fall back upon....There was not much insurance on the Pugwash property. The town was not generally insured, not having modern fire protection...and little improvement was made since the underwriters commenced a crusade against unprotected towns five years ago.

Many Pugwash residents suffered over the years from repeated visits by fire, but two prominent business names stand out above the rest: William Henry Brown and James A. Elliott. Herbert F. Elliott joined his father's business and experienced extensive losses himself. These men had to be the hard-luck citizens of Pugwash, but like their fellow townsfolk, one thousand strong, they "were never to be crushed by fire. From the ashes there rose new buildings to replace those lost."

William Henry Brown (?-1916):
Fire of July 25, 1898: lost three-storey brick store & home, warehouse, hotel.
Fire of September 11, 1901: thieves robbed store safe of $450, then set fire to premises—new brick block, warehouse, barns and contents destroyed; $15,000 losses, no insurance.
Fire of November 10, 1901: lost new home.

James A. Elliott (1826-1905):
Fire of December 31, 1890: lost two stores and adjoining buildings.
Fire of July 25, 1898: lost house and barn.

Herbert F. Elliott: (1858-1942)
Fire of December 31, 1890: lost house and barn.
Fire of November 10, 1901: lost business block, season's lobster catch, boats, fishing gear.
Fire of June 29, 1928: lost smoke-fish factory.
Fire of August 11, 1928: smoke damage to general store.
Fire of August 21, 1928: lost H.F. Elliott business block for second time.
Fire of May 12, 1929: lost home, barn, garage.

Halifax *Morning Chronicle*, January 13, 1899:

BRIDGEWATER TOWN SWEPT BY FLAMES

Fifty-Four Buildings Burned, Embracing Almost The Entire Business
Part of the Town.
Sixteen Families Are Homeless, But There is No Destitution.
Loss Between $200,000 and $250,000—Insurance May Reach $100,000.
All Merchants, Lawyers, Doctors, Livery Stable Keepers, Newspaper
Proprietors, Barbers, Etc. Have No Places in Which to Carry On Their
Callings-Lunenburg Firemen to the Rescue
No Fatalities Reported.

(Special Despatch to *The Chronicle*)

**"Burning
Bridgewater,"
January 12, 1899**

The business portion of Bridgewater has been entirely consumed by fire. From the store of Robert Winters, on the north, to Dr. Stewart's residence on the south, the flames have done their terrible work. Commercial Street is one smouldering ruins

and the prosperous stores and offices which graced it are but a stack of gaunt chimneys and glowing coals.

The whole town was peacefully sleeping when the first fearful alarm rang out but ere long the streets were filled with terrified people, many of them half clad. The fire originated in the store of E. B. Simeonson, in the basement of the Music Hall. How it caught no one seems to have any idea. About 3:30 this morning Mrs. Carter, who lives directly opposite, discovered the flames through her bedroom window and at once gave the alarm [one report had it 1:00 a.m.]. In 15 minutes the vast structure of the Music Hall was wrapped in flames and in ten minutes more a roaring raging furnace. At once it was seen that the business portion of the town was doomed. The firemen responded promptly and with bucket brigades worked hard to stem the tide of flames. [Bridgewater owned a Ronald steam engine which had been purchased in 1880 but no mention of it appeared in accounts of the fire]. A high wind prevailed and the cold was intense. Building after building caught and was consumed like tinder. Very little personal property was saved and in several instances people had to flee for their lives with but the clothes they stood in.

The fire leaped with startling rapidity from block to block, pouring its cruel torrent of devastating flame against the splendid business houses which represented the accumulations of a life work. The three newspaper offices with their entire contents were consumed. The merchants saved all their books and papers; also the lawyers their libraries and papers with the exception of H.P. Rose. Instead of saving his own books, he helped other people. A man on horseback was despatched to alarm Lunenburg and get assistance. A special train was sent from that town with its fine fire brigade and steam engine and the service rendered by them was valuable. The Lunenburg firemen worked like Trojans aided by hundreds of Bridgewater citizens; although the firemen worked heroically they were utterly unable to stem the onslaught of the flames. At daybreak this morning the whole street was a mass of flames. A second train with assistance left Lunenburg at nine o'clock and another band of workers put forth strenuous efforts to save the fine residences of the town. At six o'clock the fire was under control. There were no fatalities. Tonight the glow of the smoulder-

Looking north from the Old Town Bridge

"Large quantities of coal had been stored by parties in the burnt district and the coal is still on fire emitting a continuous glow"

ing fires is bright and a special force of constables is patrolling the town. Numerous instances of thieving was discovered and the thieves will be brought to swift justice. It was only less than a year ago that the inspector of one well known company and the Halifax agent were in Bridgewater where the company held considerable insurance and it was decided not to renew any of the insurance on Main Street. As bad as things are, however, they might still have been much worse. Most of our businessmen have already made arrangements for the building of temporary stands and operations along this line are to be commenced so soon as the ashes are out. Bridgewater will not remain down but arise again to take its place among the thriving towns of the province."

163

Surveying the damage

"Soon the streets and vacant lots were filled with household goods and the usual mixed mass of groceries, dry goods, etc. which is the result of fire."

Editorial from Halifax *Morning Chronicle*, January 13, 1899:

The fire that yesterday swept the business portion of the thriving and bustling town of Bridgewater, involving many people in heavy losses—possibly ruinous in some cases—is one of those visitations that so frequently and unexpectedly sweep over towns ill-prepared to meet such a danger….This is a happily different state of affairs from that which prevailed when Windsor was swept by flames; in the latter case the town was literally wiped out, neither shelter nor the necessaries of life, being left for those burned out. In that respect the people of Bridgewater are exceedingly fortunate….The sympathy of the whole province will go out to Bridgewater in the day of her calamity, and if substantial aid should be required to relieve suffering or want, it will certainly be forthcoming. It need not be imagined that the businessmen of Bridgewater will waste time in bemoaning their losses, serious though they be. They are plucky Nova Scotians and we have no doubt will be prepared to face the future without misgivings, even with confidence and that Bridgewater will rise from her ashes fairer than ever.

Footnote—*Morning Chronicle*, January 14, 1899:

Constable Starratt has just succeeded (9 p.m.) in arresting Frank Walters who was being wanted here on several charges of stealing, etc. The arrest was effected at an Indian camp some distance from town where it is supposed Walters has been concealed for the last two months. At the time of his arrest he was armed to the teeth with a pistol, bowie knife, sand bag and other weapons. He succeeded in striking the constable with the sand bag which fortunately broke and before he had a chance to use his other weapons the constable dealt him a blow on the head with his billy which nearly straightened him out. He is now securely locked up in jail. During and since the fire much looting has been done and it is very likely Walters will not remain long alone in his present quarters.

Digby's "Big Fire of 1899"

Conflagrations had the uncanny knack, it seems, of beginning in the foulest of weather. Such was the case at Digby on February 13, 1899, when "fire was first discovered in the basement of G.I. Letteney and Bro's large store on Water St. at about 9:45 P.M. during one of the worst northeast gales and blinding snowstorms known in Digby's history." The *Digby Courier* of February 17, 1899, reported the following:

> The snowbound DAR trains were in Digby at the time and one of them was across Sydney St., entirely blocking up the route to the fire. As soon as possible, the train was backed up and the hose reels proceeded to the nearest hydrant and a stream was turned on the burning building but it was soon realized the entire south portion of the town was in danger owing to the heavy northeast gale that was blowing and seemed to be constantly increasing in force. Many of our leading citizens were enjoying themselves at the residence of Mayor Shreve celebrating the 10th anniversary of his marriage when the alarm sounded. This broke up a very pleasant evening and the ladies and gentlemen were soon hurrying in all directions to reach home and look after their property, some of which was already surrounded by fire….The fire continued to spread and dry goods, boots and shoes, house-hold furniture, show cases, etc. were being carried out of the adjoining buildings and piled in the streets, the increasing snowdrifts covering a large portion of the already damaged goods….The vacant lots on the east side of the street greatly assisted the firemen whose attention could now be almost entirely given to the west side. Three-thirty Tuesday morning the fire was under control and confined to the burning foundations. About this time the wind blew even harder and large snowdrifts filled the streets. The crowd began to disperse and seek shelter….At daylight, Water St. presented a sad sight, one not to be forgotten….It is rumoured that some of the people who attended the fire are at present quite well supplied with dry goods, boots, shoes and groceries." Losses totalled $89,500, with forty-four buildings damaged or destroyed, twenty-four of which were not insured.

The start of the fire

Beginning of Sydney Fire, Charlotte Street, October 19, 1901.

Photo taken 2:00 p.m.

Excerpts of the 1901 Sydney Fire, taken from the *Weekly Cape Bretoner*, November 3, 1956:

Sydney had long expected a big fire and it came to pass. Saturday afternoon an alarm was sent in about half-past two for a fire in Gordon and Keith's [furniture] building on Charlotte Street, which initiated a conflagration, the worst in the history of Cape Breton, and which destroyed seventy-eight buildings and sixty-four business places, causing a loss estimated at over a half a million dollars. The loss is covered by insurance to the amount of $240,000. As to the source of the fire, from what can be gathered, it appears that the flames started from an oilstove that was being used in melting glue in a small room in the back of the building. This stove is supposed to have overturned setting some inflammable material that was lying about on fire. When it was noticed, the flames had made practically no headway and could easily have been put out if there had been any water but there was none to be had—the faucet was dry. The fire came unexpectedly as all fires do, and at an unfortunate moment for along the two very blocks destroyed, the water had been turned off to effect a connection with a branch pipe on Prince Street. It was a day suited to a big fire. The wind was high and blowing from the westward. The fire, gaining upon the boys that tried to put it out as best they could, crept rapidly into the building, got to the dumb waiter and in a few minutes was crackling upon the third storey and out through the roof. The alarm had been sent in and the firemen had responded but already it was evident that it had got beyond their control. The whole building was in flames and Capt. Carlin's other building on the left of it had caught, and also A.D. Gillis' on the other side. It was now only a few minutes since it had been discovered. These two buildings were soon enwrapped in flames and fire was spreading to the adjoining ones. By this time the [fire] engine had been stationed on the Acadia wharf and had begun its work. But the fire was beyond control. From Gordon and Keith's,

Sifting through the rubble, Prince Street

it leaped across to the Dillon Block and caught in the awnings over the stores and a few minutes later flames were encircling the building and rapidly devouring the interior. The Central Warehouse was then afire and Gillis store had fed Jost's building adjoining. The fire now was spreading in two branches-one extending along the west side of Charlotte, the other crossing over to Bentinck Street. The former worked swiftly, driving the firemen back with its intense heat and voracious appetite….The wind up to this point had still been blowing stiffly from the westward. At half past four it began to veer gradually to the south. When it thus changed, the fire was working at three distinct points—at Burns Corner, Conway's and on George Street. The wind shifting drove the fire down north from all these points….The fury of the fire was now concentrating itself upon Moore's Corner. Here there was great danger….A great deal depended upon how the fire was handled at this point. Everybody realized this and none more than the brave men who had all along steadily contested every inch of ground, falling back only at the crash of a wall or when the heat became unbearable to human life. It had been a hard struggle. The men had been fighting incessantly since half past one. Night was now coming on and rain was beginning to patter upon the faces of the men. The roofs of the opposite buildings had become wet and hose was taken off to prepare for the grand struggle when the fire would get to Moore's building. The scene now looking on at the fire from the corner of Prince and Bentinck Streets diagonally to where it was concentrating its energies at Moore's corner was one of grandeur and awe. Huge mountains of flame sped their way heaven ward lighting the gloom of the night. Penetrating the flames could be seen the frames of the structures that were being consumed like skeletons. The heat was intense. Onward and ever upward the fire sped its course, crowding in upon the corner. The flames roared and crackled with tremendous fury. Sharp tongues of living fire arose and were lost in the darkness some two hundred feet above the doomed buildings. It was an awful sight but grand. On the other side

Desolation on Bentinck Street following 1901 Sydney Fire

and in front of the fire the scene was a little different. These mountains of fire were coming down upon the heads of the firemen as they kept pouring oceans of water upon the burning buildings. At Burn's Corner, an attempt was made to clear an open space by blowing up some of the buildings...but besides wrecking the buildings no further check was put to the fire...Moore's building was treated other wise. The sills were cut so that when the interior would be destroyed the walls would fall inside and this is what happened. The walls did collapse and the fire was controlled. It was now raining quite heavily. This would be seven o'clock. Half an hour later, great was the relief when it became quite apparent that the fire was actually under control....The wind had subsided and the rain was coming down quite heavily and this aided the brave firemen as they continued at their work. By 8:30 all danger of the fire spreading any farther was over....The work of the firemen was meritorious. When Mayor Crowe saw that the fire was about to assume large proportions he immediately telephoned North Sydney and Glace Bay for assistance. The Glace Bay Brigade, comprising fifty men, arrived at quarter past three; North Sydney had reached the scene of the conflagration before this but their engine sustained some damages while being put on board the [ferry] and it was nearly four o'clock before it could be brought into action....It is estimated that upwards of thirty thousand feet of hose were stretched from the two engines and different hydrants which were attached. The work of the men as they gradually contested every inch of ground was heroic. They were to be seen in the very teeth of the fire....They clambered up the sides of the buildings, worked on the roofs and went into buildings while flames were writhing in agony on the top floors. No work could be done better with the apparatus on hand and handicapped as they were. They kept playing on the fire until driven back by an intense heat or the fear of a falling wall. All night long the firemen were on duty and kept streams of water playing on the glowing ruins...[They] had worked till nine and

Nothing to go home to on Pitt Street

ten o'clock without anything to eat. Hot lunches were prepared for them at the Town Hall and several of them taken to the neighbouring cafes for something to eat. They were both tired and hungry. It was about five o'clock Sunday morning before most of the boys were called off. For blocks surrounding the burning district the houses [had been] emptied of their contents, the occupants hurrying hither and thither before the oncoming fire. To see men and women rushing in every direction bearing whatever they could; to see teams loaded as they were never loaded before galloping up and down, and above all to see the volumes of smoke and flying cinders, and see the flames soaring above the doomed buildings, formed a picture that baffles description. It was a picture a town wants to see but seldom and one that hundreds of people who witnessed and experienced its effects will not want to have reproduced. Not until late in the evening did these people feel that their homes were safe from the devouring elements. Some of these people were fortunate, others were not. The fortunate ones were those who knew where their personal effects were, the others were those who even up to this moment have failed to locate their belongings. They simply told the truckman to take the stuff somewhere. This the expressman did, but where, no one knows, and the particular men who performed the work cannot be found by those for whom it was done. Scores of residents spent all day yesterday in looking for their furniture but they were unsuccessful. Some of them will be very fortunate if ever they will find some of their effects. These were badly damaged in their removal or ruined by the rain at night. They were simply piled on the teams in any shape. Galloping through the streets, the loads were frequently piled on the street and not seldom left there....It is highly commendable on the part of the businessmen affected that they are already beginning to show a laudable enterprise by making ends towards starting business again."

Richmond looking north towards Acadia Sugar Refinery before Halifax Explosion

Thomas Raddall, *Halifax: Warden Of The North:*

In 1917 occurred a catastrophe which had been privately feared and officially ignored ever since the foundation of the fortress, the explosion of a large quantity of munitions. On December 6, 1917 the naval authorities permitted the French steamship *Mont Blanc* to enter the harbor and pass the city in order to join a convoy being assembled in Bedford Basin. She had a devil's brew aboard: 2300 tons of picric acid, 10 tons of guncotton, 200 tons of the touchy TNT— a perfect detonator for the rest of the cargo—and for good measure 35 tons of benzol, an easily flammable liquid, in thin steel drums which were placed on deck about the hatches....Shortly after eight o'clock as *Mont Blanc* drew abreast of the Richmond terminal she was struck by the Belgian Relief steamer *Imo*, which was coming out of the Narrows. The ships drew apart without much damage but the collision had punctured some of the drums on the Frenchman's deck and at once the benzol flared...[The] ship, burning furiously drifted in to one of the Richmond piers. Someone rang an alarm to the Halifax fire department, which sent its new pumper *Patricia* towards the scene....About five minutes past nine, as most of the city schools were finishing the morning hymn, *Mont Blanc* exploded and vanished in a pillar of white smoke reaching a mile into the sky and unfolding at the top in greasy gray convolutions like an incredible toadstool. The blast rattled windows in Truro sixty miles away, and the sound traveled more than one hundred. In Halifax and Dartmouth the explosion killed more than fourteen hundred men, women, and children outright or buried them in the ruins of their homes, where they burned to death before help could reach them. An estimated six hundred others died later of their injuries. [In addition, 37 people lost their sight completely, 250 eyes had to be surgically removed, 25 limbs amputated, 4,000 people sustained various injuries, 6,000 were left homeless, 1,630 homes were completely destroyed, and 12,000 damaged]. The whole Richmond district, about one square mile in area...was smashed to flinders."

"The first thing I remember after the explosion was standing quite a distance from the fire engine," recounted eighty-seven-year-old Billy Wells in a December 6, 1967, *Chronicle-Herald* interview. "The force of the explosion had blown off all my clothes as well as the muscles from my right arm." Wells was then knocked unconscious from the ensuing thirty-foot tsunami that washed him up Richmond Hill. When the tidal wave abated, Billy became entangled in fallen telephone wires and wreckage, leaving him half drowned. He was then coated with "black rain," the residue carbon from the explosion that fell from the sky over the city. "After the wave had receded I didn't see anything of the other firemen so made my way to the old magazine on Campbell Road [Barrington Street]. The sight was awful, with people hanging out of windows dead. Some with their heads off, and some thrown onto overhead telegraph wires." Wells stumbled upon two children wandering aimlessly in the street and took them under his wing until he was able to turn them over to a couple of sailors from the warship *Niobe*. Weakened from his ordeal, he sat down to rest and was rescued by the passing salvage wagon from the Union Protection Company. A further search turned up fireman Frank Leahy, alive but unconscious and seriously injured. Both men were transported to Camp Hill Hospital, where Leahy died twenty-five days later on New Year's Eve. Billy lay on the hospital floor two days awaiting a bed and spent the next five months in hospital recuperating. LaFrance Fire Engine Company, which built the *Patricia* and returned her to working order after the explosion, presented the remaining half of the steering wheel to Billy as a memento of his experience. Although handicapped somewhat by an arm lacking muscle tone, he returned to the Halifax Fire Department as a special constable until 1926, after which he went to work at Oland's Brewery until retiring in 1948. Billy Wells died in 1971 of old age. He should have perished fifty-four years earlier when, at ground zero of a 2.9 kiloton blast, nine of his brother firemen "passed away...to a world wherein faithfulness to duty is entailingly rewarded."

**Halifax fireman
Billy Wells**

Comptroller Hines and Halifax Fire Chief Edward Condon at wheel of McLaughlin Buick Roadster, West Street Station

When the alarm sounded in West Street Station shortly before 9 A.M. on December 6, 1917, the firemen knew even before the coded sequence of numbers finished ringing that it was box #83 at Pier 6. This had become almost a daily ritual as the dock was continually catching fire when coal embers were dumped from ships' boilers. What should have been a routine response, however, quickly turned to one of urgency when the telephone rang simultaneously with the alarm. It was Constant Upham calling from his convenience store in the north end. Upham's had an unobstructed view of the harbor, and directly in front him at that moment was a large vessel spewing flames. Sensing trouble, and having one of the few telephones in the area, he notified fire stations at West Street, Brunswick Street, Gottingen Street, and Quinpool Road. Firemen from all four prepared quickly to fall out. At West Street Station, driver Billy Wells had the *Patricia*—the pride of the Halifax fire department and Canada's first motorized pumper—up and running in jig time. Wells was in a hurry to get going. His brother Claude was a fireman at Brunswick Street Station, who drove Chief Condon's McLaughlin Buick Roadster. The brothers always raced each other to dockyard fires, with Claude generally coming away with bragging rights. Unbeknown to Billy, it was Claude's day off, and Deputy Chief William P. Brunt was chauffeuring Condon's roadster. *Patricia's* crew—Captain William Broderick, Walter Hennessy, Frank Killeen, and Frank Leahy—were loaded and ready to go, with the exception of one member. He was holed up in the bathroom with a bad case of the flu and no amount of disciplinary threats from Captain Broderick would bring him out. Captain Michael Maltus jumped onboard in his place and the men sped away. For all but one, it would be their last alarm.

Albert Brunt was a call fireman with the Halifax Fire Department and a house painter by vocation. On this fateful morning, he was pushing his paint cart along the corner of Gerrish and Gottingen streets when the *Patricia* slowed for the turn. He tried to jump onto the back running board but lost his grip and fell to the street. Other than a few scrapes and a bruised ego (inflamed by derisive howls from *Patricia's* crew as they motored on up Gottingen Street), Brunt was no worse for the wear. He would soon learn just how fortuitous his tumble had been. Everyone converged on Pier 6 at the same—the *Patricia* and her crew, Chief Condon in his beloved McLaughlin Buick, fireman John Duggan with the hose wagon from No. 4 Isleville Hose Station. The chemical engine and crew from Quinpool Road would arrive momentarily; others were on their way. It was apparent that this was no piddling coal ember fire. The *Mont Blanc* lay dockside,

Patricia wrecked

ship and pier a mass of flames. The heat was stifling, forcing men to turn their faces away. Chief Condon, a man of many years experience, took charge. Hose was stripped from the *Patricia* and Duggan's wagon, a line run to the pier, and orders given to pull Box 83 again for a second alarm. Billy Wells moved the *Patricia* into position at the nearest hydrant. The time was 9:06 a.m., mere minutes from the sounding of the first alarm. Suddenly came a rumbling, muffled roar and the ground trembled, knocking the firemen from their feet. All hell broke loose as the *Mont Blanc* disintegrated in the largest man-made explosion that the world had ever seen or would see before the atomic bomb. Except for Billy Wells and Frank Leahy, the *Patricia* crew were killed outright. Wells was catapulted from the driver's seat still gripping one-half of the *Patricia*'s steel and hardwood steering wheel in his hands. The *Patricia* somehow stood firm where she was—what was left of her. The McLaughlin roadster flipped backwards, landing upside down; Deputy Chief Brunt and Chief Condon were killed instantly. Hoseman Duggan was vaporized. John Spruin, 65, a retired 18-year veteran and "legend" in the fire department was still allowed as a call fireman to answer second alarms. Responding with a hose wagon from Brunswick Street, he was hit by flying debris, knocked from the wagon, and died instantly when his head struck a street curb.

Richmond looking north towards Pier 8 after explosion

With north-end Halifax in ruins, firemen faced a herculean task. Thirty-two permanent city firefighters and 120 volunteers remained to stem the tide of fires that seemed to blaze everywhere at once, fuelled in many cases by winter stock-piles of coal in basements. Comptroller Hines commanded forces in the south section of Richmond, thinking all the while that Chief Condon was in charge to the north; it would be nightfall before he learned differently. Fire crews and station captains worked their way independently from fire to fire, priority dic-tating that isolated burns with no danger of spreading be left. The *Patricia*, the only piece of motorized equipment in the fire department arsenal, was out of commission. Filling the breach came the dependable fire horses, which saw yeoman service that day pulling seven steam fire engines, two chemical engines, eight hose wagons, and four ladder trucks. Firemen made the most significant stand in the face of fiery conflagrations at the west gate of Wellington barracks (now Stadacona) on the corner of Gottingen and Macara. Here they checked a blaze that if allowed to pass, could have spread to southern sections of the city. Aid poured in from around the province. Within one hour, a train pulled out of New Glasgow carrying a steam engine, three thousand feet of hose, and forty men. En route it picked up reinforcements in Stellarton and Truro, arriving in Halifax by the afternoon. Similar trains were despatched from Amherst, Sydney, and Kentville. While the manpower was welcomed, most of the equipment proved useless as none had standardized hose threadings to hook into the Halifax system. By late afternoon, the initial fire crisis was over. New Glasgow and Truro forces spelled off Halifax firemen that night, patrolling the north end in the teeth of a raging blizzard that compounded an already tragic state of affairs. On December 6, 1992, a seventy-fifth anniversary ceremony was held at Station No. 6 on the corner of Lady Hammond Road and Robie Street, where a nine-foot granite monument erected by the Halifax Fire Department was dedicated to the memory of the nine firemen killed that fateful day.

Great Fire at Annapolis, Royal, [?] closing up buildings with

Postcard of 1921 Annapolis Royal fire

Annapolis Royal has suffered its share of conflagrations down through the years, losing portions of the town in 1877, 1880, 1885, 1887, and 1920. In 1921 the red terror again cut a swath through the business core, ravaging the east side of St. George Street in what the *Halifax Herald* of September 8, 1921, called "the most terrible conflagration that has swept a Nova Scotia community for a quarter of a century." The following account was written by a *Herald* staff correspondent in Annapolis Royal at midnight on September 7:

Practically the entire business section of Annapolis Royal is a wide mass of ruins tonight…the whole centre of the town, roughly one-third of it, has been blotted out. Scores are homeless, the finest businesses have been destroyed and the property loss will run into figures that may total half a million dollars. The flames started in a barn back of the Queen Hotel on St. George Street. They had insignificant beginnings. One of the hotel girls, going out to the barn to feed a sick dog discovered the fire at a time when a couple of pails of water would have extinguished it. There was no water—and therein lies the tragedy of it all.

A light southeast wind was blowing; and had the water supply been adequate, there is every possibility that little damage would have resulted. Annapolis, however, has been without its water supply for some time as the result of the prolonged drought. The discovery was made at 5:40 o'clock this evening. The flames gained headway with the townspeople forced to watch them without adequate means of combating a small fire, much less a steadily-growing conflagration. Soon the barn was a roaring furnace which spread to other buildings with appalling rapidity. Tongues of flame and sparks from the blazing barn caught the nearby structures which burst out in conflagration as though they were so much tinder. What followed was an inferno.

A roaring furnace of flame

"Residences and business blocks were abandoned to the sacrifice"

Calls for assistance were sent out broadcast and the people soon began to pour in from the outlying districts. Special trains were rushed to the scene from [Kentville] and Yarmouth. The train from Kentville carried a crowd of men and a chemical engine to help in the fight. Volunteers rushed to the scene from Bridgetown and Digby. Communication with the town was cut off shortly after the conflagration had gained early headway. By eight o'clock, everything between St. George and Victoria Streets, as far south as St. Luke's Episcopal Church, had been devoured by the tremendous holocaust, which was then also sweeping north among the buildings lying along St. James Street, and as far in a southerly direction as St. Anthony Street.

People fled from the path of the flames; residences and business blocks were abandoned to the sacrifice. Meanwhile, every possible means was being employed to fight the red terror. Lacking water, the next best thing was dynamite. As fast as buildings caught and were considered doomed, they were dynamited. In this manner, the conflagration was finally brought under control about ten o'clock. A heavy blanket of fog which settled over the town earlier assisted those who were so heroically battling against stupendous odds. And all the while the Annapolis River flowed little more than a hundred yards from the scene with no pumping apparatus available to the townspeople to bring them the sorely needed deluge. [There is no evidence to suggest that Annapolis possessed fire engines at this time, although there had been a hand engine many years earlier]. Motor trucks and other vehicles were pressed into service to haul water but this was as nothing in the face of such a roaring furnace of flame. Late tonight a telephone instrument was installed on the premises of J.H. Edwards and a connection with Halifax established by way of Middleton. It is regarded here tonight as nothing short of miraculous that no loss of life resulted. There were one or two minor injuries but nothing of a serious nature has so far been reported.

Annapolis Royal rebuilds

The scene about the town outside the burned area tonight is indescribable. For more than a mile out, goods and articles of all sorts strew the roads. Looting apparently ran rampant, with no possible means of checking it, every person that could help being engaged in fighting the flames. The old fort grounds [Fort Anne; now a national historic site] are littered with all sorts of stuff, the electric light and telephone wires are down, the town, which gets its light from the same source from which it gets its water, has been plunged into total darkness. The only walls to be seen in the devastated area tonight are those of Runciman's store. The whole area has been swept practically clean. On the West side of St. George Street the buildings have been badly scorched and hundreds of window panes are broken in the buildings that escaped the flames.

It is difficult to exaggerate the plight into which this town has been thrown in a few hours. The homeless are being cared for tonight by their nearby neighbors with true Nova Scotia hospitality. Granville and other places have thrown open their doors; but while this will afford temporary relief, the housing problem in Annapolis will for a long time be most acute. Many of the people rendered homeless have lived there for years, among them elderly citizens, who have tonight seen the results of the work of a lifetime wiped out in a few brief hours. It seems almost impossible tonight to tell the exact number of buildings destroyed. With business blocks, residences, barns, out-buildings, warehouses, etc., the count will run close to sixty…Annapolis Royal is truly in a pitiful plight and in need of the assistance of all who can bring relief. Her citizens are still numbed from the shock of the horror, and as yet unable to realize the full extent of what has come upon them. Only a few days ago there was celebration and holiday-making here. Tonight there is nothing but pathos and misery and woe.

A guest of the Queen Hotel clings precariously to an aerial ladder as Halifax firemen climb to the rescue. The first sign of trouble was detected at about six o'clock in the morning on March 2, 1939, when smoke billowed from the hotel's furnace room. Within minutes, flames engulfed the fifty-year-old tinderbox, racing through the elevator shaft to upper floors, where it sealed off what few escape routes were available to the ninety guests and employees. The front desk clerk immediately notified the fire department, then tried in vain to telephone

Queen Hotel Fire, Hollis Street, Halifax, March 2, 1939

rooms to awaken unsuspecting guests of the impending danger. He completed only one call before being forced into the street by stifling smoke. (A post-fire inquiry would discover serious fire regulation violations, one being no available means for sounding a general alarm). Firemen quickly arrived but in some cases were foiled from raising ladders by overhead power lines and trolley cables. Ted Mitchell, a salesman from Bridgewater, awoke to smoke seeping under his door and a roaring noise in the hallway. He wisely chose not to investigate the source but climbed out the window, clung to the sill until his arms tired, then fell three storeys to the street below. Despite breaking both legs and an arm, he miraculously walked out of hospital fourteen months later. Many others were not as fortunate. A man who initially escaped to the street went back into the hotel looking for his wife. They both perished. At least a dozen people fled to the rooftop but were burned alive when it collapsed into the fiery inferno below. Panic reigned as screams could be heard from what seemed like every window; bed sheets were knotted together to improvise escape ropes. A desperate father threw his three-year-old and eleven-year-old children into a life net thirty feet below, then followed them to safety. An indelible image was forever etched into one fireman's memory—having climbed through an upper-storey hotel window, he was startled to see before him the silhouette of a woman kneeling in prayer surrounded by advancing tongues of flame. Repressive heat drove him back outside before he could save her.

THE
SMOKE-EATERS

By noon, firemen had beaten the conflagration into submission, and it was time to assess the grizzly toll. Twenty-eight people perished, ten of whom were burned beyond recognition; nineteen others suffered various injures. "Hollis Street looked as if it had been ripped by a tornado," wrote the *Halifax Herald*. "Debris littered the street and all lanes of traffic were blocked by fire apparatus....The skeleton walls of the once-famous hotel were reminiscent of scenes in battle-scarred France." The hotel and two adjoining buildings, valued at

Aftermath of Queen Hotel Fire

$800,000, were a total loss. Two public inquiries were held, one conducted by the Fire Marshal's office, the other by a government-appointed Royal Commission. The findings were damning. Blame was placed squarely on the shoulders of hotel owner John Simon, who had purchased the rambling five-storey complex at the bargain-basement price of $17,500 during the throes of the Great Depression. Talk of renovations failed to materialize, and safety features were non-existent. Employees were never versed in procedures to follow in the event of fire. No escape-route directives were posted in hallways or guest rooms. Exterior iron fire escapes had wooden landings that quickly burned away. Access to fire escapes ran through guest rooms that were generally locked. As mentioned, there was no fire alarm system in the building and not a single room was equipped with an escape rope. The Honourable M.B. Archibald, Justice of the Supreme Court headed the Royal Commission and did not mince words. Hotels in Nova Scotia were the responsibility of the factory inspector. Two years before the fire, he had inspected the Queen Hotel at the behest of the Minister of Labour, made recommendations, but never returned to ensure that they were carried out. Justice Archibald criticized the Fire Marshal's Office, saying it had failed to enforce existing safety regulations and recommended that the office be completely overhauled to reflect greater accountability and increased powers of enforcement. The cause of the fire was never determined; there were theories, including one of arson attributed to a disgruntled employee, but nothing conclusive.

The Halifax Fire Department did not escape Justice Archibald's scathing rebuke. His report in the *Journals and Proceedings of the House of Assembly 1940* pointed out that the department was under-manned and existing equipment outdated.

There was a scarcity of ladders of sufficient length to reach the upper floors of the building...[The] aerial ladder is twenty years old, and from the evidence of the firemen and the Chief of the Department, it is apparent that the ladder is unsafe [men were warned they used it at their own risk]....The presence of overhead live wires, combined with the failure to provide the Fire Department with more efficient, up-to-date and speedy wire cutting apparatus, greatly hampered the firefighters during this fire, and interfered with the work of rescue of occupants of the hotel.

Queen Hotel, a shell of its former self

Despite the shortcomings of fire department administrators, city firemen gave heroic service. Two smoke-eaters scaled a ladder amid shooting flame from windows to rescue a woman who moments earlier had stretched for a ladder, missed, and found herself clinging to life by her fingertips on a narrow ledge. The firemen barely had time to slip a rope under the woman's arms before she passed out, then lowered her to safety. And acts of courage were not reserved for the professionals. Clyde MacIntosh was a day desk clerk who lived in a fourth-floor room of the Queen Hotel. He was awakened by the smell of smoke and quickly climbed onto the fire escape, where he proceeded to bang on neighbouring windows; MacIntosh assisted nine people to safety despite burns to his feet from repeated trips on the red-hot iron rungs of the fire escape. His last rescue involved an unconscious guest whom he carried over his shoulder. Not yet finished, MacIntosh returned to the hotel's third floor looking for more survivors but succumbed to smoke and fell to the street. Incredibly, he survived with only minor injuries.

THE
SMOKE-EATERS

Bedford Magazine explosion, 1945

Civilians and naval personnel watch the fireworks from North End Halifax

The east shore of Bedford Basin was chosen in 1927 as the site for a series of magazines to be used by the Canadian armed forces. During World War Two, it was taxed to its limit simply handling the incredible volumes of ordnance required by the Royal Canadian Navy. With victory assured in Europe by May 1945, there was a push to decommission many of the country's 350 warships and the Bedford Magazine was swamped with naval vessels needing to be de-ammunitioned. Between May 1 and the fateful day of July 18, 1945, no less than eighty-three ships dumped an array of depth charges, TNT, and ammunition at the Bedford depot. Much of it was stored outside in piles six feet high, the reinforced bunkers filled to overflowing.

This powder keg blew on July 18, 1945. What caused the initial explosion was never determined, but it mattered little. The South Jetty disappeared in a huge mushroom, taking with it the lone fatality in the disaster—naval seaman Henry Craig from Windsor, Ontario, who had drawn night watch. Other personnel had fortunately gone home for the day; only five minor injuries were initially reported. The isolated location of the magazines prevented a higher death toll, and destruction around the blast site was limited for the most part to four hundred acres of scrub brush. Halifax took much of the brunt, as shock waves skipped across the water and hit the low areas. The initial blast was only the beginning. According to a later military report, "Fairly heavy explosions occurred regularly until almost midnight, when a very heavy detonation took place. Extremely heavy explosions were felt at 0100, 0200 and 0400 the following morning." Vibrations were felt over two hundred miles away in Yarmouth; people in Truro and New Glasgow watched the red glare in the night sky bounce off cloud cover.

Great Fires & Disasters

Original Mount Saint Vincent Mother House

Mount Saint Vincent was established at Rockingham outside Halifax in 1873 as an academy by the Sisters of Charity. The original intent was to train novices and sisters to be teachers, but its mandate soon changed to include post-secondary education for other women as well. In 1914, Dalhousie University and the Mount signed an agreement whereby students enrolled in a bachelor's degree program for two years at the Mount, then finished the remaining two years, and received their degree, at Dalhousie. In 1925, Mount Saint Vincent was legislated degree-granting status by the provincial government, giving it the distinction of being the first "independent women's college in the British Commonwealth." The college suffered a financial holocaust (but no loss of life or personal injuries) on a frigid January night in 1951, when fire caused $4 million in damages, destroying the

Mount St. Vincent, Halifax, N.S.

main complex known as the Mother House. With temperatures at -25 degrees celsius, more than four hundred professed sisters, novices, postulants, and students were driven from their dormitories, taking time in many cases to don habits and veils before evacuating in orderly fashion through smoke-filled corridors to fire escapes. Once safely outside, the women escaped the bone-chilling cold by staying in small cottages on the property until a motorcade of buses, taxis, and private automobiles moved two hundred sisters, novices, and postulants into Halifax convents. All were later billeted at St. Joseph's Orphanage on Quinpool Road, where as many as sixteen women to a room lived for thirteen months. With little time to save personal belongings, such things as toiletries and extra clothing were sparse. The Red Cross provided everyone with a toothbrush, toothpaste, soap, and comb; extra habits and clothing of odd sizes and various colours were scrounged from Sisters in the congregation and the community. Although classes resumed on campus in the fall of 1951, the Mother House wasn't rebuilt and opened until 1958.

When firemen from Halifax and surrounding communities arrived upon the scene, the Mother House was already beyond saving. Confusion ensued when statues within the building were mistaken for people. One fireman was coaxed by a sister to rescue a Stradivarius violin from the music room; the instrument had belonged to her father, a concert violinist. Only a station of the cross in the courtyard and a hand-painted ornament survived.

The following letter (dated April 7, 1951) was received by Fairview Fire Chief Leo Nelson.

Mother House burns, January 31, 1951

Dear Mr. Nelson:

In the difficult days and weeks which have followed on the total destruction of our dear Mount Saint Vincent, it has been impossible to find time to acknowledge on paper our debt of gratitude to you and your men for your services on that occasion. Be sure that despite the delay of this letter, your splendid service has been spoken of many times by the Sisters, and remembered by them in prayer. Thanks to your gallantry and hard work, our loss was less than it might have been. We owe the saving of at least one building to your promptness and efficiency.

We have learned that you and your men have declined any compensation for your labor as firefighters. This fine gesture on your part is very much appreciated, not only by me but by all the Sisters who were at the Mount that night. Were it in our power, we would compensate each man a hundredfold; but since you have given your services free, we can only beg God to compensate you fully, as you deserve.

Please convey to each member of your force our sincere gratitude, and may God bless you all!

Very sincerely yours in Christ,
Mother Stella Maria
Mother General

A book on firefighting would be remiss without acknowledging the victims of fire. Many are the acts of heroism when people have shown a total disregard for personal safety in the face of almost certain death. The story of Mary Elizabeth Crowley serves as testament to all those who, because of space, must remain nameless but have paid the ultimate sacrifice so others could live. During the evening of October 14, 1869, Cornelius Crowley awoke at ten o'clock to the crackling sound of fire somewhere within his house. Seeking help, he raced to

Monument erected July 1870 in memory of Mary Elizabeth Crowley, Pugwash

the barn, where his two eldest sons slept. Within minutes, flames had engulfed the dwelling, preventing Mr. Crowley from re-entering to help his family. Mrs. Crowley, with a baby in her arms and two children in tow, had managed to escape, but three others remained trapped on the second floor. Twelve-year-old Mary Elizabeth, ignoring pleas from her parents to save herself, first carried her nine-year-old brother to a window, from which he leaped unharmed. Mary then returned for her seven-year old sister Catherine, but the frightened young girl refused to jump. With flames encircling them, Mary pushed Catherine out the second storey window, then followed, holding onto the sill before dropping heavily to the ground sixteen feet below. Gaining her feet, Mary whispered in a faltering voice before collapsing, "I am done, mother, but I have saved my brother and sister from being burnt up." Sadly, both girls died a short time later. News of the tragedy reached the floor of the Nova Scotia Legislature, where a resolution to erect a monument to her memory in St. Thomas More Roman Catholic Cemetery was unanimously passed on March 23, 1870. The inscription reads:

Mary E. Crowley lies beneath this sod, a victim to fraternal love, having rescued a younger brother and sister from the flames of her parents' dwelling, she exclaimed, 'Mother, all is over with me now, but I have saved my brother and sister.' She expired 24 hours after Oct. 15, 1869, aged 12 years. Greater love no man hath known. R.I.P.

The monument is claimed to be the first public memorial erected in honor of a Canadian-born female.

A FIREMAN'S PRAYER

When I am called to duty, God
Wherever Flames may rage,
Give me the strength to save some life
Whatever be its age.

Help me embrace a little child
Before it is too late,
Or save an older person from
The horror of that fate.

Enable me to be alert and
Hear the weakest shout,
And quickly and efficiently
To put the fire out.

I want to fill my calling and
To give the best in me,
To guard my every neighbor
And protect their property.

And if according to your will
I have to lose my life,
Please bless with your protecting hand,
Those I've loved in life.

-AUTHOR UNKNOWN

RULES and ORDERS
To be observed by the Members of the
UNION FIRE CLUB

First instituted at Halifax on the 14th Day of January, 1754, and thence continued to the 14th Day of January, 1759: At which Time the former Rules and Orders, together with the several Bye-laws and Regulations since made for the better Order of the Society were taken in Consideration, and the same collected into the Fourteen following Articles, which are agreed to by the Society, to stand and be as Rules and Orders to which the Members are subject.

1st That every Member shall be provided with Two Leather Bucketts [sic], mark'd with their Names on one Side, and Union Fire-Club on the other; and two Bags, each made of four Yards of Canvas: That said Bucketts shall be hung up, with the Bags in them, in some convenient Place of each of the Members Houses, so as to be ready on all Emergencies.

2dly. That said Bags and Bucketts shall not be employed on any other Occasion than that of Fire; and that every Member who shall have his Bucketts out of the way, or have his Bags out of his Bucketts or suffer them to be used for any other Service, shall forfeit for every such Offence, Five Shillings.

3dly. That upon the Cry of Fire, the Members of the Society shall immediately repair to the Place where such Fire is, with their Bucketts and Bags; the Bucketts to be delivered to be made use of as Occasion shall require and they and their Servants to assist with their Bags in removing the Effects of such Persons as shall be in Danger of suffering by the Fire; and such Bucketts as may be lost at any Fire shall be replaced or made good to the Member to whom they did belong, out of the common Stock of the Society.

4thly. That the Ladders and Firehooks belonging to the Society be lodged at the following Houses, Viz.
One Firehook and two Ladders at the House of Benjamin Greene Esqr.
One Firehook and Two ladders at the House of Thomas Saul Esqr.
Two Ladders at the House of Charles Proctor Esqr.
Two Ladders at the House of Malachy Salter Esqr.
And two Ladders at the House of Mr. Franklin
To be ready for use whenever a Fire happens, and not to be made use of on any other Occasion; and those Gentlemen are desired to report to the Two Members who visit the Bucketts and Bags, or to the Secretary of the Society, whenever the said Ladders and Firehooks shall want Repair, in order that they may be repaired accordingly.

5thly. That the Members shall make Inquiry into the Condition of the Chimnies [sic] of the Houses (they shall suspect to be in want of Repair) in the Neighbourhood in which they live, and when any of them shall be faulty, and that Person who inhabits such House, shall, upon Application being made to him, neglect or refuse to cause the same to be repaired, a Report thereof shall be made to the Society, in order, that proper Steps may be taken to oblige them to it.

6thly. That the Society shall meet on the Evening of every first Tuesday in each Month, and at all such other Times as shall be found necessary, and also on every fourteenth Day of January being the Anniversary of the Institution of the Society.

7thly. That such Members as shall not attend to the Meetings of the Society, having had due notice thereof, shall forfeit, and pay the Sum of Two Shillings and Six Pence for every Time of absence, unless prevented therefrom by Sickness or being out of Town; And in order the better to support the Use and Intent of this Society, every Member who shall absent himself from the Meetings thereof for three Months suceffively [sic] unless by Cause of Sickness or absence from the Town shall be dismissed from the Society, and…[not legible]…Bucketts to the Treasurer, who shall pay for the same a reasonable Price.

8thly. That the disposing of Money imposing Fines, and all other Matters and Things relating to the Society (except in the Case of admitting Members) shall be determined by the unanimous Consent of the Members present at any of their Meetings; provided the Number of such Members present by the Majority of the Members in Town; without which no Determination shall have Effect.

9thly. That the Method of admitting Members shall be by Ballot, and that when there shall be under Twenty Members present, Two Negatives shall exclude the Person proposed from being admitted; and when there shall be Twenty or more Members present, Three Negatives shall be required for that Purpose.

10th. That there shall be a President for each Month, and that each Member shall take that Office on him in his Turn, as he stands in the List of Members of the Society; of which he shall be acquainted by the Secretary the preceeding [sic] Meeting, or, if then absent, the next Day.

11th. That in the same Manner two of the Members shall each Month visit the Bucketts and Bags belonging to the Society, and see that they be in good Order as directed by the First and Second Articles of these Rules; as also the Ladders and Firehooks, which Latter they shall cause to be repaired when in Want thereof; and report the Whole to the Society at the next Meeting; And in Default thereof to forfeit each Two Shillings and Six Pence.

12th. That Two of the Members shall be chosen at the Anniversary Meetings on the fourteenth of January; the one to act as Treasurer, and the other as Secretary.

13th. That the Treasurer shall receive from the Secretary all Monies belonging to the Society, and apply the same to such Purposes as shall be determined by it, as is directed in the Eight Article.

14th. That the Secretary shall give Notice in writing to the Members, of the Monthly Meeting, or of such other Meetings as shall be agreed on by the Society, and shall collect and receive all Fines and Forfeitures as are set forth in these Rules and Orders or shall, or may thereafter be set forth by any Additional Rules, and shall pay the same to the Treasurer.

15th. That every Evening the Society meets, the Bill of Expence [sic] shall be called for by the President at Ten o'Clock.

UNION ENGINE COMPANY Of HALIFAX
CONSTITUTION & BYE-LAWS
1845

1) This Company shall consist of 80 members including the Captain, 5 first and 5 second Lieutenants, a Secretary, and a Treasurer. The whole to be divided into five divisions, each to have one 1st and 2nd Lieutenant. Each 1st Lieut. to have charge of an engine. In his absence, the 2nd; and in the absence of both the 1st and 2nd Lieutenants the senior member of each Division to have charge. The whole to be under the direction, and subject to the inspection of the Captain and no officer shall act as such until approved of by fire wardens or other competent authority.

2) This Company shall meet on the third Tuesdays of April, May, June, July, August and September, in each year, for the purpose of examining or working the engines, and keeping them in good order, at 6:15 p.m. Every member, upon neglect thereof, shall pay a fine of 50 cents—sickness or absence from the city upon necessary business, excepted.

3) At the monthly meeting in October the Company is to meet at 3 p.m. precisely, for cleaning and putting the engines in good order for winter, and every member not attending shall pay a fine of $1.

4) After working the engines, each and every member shall repair to the Engine House, in the months of April to September, inclusive, at 8 p.m. precisely; and in the months of October to March inclusive at 3:15 p.m. precisely, or pay a fine for each neglect. Any member absenting himself three successive monthly meetings from the room shall be excluded.

5) At every monthly meeting, one or more members shall be appointed for each Division to take care of their respective engines and apparatus, and in the winter season they must clear away the snow from the door of the engine houses, so that there may be no obstruction in the way of the engines in case of a fire. This shall be done before 9 a.m. or before 9 p.m. under a penalty of 50 cents for each and every member, and for every neglect.

6) Each member on hearing an alarm of fire, shall immediately repair to his engine house. If he finds that his engine is gone before he gets there, he shall repair to the fire and assist his brethren. After the fire is extinguished he is to assist in getting back the engine to the engine house, but if the engine should be detained by order of the fire wardens or other authority, no member is to absent himself without permission from the officer commanding the engine to which he belongs. For disobedience he shall pay a fine of $1. and every member who does not repair to the engine to which he belongs after it has gone to a fire, shall also pay a fine of $1.

7) If after a fire the Captain or officers think it necessary to examine and clean the engines they shall appoint a time and place for that purpose and every member not attending shall pay a fine of $1.

8)   Any member absenting himself from his proportion of duty by repeated negligence, or contempt, or who shall expose the business of the Company to any person who is not a member, may be finally excluded from the roll of the Company by a majority of votes.

9)   When any person is proposed to become a member of this Company, he shall be balloted for when, if there be two-thirds of the members of the Company, who are present, in his favor, his name shall be minuted in the books for one month, and then only to be admitted by a majority of votes by ballot. Upon his admission he shall pay $1. entry money, and before the next meeting he shall furnish himself with a fire cap, such as shall be approved by the Company. In default thereof he shall pay a fine of $1.

10) At the working of the engines in the months of April and October, all the members of the Company are to wear their fire caps which are to be inspected by the Lieutenants of each division. The owner of any cap not found clean and in good order, shall be find 20 cents.

11) The officers shall have the power to call special meetings when it appears to them to be proper to do so, and any member who does not attend to his engine, should it need to be moved at any time, after being warned by the officer commanding shall pay a fine of 50 cents—sickness or being out of the city on necessary business excepted.

12) Any member leaving the Company at a monthly meeting, before the business of the evening is over, without the consent of a majority of the Company, shall pay a fine of 50 cents.

13) The Secretary, in consideration of the fact that he has considerable trouble, shall be exempt from every expense and attendance at the engine except in case of fire but he shall attend at the rooms where the business of the Company is transacted.

14) In case repairs are required by any of the engines the Captain is to apply to the Fire-wardens of the City of Halifax to have them done.

15) The limits of the City for fire purposes shall be the same as prescribed in the Act of Incorporation of the City.

16) In the event of the Captain being absent at a meeting of the Company or at a fire the Senior Lieutenant shall take command of the Company and engines and shall proceed agreeably to the foregoing rules.

17) Any member or members of this Company meeting on any jury (Coroner's inquests excepted) or doing militia duty of any kind shall pay a fine of $4 for each and every offence.

18) Any member interrupting another while addressing the chair, or swearing, or using abusive or profane language at the time of performing the business of the Company shall pay a fine of 25 cents for each and every offence—the Captain to be the judge whether it is an interruption or not.

19) In order to facilitate the transaction of business no member shall be permitted to address the chair on any single subject more than twice at one meeting.

20) Any member of the Company who shall be accused of a breach of any of the foregoing Rules, shall, when so accused, be allowed ten minutes for an explanation, after which the chairman shall put it to the Company whether the party be guilty or not. Such decision to depend on a majority of the company present and to be given, in all cases, without discussion. Should the party so accused be proved guilty and refuse to comply with the Rule applying to his particular case, such member shall be expelled from the Company.

Appendix 3

FUN AND GAMES

Acadian Recorder, August 12, 1848

"Engine Company's Holiday"

On Tuesday last, the Steamer Unicorn started at 6 o'clock in the morning on an excursion projected by the Union Engine Company to Lunenburg and Chester. The company numbered upwards of 400. As the day was fine, the wind light and the water hardly ruffled, the run to Lunenburg was delightful to all but those whom the qualms of sea sickness overcame for awhile. On the arrival of the Unicorn at Lunenburg a salute was fired from some large cannon, and men, women and youth from the town and vicinity assembled in dense masses on the wharves to greet the visitors. Having landed in safety, the 7th Fusileers Band played through the town, and the company separated into small parties to visit old friends and relatives, to survey the public edifices and surrounding scenery, to get refreshment at the hotels or to associate with the inhabitants, whose proverbial hospitality was equally extended to acquaintances and strangers on the occasion. A brief stay being thus pleasantly enjoyed the signal for returning was given, much to the regret of the visitors. From Lunenburg to Chester the passage was exceedingly agreeable. At Chester the artillery of the town received the party with a glorious salute—as well fired as it could be by a company of regulars. All were highly pleased with the scenery of Chester and many were most agreeably entertained by some of the inhabitants. Another embarkation was at length required and as everything that was expected was seen, an impatient wish to hasten homeward, made the rest of the passage very tedious to most of the company. Contrary to orders, some persons improperly plied the crew of the Unicorn with intoxicating liquors until they became incapable of performing their duty, and accordingly the fire was suffered to burn too low to generate the steam in sufficient quantity to propel the vessel. A considerable delay was the consequence. This disagreeable circumstance was, however, obviated as soon as it was detected, and the Unicorn arrived off Ives' Wharf [Halifax] about midnight, but here the impatient company were doomed to a worse annoyance for though the vessel reached so nigh that a rope could be thrown to the wharf, yet she could not be made to budge a single inch nearer by any means, and thus all on board were obliged to remain helpless but provoking, tantalizing durance for at least an hour and a half. It is insinuated that a misunderstanding between Capt. Meagher and Mr. Scott, the Agent of the Unicorn, was the occasion of the unpleasant finale, but nothing of the kind took place. Both the Captain and Mr. Scott kept silent while they were in difficulty, knowing that a waste of loud orders, and adopting all sorts of suggestions would not help them out of the "fix" they unfortunately got in. There were but few overcome with strong drink on board, but the excursion would have suffered no diminution of its attractions had all sorts of intoxicating beverages from wine down to rum, been totally excluded from the vessel…

The Nova Scotian, February 6, 1857

"FIREMEN'S SLEIGH RIDE"

This annual affair came off on Tuesday last. Some half dozen sleighs drawn by teams of eight, six, four, spans and tandems, containing nearly one hundred Firemen and their friends, drove through the principal streets of the City. The effect was very fine, the sleighs being decorated with the elegant banners and insignia of the Union Engine Company. The weather was all that could be desired, the party in their happiest mood, and the going first rate. The leading sleigh drawn by eight horses carried the Union Company's Banner presented some years since by the late William Caldwell, Esq., for many years the honored Captain of that Body; and the cavalcade was closed by a tandem team elegantly decorated, driven by Mr. J.W. Wills, and in which was also seated the Vice Chairman of the Company. The gay party took the Campbell Road for Blois' Hotel, Sackville, soon after 11 o'clock, stopped to bait at Davy's Four Mile House, and arrived at their destination without any accident by breaking down or otherwise. Here luncheon was served in good style and enjoyed by the host of hungry pleasure seekers. The party amused themselves after the most approved fashion until 3 1/2 o'clock when dinner was announced. The company had by this time been considerably reinforced by the arrival of the trains, including the Hon. Joseph Howe, and other celebrities. Nearly one hundred and twenty sat down to a sumptuous entertainment provided by Mr. Blois for this occasion. Many of our most estimable citizens were present and participated in the pleasures of the day. It is but justice to the caterer for the Firemen to state that the dinner has been pronounced by competent judges to have been one of the best ever served up in these parts. Capt. Caldwell occupied the Chair, supported on his right by His Worship the Mayor, and on his left by the Hon. Joseph Howe; while the Vice Chair was filled by Lieut. John McIlreith, who was also well supported. After the cloth had been removed, all the usual loyal and patriotic toasts were drank with the enthusiasm characteristic of Halifax Firemen. The health of the Mayor and Corporation elicited a happy reply from His Worship; that of the sister Company, the Axe Firemen, brought Capt. Roome to his feet; nor were the Chairman and Fire Wards of the City forgotten. Much regret was expressed at the absence of G.A.S. Crichton, Esq., the able and zealous Chairman, who was prevented from attending, owing to the death of a near relative. The health of the Hon. Joseph [Howe], proposed from the Chair, was most uproariously drank—cheers upon cheers following each other until the rafters fairly rang again. Mr. Howe made a most felicitous response. We regret that our space precludes the possibility of furnishing even an outline of the many good things, solid and sensible, uttered by the Hon. Gentleman, all of which were received with repeated bursts of applause. There were several good songs sung, interspersed with recitations, volunteer toasts and impromptu speeches. Thus the time sped on right merrilie until the hour for returning to home had arrived. Soon after 9, the party embarked for home, which was reached without accident at about 10 1/2 o'clock, the calvalcade coming in as they went out by the Campbell Road, with torches lighted, music playing, and banners waving, the whole having a very beautiful effect. After passing through several of the principal streets the party was set down at the Engine Hall, where they spent an agreeable hour in the service of Terpsichore. Nothing occurred to mar the harmony of the day, and the Festival of 1857 has been pronounced the best the Firemen of Halifax have ever held, which is certainly saying a good deal. Great good credit is due Mr. Veith for the very efficient manner in which he conveyed the company to and from the scene of revelry. The Committee, comprising the Second Officers of the "Union", were unremitting in their exertions to make every body feel at home, and they succeeded to their heart's content. And thus happily ended the Firemen's Festival for the winter of A.D. 1857.

Acadian Recorder, August 10, 1861

"PICNIC OF THE FIRE PROTECTION SOCIETY"

[When members of the Union Engine Company resigned en masse in 1861 because of a dispute with city council, they re-organized themselves into the Union Protection Company and carried on their merry ways. This was the first picnic of the newly formed company.]

This association, late the "Union Engine Co.", with their guests, numbering over one hundred and sixty persons, embarked on board the steamer Micmac on Thursday morning, to enjoy a day's sport at Belmont, the residence of J.W. Ritchie, Esq. The steamer left the dock shortly after 10 o'clock, and proceeded some distance up the Basin, saluting the flagship on the route; and then turning, steamed down the harbor nearly to the Lighthouse—thus giving the company a pleasant excursion on the water, previous to landing them at the beautiful grounds on the borders of the North West Arm, which had been selected for the scene of the day's festivities.

After landing, the first piece on the programme was an invitation to partake of a bountiful supply of substantials and delicacies which were very acceptable—the bracing air on the water having sharpened the appetites of all; and this timely attention to the wants of the company was hailed as a guarantee that the committee of management had left nothing undone that could administer to the pleasures or comfort of the party.

The refreshment tables were placed under the shade of large trees and were kept well supplied with creature comforts. When we say that this department was under the management of Hesslein and the duty performed in his best style, no other description is necessary.

A platform had been laid for the use of the dancers and here and there a small tent afforded protection from the sun and added much to the picturesque appearance of the scene. The day was spent in dancing, boating upon the Arm, promenading the Belmont woods, feasting…and in such other ways as people determined to enjoy themselves were enabled to devise. The Volunteer Battalion Band played during the day and the gay party marched into town to its music and finished the day's enjoyment at Mason's Hall, where dancing was kept up, to the music of Addimore's Quadrille band until midnight.

Unidentified newspaper source, September 24, 1863

"VOLUNTEER ENGINE COMPANY'S PICNIC"
(formerly Halifax Union Engine Company)

Last Tuesday the beautiful grounds at Woodside [Dartmouth] were the scene of one of those delightful rural fetes that break in upon the usual monotony of city life, and are remembered with pleasure by all who have taken a part in them. The Volunteer Engine Company, in this respect, have the satisfaction of having given the most agreeable picnic for many seasons. The steamer left Power's Wharf at 10 A.M. with about 360 of the Company, with their ladies. During the afternoon a second boat took over about 150 more, consisting principally of guests and firemen. The grounds as the boat approached presented the most animated and lively appearance: the brilliant red uniforms of the men contrasted pleasingly with the light dresses of the lasses, as each moved about on the green slope. Games of base, quoits, and foot-ball were carried on with great spirit, and we doubt if the green shades of Woodside ever echoed back the shouts of a happier company. A dainty lunch was served to the last comers; and at 8 P.M. a handsomely arrayed, and well filled table was laid, at which fully 500 dined. Capt. Lyons did the duties of host in a happy manner, in which he was well seconded by Messrs. Phelan, Murphy and other officers of the Company. The health of Her Majesty was given by the Captain and drunk with all the honors. Several good dancing floors were laid which were at all times crowded. The Artillery Band furnished the music, and is highly spoken of by all who were present. Some amusing sack races took place for a fireman's hat, which after considerable tumbling and fun was won by Mr. Jas. Dareen. As the twilight set in, the company re-embarked and making a trip round the war vessels, the band played the French and English national airs. At nine o'clock, agreeably to programme, the ladies assembled at Masonic Hall in ball costume. Dancing was kept up until a late hour and all separated with the consciousness of having spent a joyous day. The whole affair was characterized by the most pleasing order and decorum and reflects the greatest credit upon the committee who were unremitting in their exertions.

Unidentified newspaper source, August 9, 1888

"FIREMEN'S BASEBALL"

Yearly on August 8, if the weather is favorable, the U.P.C. [Union Protection Company] enjoy their annual hodge-podge and yesterday they went to the "Hawthorne House", St. Margaret's Bay road and enjoyed a day's outing that will be memorable for its many good features. Mine host Wilson was indefatigable in his efforts to please both in the cuisine and the accommodation of the party that numbered between 70 and 80. A field on the opposite side of the road from the house had a diamond whitewashed on it and during the early part of the day two teams played a close game, the score being 9 to 7 according to some, and 9 to 11 according to others. When the afternoon contingent arrived, a grand baseball contest was arranged for a meerschaum cigar holder presented by J.R. Saunders for the man who made the most runs. Four innings were played as follows: [box score was given] Winsor's Nine 6, Sellon's Nine 12. Mr Sterns and Mr. Doane tied for the smoking utensil but as the latter does not smoke, the former was the recipient. It is by special request that the record of errors are not published; they would look very formidable. The umpire gave great satisfaction, and was perched on a boulder about four feet high just behind the pitcher's box where he could see all over the field and particularly down in the valley where the home plate was supposed to be.

Addendum:

In 1906, the Union Protection Company staged "a star game of baseball" for their annual August 8 hodge-podge "for which an umpire had been especially secured from Montreal in the person of Mr. Marcus Hirsch. He showed a thorough knowledge of the game and his decisions were not questioned."

Halifax Morning Chronicle, April 15, 1878

Yesterday morning a fire broke out in a building in Barrington Street extension which turned out to be one of the most disastrous that has occurred in this city for some years. About ten minutes past three, policeman William Keating left the Police Station and proceeded along Barrington Street north towards his beat. At the corner of Cornwallis Street he met policeman M. Sullivan and stood talking to him for a minute or two, when they saw a sudden flash of light followed by a red glow, as from a fire, south of them. They ran in that direction and saw flames bursting from the roof of a large wooden building on Barrington occupied by Messrs. H.C. Evans & Co., commission merchants. They sounded an alarm from box 35 in Hurd's Lane. Keating then went to the burning building and bursting open the door found that the most of the fire seemed to be rising from the back part of the building among some barrels. Some of them were rolled out and were afterwards found to be barrels of kerosene.

The firemen responded to the alarm in a few minutes, but the upper part of the wooden building was one mass of flames, which had spread to a building back of it on Water Street, occupied by Mr. A Fordham as a leather finding store in the basement, and by a family named Purcell in the upper stories. Through the latter building the fire spread so rapidly that though the Union Protection men worked well very little of the stock could be saved. The stock in both buildings was of a very inflammable nature—one had butter, nuts, matches, brooms, kerosene, etc., and in the other were barrels of shoemaker's wax, pegs, lasts, leather and other shoe finding material. In fact a mass better fitted to make an immense bon fire could hardly be got together. But the engine and axemen worked well and, having a plentiful supply of water, in a few minutes the effect of their work began to show and it seemed as if the whole fire would be extinguished in a very short time. Then a catastrophe occurred which entirely changed the aspect of affairs. The ladders had arrived and were about being erected against the front of the building when a loud explosion was heard; sparks and burning timbers were hurled in every direction, and the building

Appendix 4

A FIREMAN'S LOT

THE
SMOKE-EATERS

was shaken to its foundation. The flames now leaped from box to box through the building, their forked tongues licking up the inflammable material, and burst forth with redoubled fury, seeming to defy all human efforts to stay their progress. As the dense volume of black smoke, sparks and lurid flames shot upward the firemen's task was indeed a severe one. But they never flinch; appalled neither by the mysterious explosion nor its consequences they stand their ground, and the steady, incessant streams from branches held in strong, willing hands, once more begins to tell on the burning building when another accident occurred, followed by consequences which will make it memorable for our firemen for many a day.

The explosion referred to, shook the building, as just stated, to its foundation but as it still appeared comparatively safe in the lower story, several of the Union Protection Company continued removing the office furniture, and two of them, Mr. William Howell and Mr. Edward Fredericks, were together in the office when the building was seen to sway, a cry of warning burst from the crowd, a loud crash was heard, and the two floors, loosened by the explosion, fell through to the cellar, burying the two men in the ruins, while the shop front of the office fell out on to the sidewalk. The walls of the building and the roof still remained, supported by the chimney, but looked as if they would fall at any moment. If the firemen had worked well before, they fairly surpassed themselves now. While some continued playing on the flames with the hose, others seized chains and grapnels and began clearing away the burning ruins. For it was not then known who were buried, as several were in the building but a moment before. Presently a faint cry rising from the smoking ruins proclaimed that at least one man lived.

Then two firemen named William Tierney, a Lieutenant in No. 5 Division, and Edward Phelan, a Lieutenant of No. 1 Division—whose heroic conduct through this eventful morning is deserving of a substantial recognition at the hands of the public—heedless of the danger, went down into the cellar under the ruins, and remained there working for hours, though the smoke was stifling and they were completely surrounded by fire at times. Once they were so long coming to the surface that it was thought they were suffocated, but suddenly a shout was heard and the dead body of young Fredericks was handed up. Sorrowfully his late comrades placed it on the waggon and carried it to the North End Protection Company's Hall. The body was not much bruised but the breast on one side was crushed in, and there was a gash on the forehead, supposed to have been caused by a heavy iron copying-press falling on him. From the nature of his injuries it is evident that he died instantly.

The work at the building continued. It was found that Mr. Howell was alive, and was held fast between the two floors, which had fallen together. Tierney, one of the men before referred to, with a saw and axe, cut a hole through the lower floor beneath, an extremely difficult task owing to the narrow space in which he had to work, to say nothing of the danger. Through this hole he held communication with Howell and found him lying face down-wards, very weak but still sensible. He cleared the debris away to allow him to breathe more freely. Other firemen were now working in the cellar, and the broken timber and rubbish were rapidly being cleared out, when the roof and walls fell in, still burning, but protected by the floor, those in the cellar fortunately escaped unhurt. Among them was Dr. Moren, the City Medical Officer, who had gone down with a drink of cordial to Howell. The rubbish was soon cleared away sufficiently to allow Howell to be extricated; and, after having been jammed down on his face, and held in that position, in stifling smoke, with heavy beams on him, and alternately half drowned and half roasted for over three hours, he once more breathed the fresh air. A mighty shout burst from the attending crowd as he was lifted to the surface, and he was placed on the waggon and borne away. Cheer on cheer went up and strong men wept tears of joy....

Mr. Edward Fredericks, the man who was killed, was about 26 years old and was very well known as the proprietor of the Brunswick Street drug shop. He was Lieutenant of the North-end branch of the Union Protection Company, with the members of whom he was very popular. He was unmarried, and lived with his mother, a widowed lady. The cool manner in which the firemen worked under such adverse circumstances was highly creditable to them and caused much wonderment to the spectators. One of the axemen was on the roof of the brick building at work; the roof was expected to fall in every moment, but he continued as though there was no danger. A portion of the roof above him did fall in and sent a shower of burning embers all about. He stopped work for a moment, and coolly picking up one of the embers, lit a cigar with it and then resumed work.

Middleton Outlook, April 10, 1930

Saturday morning, April 5, about 3 o'clock, Middleton folks were called from their slumbers, to witness one of the costliest fires for some time. The Armdale Theater Block and Mr. John H. Potter's residence were totally destroyed by this fire. The Canadian National Railway Telegraph Office, the Highway Office, and the various Oddfellow lodges located in the theater block lost all their equipment, records, etc. The fire originated in the theater and when first noticed was a mass of flames. With a high wind blowing, the flames soon spread to Mr. Potter's residence and soon demolished it. Mr. And Mrs. Potter escaped with very scant wearing apparel, and but little of their furniture was saved. The nearby residences and buildings caught on fire and it was with difficulty the brigade and volunteer helpers kept the fire to the two buildings mentioned....The estimated loss from this fire is upwards of $40,000....It is a very desolate scene greets the eye, on the place that held the fine theater building and handsome residence...

A serious accident occurred at the fire when Mr. Harold Ray, one of the firemen, was badly hurt by the falling theater wall. He had an arm and leg broken, also receiving severe spinal injuries. He was taken to the hospital, and is still in a serious condition, but everything is being done, and from reports as we go to press, he is resting quite comfortable. We all hope for a speedy recovery from his unfortunate incident.

THE
SMOKE-EATERS

FIRE DEPARTMENT LETTER TO TOWN COUNCIL, May 28, 1930

To The Mayor and Councillors of the Town of Middleton:

At a regular meeting of the Middleton Fire Department, held on Wednesday, May 28th, 1930, the following resolution was unanimously passed and ordered to be presented to the Mayor and Councillors of The Town of Middleton.

Where Nozzleman Harold Ray was seriously injured in the performance of his duties as a member of the Department, on the morning of April 5th, 1930, necessitating a long and painful stay in hospital, and, whereas, he is still in a serious condition at home, unable to work at his usual occupation, THEREFORE,

RESOLVED, That the Fire Department is of the opinion that The Town of Middleton is morally, if not legally, responsible to Nozzleman Ray to compensate him for whatever costs he may incur during the period of his disability as well as for whatever losses he may incur through inability to attend to the duties of his vocation, and, further, the said department recommends the following:

1) That The Town of Middleton be responsible for payment of all doctor and surgical bills incurred during the disability of Nozzleman Ray;
2) That The Town of Middleton be responsible for payment of all Hospital bills inurred, including nursing and such other expenses which may have been incurred necessary to his welfare.
3) That The Town of Middleton pay to Nozzleman Ray a sum of $19.00 per week—the amount of his wages lost—from the time such wages ceased until such time as he is able to resume his ordinary occupation or until gainfully employed;
4) That, further, the above recommendations be carried out forthwith.

The Fire Department believes the above recommendations to be only fair to Fireman Ray, who was carrying out his duties in a careful manner, and further that Fireman Ray and Officers or Members of the Department were in no way responsible through lack of caution for the regrettable accident which occurred. Finally, the Department respectively requests that the Town Council take immediate action in connection with this resolution.

Respectively Submitted,

K.P. Johnson, Secretary, Middleton Fire Department

Middleton Outlook, February 12, 1931

The death occurred at the Victoria General Hospital, Halifax, on Friday, February 9 of Harold E. Ray, after an illness of ten months. Injured internally at the fire that destroyed the Armdale Theater in April of last year, the late Mr. Ray suffered much but bore it all with patience and fortitude.

Born at Bear River thirty-seven years ago, the deceased spent his early life in that place, moving to Middleton to make his home about ten years ago. Here by his genuine worth and quiet manner he has won the esteem and respect of all who knew him, and none were his enemies. During the time he has lived in Middleton, the late Mr. Ray has been an active member of the Band, the Fire Brigade, and Sunbeam I.O.O.F. He has been a consistent Church attendant and supported every movement to the good.

The unusually large attendance at the funeral service held Monday in the Baptist Church was a testimony to the high esteem in which the deceased was held.

Bibliography

Acker, Sarah & Jackson, Lewis. *Historic Shelburne*. Halifax: Nimbus Publishing. 2001.

Akins, Dr. T.B. *History of Halifax City*. Halifax: Nova Scotia Historical Society. 1895.

Baird, Donal M. *The Story of Firefighting in Canada*. Erin, Ont.: Boston Mills Press. 1986.

———. *A Canadian History of Fire Engines*. St. Catherines, Ont.: Vanwell Publishing. 2001.

Bear River Historical Society. *Water Under The Bridge*: Bear River, N.S., 1920-1980. Lockeport: Community Books. 2001.

Beed, Blair. 1917 *Halifax Explosion & American Response*. Halifax: Tours Visitors & Convention Service. 1998.

Benson, Denis A. & Dodds, Donald G. *The Deer of Nova Scotia*. Halifax: Dept. of Lands & Forests. 1977.

Brown, Roger David. *Blood On The Coal: The Story of the Springhill Mining Disasters*. Hantsport, N.S.: Lancelot Press. 1976.

Calnek, W.A. *History of the County of Annapolis*. Toronto: William Briggs. 1897.

Cameron, James M. *The Pictonian Colliers*. Halifax: Nova Scotia Museum. 1974.

Campbell, Rev. J.R. *A History of County of Yarmouth*. Saint John: J & M McMillan. 1876.

Caplan, Ron. *Cape Breton Lives*. St. John's, Nfld.: Breakwater Books. 1988.

Centennial Committee. *Gateway To The Valley*. Windsor: Self-published. 1977.

Cochrane, Tony. Editor. *Echoes Across the Valley: A History of Kingston and its Neighbours*. Vol. 2. Hantsport, N.S.: Lancelot Press. 1994.

Colchester Historical Society. *Historic Colchester: Towns & Countryside*. Halifax: Nimbus Publishing Ltd. 2000.

Davison, James Doyle, Editor. *Mud Creek: The Story of the Town of Wolfville*. Wolfville Historical Society. 1985.

DesBrisay, Mather Byles. *History of the County of Lunenburg*. Toronto: William Briggs. 1895.

Friends of the Desbrisay Museum & Bridgewater Heritage & Historical. *1899-1999 One Hundred Years-A Pictorial History of Bridgewater*.

Hart, H.C. *History of the County of Guysborough*. Belleville, Ont.: Mika Publishing. 1975.

Jackson, Elva E.; *North Sydney Nova Scotia, Windows On The Past*. Belleville, Ont.: Mika Publishing Co. 1982.

Johnson, Ralph S. *Forests of Nova Scotia*. Halifax: Four East Publications. 1986.

Kitz, Janet F. *Shattered City: The Halifax Explosion & The Road To Recovery*. Halifax: Nimbus Publishing. 1989.

Kroll, E. Robert. *Intimate Fragments: An Irreverent Chronicle of Early Halifax*. Halifax: Nimbus Publishing. 1985.

MacKinnon, J.G. *Old Sydney*. Sydney, Cape Breton, N.S.: Don MacKinnon. 1918.

Martin, John P. *The Story of Dartmouth*. Dartmouth, N.S.: self-published. 1957.

Metson, Graham. *An East Coast Port...Halifax at War 1939-1945*. Toronto, Ont.: McGraw-Hill Ryerson Ltd. 1981.

Miller, Thomas. *Historical & Genealogical Record of First Settlers of Colchester County*. Halifax: A. & W. MacKinlay. 1873.

Monette, Kimberley. *A Century of Service*. Kentville, N.S. Kentville Volunteer Fire Department. 1991.

Mosher, Edith. *North Along the Shore*. Windsor, N.S.: Lancelot Press. 1975.

Nova Scotia Archives & Records Management. *Halifax and its People 1749-1999*. Halifax: Nimbus Publishing. 1999.

Parker, Mike. *Historic Dartmouth: Reflections of Early Life*. Halifax: Nimbus Publishing. 1998.

———. *Historic Lunenburg: The Days of Sail*. Halifax: Nimbus Publishing. 1999.

———. *Historic Digby*. Halifax: Nimbus Publishing. 2000.

Quinpool, John. *First Things In Acadia*. Halifax: First Things Publishers Ltd. 1936.

Robertson, Marion. *Kings Bounty: A History of Early Shelburne, Nova Scotia*. Halifax: Nova Scotia Museum. 1983.

Ruff, Eric & Bradley, Laura. *Historic Yarmouth*. Halifax: Nimbus Publishing. 1997.

Ryan, Judith Hoegg. *Coal In Our Blood*. Halifax: Formac Publishing Co. Ltd. 1992.

Sherwood, Roland H. *Pictou's Past*. Hantsport: Lancelot Press. 1988.

Sheppard, Tom. *Historic Queens County*. Halifax: Nimbus Publishing. 2001.

Smith, James F. *The History of Pugwash*. North Cumberland Historical Society. 1978.

Smith, Richard. *Windsor Fire Department, 120 Years Of Dedicated Fire Service*. Windsor: Martin Printing, Windsor. 2002.

Stephens, David E. *Truro: A Railway Town*. Hantsport, N.S.: Lancelot Press. 1981.

Sweeney, E.M. *From Little Boats: A Short History of the Township of Yarmouth*. Tantallon, N.S.: Four East Publications. 1993.

The University Women's Club of Truro. *Cobequid Chronicles: A History of Truro & Vicinity*. Truro: 1975.

Wigglesworth, Armand F. *Anecdotes of Queens County Nova Scotia*. Liverpool: A.F. Wigglesworth & Memory Lane. 1994.

Wilson, Isaiah W. *A Geography & History of the County of Digby*. Halifax: Holloway Bros. 1900.

Wise, David Burgess. *Fire Engines & Firefighting*. London: Octopus Books. 1977.

Withrow, Alfreda. *St. Margaret's Bay, An Historical Album*. Halifax: Nimbus Publishing. 1997.

Wright, H. Millard. *The Other Halifax Explosion*. Halifax: Self-Published. 2001.

BOOKLETS, PAPERS:

Annual Reports of City of Halifax Fire Department 1900-1916.

By-Laws of Bridgewater Fire Company 1913.

By-Laws of Tatamagouche Hook & Ladder Company 1902-1906.

By-Laws of River John Hook & Ladder Company 1869.

Cleveland, Paul. *History of the Yarmouth Fire Department*. Yarmouth: Firefighters' Museum of Nova Scotia. 1987.

City Firefighters Benevolent & Protective Association Journals. Halifax: 1944, '45, '46, '53, '60, '64, '67.

Constitution & By-Laws of Sydney Volunteer Fire Department, 1910.

Halifax Fire Department. *An Historical Celebration: 225 Years of Firefighting In Halifax*, 1768- 1993.

Harvey, D.C. *Notes On Firefighting In Nova Scotia*. Halifax: Archivist.

Mullane, George. Historical Notes taken from *Acadian Recorder* respecting Fire Protection Service, Halifax 1749-1950.

Rudachyk, B.E.S. *The Most Tyrannous of Masters: Fire In Halifax, Nova Scotia 1830-1850*. (Read before the Royal Nova Scotia Historical Society, February 5, 1982.)

Rules of the Glace Bay Volunteer Fire Department circa. 1901.

Rules & Orders of the Friendly Fire Club 1784, Shelburne. Reprint. Halifax: Petheric Press. 1982

Town of Glace Bay Volunteer Fire Department 75th. Anniversary Souvenir Booklet.

Truro Fire Brigade: A Brief History 1868-1910. Truro: Midland Printing Co., Truro. 1910.

Whynot, Capt. Reid. *A Brief History of the Bridgewater Volunteer Fire Department 1876-1988*. Lighthouse Publishing. 1988.

NEWSPAPERS:

The following newspapers, circa 1840-2002, provided valuable research material. Many of the clippings used are contained in archival and museum holdings while others were obtained from private collections. Unfortunately, the latter were not always identified by title and date. Sources have been given throughout the text when available.

Halifax Morning Sun, Daily Echo, Acadian Recorder, Halifax Evening Express, Halifax Reporter, Halifax Mail, Morning Chronicle, Halifax Chronicle-Herald, Evening Mail, Mail Star, Halifax Daily Star, Amherst Daily News, The Casket, Weekly Cape Bretoner, Cape Breton Post, Outlook, Liverpool Advance, Digby Courier, Truro Daily & Weekly News, The Spectator, Annapolis Journal, Weymouth Bridge, Pugwash Harbour Light.

Image Sources

Admiral Digby Museum: page 165

Beaton Institute: pages 6 (86-80-16178), 27 (81-250-5320), 62, 63, 71 (77-394-528), 137 (75-31-38), 140 (84-453-14553), 166 (85-68-15768), 167 (83-6369-13669), 168, 169

Bridgewater Fire Department: pages 12, 37, 41, 43, 76, 162, 163, 164

Colchester Historical Society Museum: pages 36 (P89 #63.1), 120

Cumberland County Museum & Archives: pages 8 (79-119-27), 21 (79-119-88), 35 (79-13-17), 122 (79-112-3)

Dartmouth Heritage Museum: pages 17 (93.15.465), 24 (93.15.464), 73 (George Craig), 78 (92.7.60), 116 (94.9.41), 142, 148

Firefighters Museum: page 5

Halifax Regional Fire & Emergency Service: pages xxii, xxix, 1, 3, 4, 9, 11, 15, 23, 25, 28, 31, 32, 33, 38, 39, 42, 45, 47, 48, 55, 65, 68, 75, 85, 86, 87, 88, 89, 92, 93, 94, 96, 99, 108, 109, 111, 112, 127, 131, 132, 136, 139, 141, 146, 150, 151, 171, 172, 173, 180, 183

Historic Restoration Society of Annapolis County: pages 175, 176, 177

Kentville Fire Department: page 60

Maritime Command Museum: pages 49, 50, 181

Museum of Natural History: page 106 (75.70.3)

North Cumberland Historical Society: pages 158, 159, 160, 161, 184

Nova Scotia Archives and Records Management: pages ix (Notman 16804), xxxii (Tom Connors 6602), 16 (Thomas Hill 26), 22 (Notman 64711), 26 (acc. 9149), 34 (Notman 46308), 52 (Civil Emergency 21), 54 (Civil Emergency 29), 57 (Bollinger 50302-6), 61 (Bollinger 50302-16), 66[lower] (Loc.53.1), 67[right] (Loc.53.1), 74 (Don Cunningham 1996-365), 77 (Tom Connors 630), 79 (Tom Connors 629), 91 (Tom Connors 654), 95 (Bollinger 50302-2), 97 (Civil Emergency 92), 98 (Civil Emergency 91), 103 (Civil Emergency 41), 110 (Tom Connors 648), 114 (Bailly Family 3), 126 (Tom Connors 663), 129 (Loc.53.1), 130 (Tom Connors 639), 133 (Loc. 53.1), 134 (Halifax Fire Photos), 144 (W. Chase Album 5, 61), 145 (Civil Emergency 10), 152, 170 (Halifax Explosion), 174 (Halifax Explosion)

Private Collections: Donal Baird: pages 70, 72, 100; Ray Beck: pages 40, 81, 113, 121, 128, 178, 179; Cliff Campbell: page 44; Gary Castle: pages 53, 84, 147; Elroy Hill: page 104; Howard MacKinnon: page 29, 124; Bill Mont: page 14, 101, 102; Steve Nearing: pages 10, 30; Bill Nelson: pages 56, 182; Mike Parker: pages 90, 107; Tom Sheppard: page 153; Harold Stewart: page 105; Peter Turnbull: page 13; Bob Watt: page 80

River John Fire Department: page 64

Shearwater Aviation Museum: page 51

Shelburne County Museum: pages 2, 115

Truro Fire Brigade: pages 7, 18, 19, 20, 46, 67[left], 82, 83, 119, 143

West Hants Historical Society: pages xvii, 154, 155, 156, 157

Windsor Fire Department: pages 58, 59, 66[upper], 123, 135, 138

Yarmouth County Museum: pages 117, 118